UNDERSTANDING SOCIAL POLICY

UNDERSTANDING SOCIAL POLICY

Fifth Edition

Michael Hill

BLACKWELL
Publishers

First published in 1980 by Basil Blackwell Ltd and Martin Robertson & Co Ltd.

Second edition 1983
Reprinted 1985, 1986, 1987

Third edition 1988
Reprinted 1989, 1992

Fourth edition 1993
Reprinted 1993, 1994, 1995

Fifth edition 1997

2 4 6 8 10 9 7 5 3 1

Blackwell Publishers Ltd
108 Cowley Road
Oxford OX4 1JF
UK

Blackwell Publishers Inc.
238 Main Street
Cambridge, Massachusetts 02142,
USA

British Library Cataloguing in Publication Data

A CIP catalogue record for this book is available from the British Library.

Library of Congress Cataloging-in-Publication data
Hill, Michael J. (Michael James). 1937–
    Understanding social policy / Michael Hill. — 5th ed.
        p.   cm.
    Includes bibliographical references and index.
    ISBN 0-631-20039-8 (pbk.)
    1. Great Britain—Social policy. 2. Welfare state. 3. Welfare economics. I. Title.
HN390.H52   1997
361.6'1'0941—dc20
                                                    96-23265
                                                    CIP

ISBN 0-631-20039-8 (pbk)

Typeset in 10½ on 12½ pt Times
by Ace Filmsetting Ltd, Frome, Somerset
Printed in Great Britain by Hartnolls Limited, Bodmin, Cornwall

This book is printed on acid-free paper

CONTENTS

Preface

This book is an introduction to the study of social policy. It is based on the view that those who study this subject need to consider the way in which policy is made and implemented, as well as to learn about the main policies and their limitations. It has been written for people who have had no previous training in the social sciences, with the needs of social workers, health visitors and other social policy 'practitioners' very much in mind, as well as those of undergraduates.

The preparation of the fifth edition of this book has involved a substantial revision, as did its predecessors. The process of change to social policy which Margaret Thatcher initiated in the 1980s has continued. This edition has been completed in the run-up to a general election which the Conservatives may lose. Some efforts have been made, therefore, to explore the contemporary trajectory of policy and the ways a future government may change it. The basic shape of the book has been kept the same, except that the chapter on health policy has now been put before the chapter on personal social services.

At this stage in the history of a textbook it is impossible to acknowledge satisfactorily all the people who have helped to shape the author's approach. However, I have been particularly grateful for the very active editorial stance taken by Jill Landeryou of Blackwell. An early version of the manuscript was sent by her to three readers. All contributed useful suggestions, and one – Jack Hampson – was particularly helpful.

The book remains dedicated to my wife Betty who, when she was a health visitor student, first helped me to identify the gap in the market. Nowadays her active involvement in Newcastle Community Health Council, the North East Alzheimer's Disease Society and the Labour Party makes her an invaluable source of comments and encouragement.

She has collected material for this edition, and has commented on the draft manuscript. I am happy that I have been able to share with her the fruits of its success.

WHAT IS SOCIAL POLICY?

INTRODUCTION

This is a book about British social policy. Social policy may be defined as policy activities which influence welfare. Whilst non-state bodies may be described as having 'policies', a generic expression like 'social policy' is primarily used to define the role of the state in relation to the welfare of its citizens. That is how it is used in this book.

However, this usage raises two key questions:

1 Since the welfare of citizens is affected by their own actions and by the actions of others, what is it about the role of the state in relation to welfare that is different?
2 What are the kinds of actions which have an impact on welfare?

One, perhaps simpler, way to answer the question 'What is social policy?' is to provide a list of the areas of public policy included under that heading. This simpler approach will be adopted here. But the issues identified above cannot be ignored altogether. It is necessary to look a little at the rationale for the policy areas chosen. In doing that, this chapter will also throw some light on some of the main concerns of the study of social policy.

WHICH POLICIES?

The policy areas covered in this book are set out in the titles of chapters 5–10. The first three of those chapters deal with policy areas that everyone seems to include within their definition of social policy – social security, health and the personal social services. Chapter 10 looks at housing policy. Most books and courses on social policy deal with housing, though with some uncertainty about the extent to which they are concerned with the private sector. There are important questions in relation to housing policy that concern the extent to which a free market can operate, in relation to the private sector, and the extent to which housing which is publicly subsidized can be managed as if it were a private business concern. This chapter, together with the chapter on employment policy (chapter 9), has to give particular attention to the issues, seldom far away in any discussion of social policy, of the impact of economic policy and of the relevance of economic and commercial considerations.

Whilst housing and employment are two policy areas where social and economic issues are particularly mingled together, they are not alone; social issues arise, for example, in relation to many aspects of environment policy and transport policy.

A chapter on education policy is included in this book (chapter 8). This is often not examined by social policy texts. The very fact that it is difficult to find reasons either for including it or for excluding it tells us something about the peculiarly arbitrary process involved in categorizing policies as 'social'. Clearly, the field of education is one in which there is a considerable amount of public expenditure upon services that contribute to public welfare. But is the hallmark of social policy expenditure its contribution to public welfare, and what does this really mean? If education policy is included, why not also include leisure policy or environment policy? In fact, the inclusion of education, and the exclusion of leisure and the environment, is the consequence of a comparatively arbitrary decision based upon a conventional view of the limits to social policy which is clearly open to challenge (see Cahill, 1994, for such a challenge).

In the introduction one of the problems about a straightforward definition of social policy which equates it with state activity to influence public welfare was mentioned: namely, that it is important not to let this lead to the false assumption that it is only state activity which influences or promotes welfare. But there is another problem. To see policies as having objectives involves confusing the character of the policies with the motives and purposes of the people who advocate, adopt and implement them. Policies proclaimed to be 'social' may advance welfare; but they may also be instruments for securing other objectives, which may be detrimental to people's well-being.

Several influential discussions of social policy have suggested that welfare policies are promulgated not from humanitarian concerns to meet need, but as responses to social unrest. Piven and Cloward, for example, argue as follows about social security policies:

The key to an understanding of relief-giving is in the functions it serves for the larger economic and political order, for relief is a secondary and supportive institution. Historical evidence suggests that relief arrangements are initiated or expanded during the occasional outbreaks of civil disorder produced by mass unemployment, and are then abolished or contracted when political stability is restored. . . . this view clearly belies the popular supposition that government social policies, including relief policies, are becoming progressively more responsible, humane and generous. (Piven and Cloward, 1972, p. xiii)

Piven and Cloward are primarily concerned to explain relief policies in the United States, but they draw on English data too, and they clearly intend their analysis to apply to other countries. Other writers have analysed British policies in similar terms. In particular, Marxists have argued that advanced capitalist societies require an infrastructure of welfare policies to help maintain order, buy off working-class protest and secure a work-force with acceptable standards of health and education (see, for example, O'Connor, 1973; Gough, 1979). Other radical analyses of social policy have seen social policy as sustaining not only class-based patterns of domination, but also patriarchy and racial inequality (see Williams, 1989).

Clearly, perspectives like these give a very different meaning to 'welfare'. Policies that promote welfare are explained in terms of social control; they are measures to combat disorder and crime, just like police and penal policies, or measures to legitimize and prop up the capitalist system. But it is not necessary to accept totally this interpretation of public policy in order to agree that there may be circumstances under which social control motives mingle with humanitarian motives in creating what we describe as 'social policies'. Moreover, the more extreme interpretations of the origins of social policies that have been mentioned do not exhaust the range of possibilities. Contemporary studies of both policy-making and policy implementation suggest that we need to give attention to some very complex relationships between the mixed goals of those able to influence policies and the varied consequences of their interventions. Outcomes may be the unintended results of policy inputs. Most policy is incremental in character, involving marginal adjustments to what has gone before and being motivated to correct what are seen as undesirable consequences of previous policies. Accordingly, social policy need not be interpreted in terms either of the continual evolution of a welfare state inspired by humanitarian ideals or of a conspiracy to manipulate a powerless proletariat. Yet the rejection of these interpretations need not imply either that individuals with altruistic motives play no part in the evolution of policy, or that manipulative and social control-motivated actions are not involved in the policy process.

This discussion implies three things for the definition of social policy:

1 that the policies that are identified as 'social' should not be interpreted as if they were conceived and implemented with only the welfare of the public in mind;
2 that other policies, not conventionally identified as social policies, may make a comparable, or even greater, contribution to welfare;
3 that public policy should be seen as a whole in which social policies are significantly interlinked with other policies.

Just because it is convenient to single out some policies for special attention, and just because there are courses on social policy that require the study of a specific and limited range of public policies, we should not therefore fall into the trap of seeing these as the main government contributions to welfare, or the 'general good'. Let us look at the implications of these arguments a little more by examining the implications, for welfare and for social policy, of policy developments in those important policy areas that no one defines as social policy: foreign and defence policy, and economic policy.

It is important to recognize that the origins of the modern nation-state lie in the achievement of a monopoly of force within a given territory. The central policy preoccupations of the government of any insecure nation are with the defence of its boundaries, the recognition of its integrity by other nations, and the maintenance of order within its territories. It is only too easy for British students of public policy to lose sight of the importance of these issues. They are the daily fare of our news bulletins, but we rarely stop to think about their relevance for our own state. Incomprehension over events in Northern Ireland and a propensity to underestimate the intensity of the feelings of some people in Scotland on the issue of devolution stem from a tendency to take the integrity and security of the nation for granted. Yet, without a secure nation-state the scope for development of what is convention-ally identified as social policy is severely limited.

These facts have three implications for the study of social policy:

1 Social policy expenditure has to compete with other public expendi-ture dedicated to the defence of the realm. The case against heavy defence expenditure cannot rest simply on arguments that some of that money would be better spent on social policy; it is necessary to prove that some of that expenditure is inappropriate or irrelevant, or to face the argument that without it no social policy would be secure.

2 The forms of this defence expenditure have a wide range of social effects in creating employment, disrupting family life and so on. Readers may like to think about the sort of policy interactions involved by asking themselves what would be the effects upon social life and social policy of the reintroduction of a two-year period of compulsory national service. The important effects they should be able to identify will nevertheless be insignificant by comparison with the effects of mobilization for war itself.

3 While social policies do not have much of an impact on relations with other states, it is important not to lose sight of the contribution they make to integration and harmony within the nation. It is this that has led students of social policy to draw attention to the significant impact of war upon policy. Thus Titmuss argued: 'The aims and content of social policy, both in peace and in war, are thus determined – at least to a substantial extent – by how far the co-operation of the masses is essential to the successful prosecution of war' (Titmuss, 1958, p. 86).

The development of the role of the British state in the nineteenth and twentieth centuries is often portrayed as the establishment of 'the welfare state'. To present it in this way is to emphasize social policy developments. But it is perhaps more important to give attention to the growth of the British economy over that period, and to the role played by government in relation to that economy. Two apparently conflicting political interpretations of these events lead us to ask some broadly similar questions about the relationship between social policy and economic policy.

To the followers of the 'classical economists', who argued that the economy would make the greatest possible contribution to public welfare if competition were to remain unshackled, the period between the middle of the nineteenth century and the present day has been marked by extensive government interference with the economy. Some of this interference has been seen as necessary, where competition has been impossible or illogical. Some of it has been seen as justifiable, because it seeks to ensure competition and prevent monopoly. But much of it has been regarded as stemming from forces eager to interfere with and undermine the market economy, shifting the locus of decision from the market-place to the political arena.

Theorists influenced by Marxism, on the other hand, interpret the same evidence the other way round. They argue that as the industrial economy has grown, so the 'contradictions of capitalism' have increased. Government intervention has been prompted in their view by a desire to save capitalism, not by a desire to undermine it.

Regulation has been introduced to prevent the logic of competition from destroying the system. State interventions to protect the working class have been designed, according to this view, to stave off revolution and help the capitalist system to survive. Late capitalist society, it is argued, experiences a form of 'welfare capitalism' in which those who originally gained so much from competitive industry are still dominant in our society.

Both these views of the relationship between government and the economy stress the extent to which social policy should be seen as dependent upon, or even a derivative of, economic policy. The key internal political issues of our age are who controls our economy, and how the rewards that stem from our industrial achievements are to be distributed. The implications for social policy are as follows:

1 that the main determinants of welfare are economic;
2 that the government's role in diverting resources into social policies must be seen to be closely interrelated with – even dependent upon – the role it plays in the management of the economy;
3 that social policies will be determined by views about the way the economy does, or should, operate.

Specific social policies need, therefore, to be understood in terms of their relationships to economic policies.

The following are some examples of important questions frequently asked about social policy which are essentially about the relationship between social and economic policy:

Are social security policies redistributive?

How far do the redistributive effects of social security operate beyond minimal insurance limits?

How does any redistribution by this mechanism compare with redistribution that occurs through other economic mechanisms – the effects of competition, the impact of unemployment and the results of wage bargaining, for example?

What are the effects of public housing upon the housing market?

How far are market forces in this area more influential than state intervention in determining who gets what housing?

It is important to take a wide view of social policy development, relating it to economic policy. Social policy expenditure amounts to about two-thirds of all public expenditure (see chapter 11). To what extent are there limits to the growth of public expenditure in a mixed economy, and therefore what impact may such limits (or the belief that there are such limits) have upon social policy expenditure? Similarly, what is the impact upon the economy, and also upon the whole political system, of the pattern of employment that has emerged as social policy has become 'big business'? Unlike those stressed above, these are questions about the impact of social policy upon economic policy, rather than the other way round. Nevertheless, the key decisions about resources for the social policy sector will be regarded as economic policy decisions.

It has been suggested, then, that, while certain policy areas, subject to a few difficult boundary problems, are defined as social policy, any proper understanding of the forces that determine outcomes in these areas must rest upon considerations of other policies not included within the conventional social policy rubric.

But the introductory comment on the definition of social policy also indicated that the state is not the only body which may have 'policies', and that social welfare depends upon much more than state action. Our welfare depends also upon our own actions, our job opportunities, the support we get from families and friends, and upon the activities of a range of non-state institutions (churches, charities, community organizations, trade unions and so on). An examination of *state* social policy, as in this book, must have regard to the things the state does to support or interfere with these other sources of social welfare. Much ideological debate about social policy is about what the state should or should not do to influence the activities of individuals as economic actors, to affect the roles played by families or to alter the legal framework within which voluntary organizations operate. Whilst the ideological 'colour' of much of that debate derives from alternative views about the management of the economy, considerations regarding the implications of policies (or their absence) for gender and ethnic divisions in society are also important.

STUDYING SOCIAL POLICY

Social policy may be studied in a number of ways. We may merely set out to determine the main policies in the areas in which we are interested; for example:

What is the system of social security?

What benefits does the health service provide?

How has the government intervened in the housing market?

These and similar questions need to be answered by those who want
to understand social policy. They can also be related to many other
points about the way the services are organized and administered.
Hence the simplest approach to the study of social policy is to describe
the policies and institutions that together make up the system of social
services.

Many accounts of the system of social policy include comments on
the strengths and weaknesses of specific policies. They relate what there
is to what, in the authors' views, there ought to be. The study of social
policy, as it has developed in Britain, has been concerned to examine
the extent to which the welfare state meets people's needs. Often,
indeed, students of social policy go further, and explicitly analyse the
extent to which it contributes to social equality. In this sense an
academic discipline has been built up with an explicitly political stance.
Social policy is seen as concerned with the alleviation of social ills;
its objectives are accepted at face value; and it is analysed in terms
of its success in achieving them. Many who have written about social
policy have done so from the standpoint of Fabian socialism, concerned with incremental social change to create a more equal society.
Few challenged this perspective until the 1980s, when Conservative
political thinking shifted sharply to the 'right', to express much more
directly suspicion of the claims of the state to regulate many aspects of
our lives and to portray welfare policy as a threat to economic
enterprise.

There has been an extensive debate among social scientists about the
extent to which the analysis of society and of social institutions can be
'value-free'. Broadly, there is today a consensus that there are limits to
the extent to which those who study and write about society can set
aside their own commitments and prejudices. Some go on to argue,
however, that value-freedom within the social sciences as a whole may
be achieved by the interplay of arguments and evidence, each biased in
different ways but contributing to the advancement of unbiased
knowledge as a whole. Others are more sceptical about the extent to
which a body of systematic unbiased knowledge can be built up, and
argue that the value problem is ubiquitous. The study of social policy
has been particularly conspicuous for the specific political or value
commitments of those who write about it.

The strong normative bias in the study of social policy has led at times
to a greater preoccupation with criticism of policies than with attempts
to discover why they take the forms they do. In practice, if one believes
that policies are wrong or ineffective, it is important to understand why
this is so, particularly if one's objective is to change them. The view that
it is sufficient to point out that policies are 'wrong' is often linked with

a view of policy-making according to which men and women of good will are believed to be responsible and anxious to rectify the unwitting mistakes made in the past. This approach to the understanding of the policy system was criticized above.

At this stage, as an author who is arguing that the study of social policy in Britain has been strong on criticism and value-judgement, but weak on analysis, I should make my position clear. Since I believe that students may be aided in drawing their own conclusions if writers make their own value biases explicit, it is particularly important to do this. Broadly, I am deeply concerned about the content of social policy, and have contributed (particularly on social security and housing policies and on measures for the unemployed) to the 'Fabian' critique of policy outlined above. I should not pretend that my personal motivation in studying social policy is not linked with a commitment to non-revolutionary movement towards social equality. However, I feel strongly that a concern to influence the content of social policy must be supported by an understanding of how social policy is made. In this book, therefore, I am concerned with what social policy is, how it was created and how it was implemented, as well as with its weaknesses and arguments about what it should be.

An understanding of the factors that influence the character of social policy must rest upon several foundations. Some attention must be given to the social and economic conditions that create the need for social policies. This is a difficult chicken-and-egg issue. One cannot simply look at the kinds of problems thrown up by particular social structures and economic situations and analyse policies as responses to those problems, since policies themselves influence the character of the societies in which they are adopted. For example, government provision of housing may be seen as a response to the inadequacies of the market as a provider of houses, but it has also transformed the character of that market. Interactions between policies and society are complex. It is important, therefore, to draw upon economics and sociology to help with the understanding of what occurs. It is also necessary to keep in mind the historical dimensions to these issues.

But social policy-making must also be seen as a political process. It has already been stressed that social policy cannot be analysed on its own, without reference to other activities of the state. Policies must be understood as products of politics, and attention must be given to the policy creation roles of politicians, civil servants, pressure groups and the electorate. Policies must also be seen as to a considerable extent products of other policies. There is a cumulative process to be analysed in which policies create needs for other policies, opportunities for other policies, and new social situations for further political responses. It will be clear that to understand social policy, considerable attention must be given to the findings of political science.

An often neglected part of the study of policy is the examination of its implementation. The actual impact of any policy upon the public will depend upon how it is interpreted and put into practice. The implementation process throws light on the strength and weaknesses of a policy, and experience at the implementation end (by junior officials and the public) gets fed back into the policy process to influence future policy change. An understanding of these issues requires the student of social policy to give some attention to organization theory and to the study of administrative law.

A particular characteristic of a state in which extensive social policies have been adopted is that it tends to be bureaucratic. The organizational complexity of such a state necessarily complicates the implementation process. Recent interventions in British social policy have involved the design of new approaches to policy delivery which aim to break out of the traditional bureaucratic approach, creating more flexible organizations and new kinds of public/private partnerships.

The portrait of the study of social policy as presented in the last few paragraphs shows that it is a subject that draws upon a number of different academic disciplines. The problem of defining the extent to which it is necessary to delve into these disciplines is like the problem discussed earlier of ascertaining the boundaries between social policy and other kinds of public policy. There is a need to make what we can of an essentially applied subject, hoping that we can gain what is required from other disciplines without going too deeply into them. The boundaries between all the social sciences are unclear. Sometimes this is a necessary feature of subjects that put some parts of the human experience under the microscope and must abstract this from other parts. But in other cases it is a result of historical accidents in the development of the disciplines, and if the study of society were to be initiated all over again, it would surely be divided rather differently. The study of social policy particularly hives off a specific area of social activity in a way that must violate subject boundaries. If it is important to understand a number of practical policies, because of a concern about their effects upon society, it is necessary to accept studies that cannot be defined in terms of a discrete intellectual discipline.

In setting out to examine what social policy is, and how it may be studied, some answers have been suggested to the question, 'Why study it?' Many who are required to study social policy are, or expect to be, involved in its implementation. The part of a social policy course that is concerned with describing and analysing policies and the institutions responsible for them has a clear face value to the social policy 'practitioner'. But, equally, it is important for such a person to understand something of the way in which social policy works, and the internal and external forces that shape policies.

It may also help to understand other agencies to which a 'practitioner' has to relate, particularly as a great deal of policy depends, or is intended to depend, upon successful co-operation between organizations. It has been stressed that no policy area is discrete, that policies in one area affect those in others. This is particularly true of social policies, whose impact upon the public depends upon the way they interrelate. Successful treatment of the sick requires attention to their housing and income maintenance problems; the care of the neglected child depends upon co-operation between health service workers, personal social services staff and schoolteachers; the homeless often face income maintenance problems as well as housing problems; and so on – the examples are legion.

Hence the most obvious case for studying social policy is a need for the staff of the various social services to understand the system in which they operate. But that is not all. A characteristic of many of the people who are drawn to work in the social services is a strong commitment to those services. Hence it is not surprising that the study of social policy has been deeply concerned with the improvement of policies. Many staff care considerably about the inadequacies of the policies they administer. But achieving policy change is never an easy process, particularly if one is a comparatively junior participant in a large organization. To make a contribution towards this end requires not only knowledge of alternatives and commitment to putting them into practice, but also an understanding of how social policy is made and implemented.

These arguments for studying social policy have been addressed to people likely to be employed in delivering benefits and services. I say 'employed'. However, recent changes to social policy have increased the extent to which private and voluntary organizations are involved in the delivery of social policy. As noted above, they have also made it very evident that many social welfare services are not delivered by state agencies, but are left to the slender resources of families, neighbourhoods and communities. Hence this is a book for all concerned citizens who want to influence social policy. Its underlying justification is that participation in policy-making, for a group of services of considerable importance to us all, must rest upon understanding: understanding of what the policies are, of how they are made and implemented, and of the implications of the many prevailing suggestions on how to change those policies.

SUGGESTIONS FOR FURTHER READING

A deeper exploration of the rather arid debate regarding the boundaries of this subject is not recommended. However, Cahill's *The New Social Policy* (1994) offers a valuable survey of the ways in which the traditional concerns of social policy analysis might be widened.

A good way to get into the key issues about social policy is to investigate the various ideological perspectives on its role in society. George and Wilding's *Ideology and Social Policy* (2nd edn, 1994) offers an excellent overview of this subject. Lois Bryson's *Welfare and the State* (1992) and Fiona Williams's *Social Policy* (1989) offer introductions to the ideological debate, with a strong emphasis upon the need to take into account issues about gender, class and race.

Good overviews of the competing perspectives on social policy can be found in two books by Mishra (1977 and 1984). A reader edited by Loney (1987) provides good examples of some of the key views.

CHAPTER 2

THE HISTORY OF SOCIAL POLICY

INTRODUCTION

This chapter deals with some of the key events in the development of British social policy, relating them to social, economic and political trends in our society. It is important to have a historical perspective, particularly on the relationship between social and political change, in order to understand the character of British social policy today.

At one level the story is simple. The growth of state involvement with the social welfare of its citizens can be related to the development of an industrial society and its subsequent maturation – or perhaps decline – into what some writers have described as 'post-industrialism' or 'post-modernism'. Alongside this industrial development are political developments, associated with the extension of suffrage, involving citizens more thoroughly in the activities of the state. Accompanying these are changes to social life, particularly family life, and changing views of the respective responsibilities of the individual, the family and the state for remedies to social problems. The result is a package of developments – of the state's role, the character of the economy, the nature of political processes and of ideologies – which those without a very dogmatic belief about the motive forces in political development find difficult to disentangle in cause–effect terms.

This version of the story of the development of the state's role in social welfare can be applied to a number of industrialized nations – to the United States, to most of the other countries of western and northern Europe and to Australasia – as much as to Britain (this theme has been widely analysed; see in particular Ashford, 1986; Esping-Andersen, 1990; Hill, 1996). But while these 'broad brush' features of the story must not be forgotten, it is important also to try to single out characteristics of Britain's development that help to explain the particular shape of its social policies. A proper understanding of this subject requires consideration of the general factors, which may apply to a distinct group of nations; the special factors, which are perhaps unique to one nation; and, furthermore, a number of factors that do not fall neatly into either of these categories. Included in this last group is, for example, the 'insurance principle' in social security, adopted in a variety of ways by various governments who clearly attempted to learn from each other's experiences (see Heclo, 1974; Baldwin, 1990).

DEVELOPMENTS BEFORE THE TWENTIETH CENTURY

In dealing with the relationship between past events and contemporary policies, it is always very difficult to know how far back to go in time. To understand British social policies, some consideration of the history of the poor-law, with its roots in Elizabethan legislation, is necessary. The Tudor age saw considerable population movements, with changes in agriculture, the growth of towns and some rudimentary developments in manufacturing. The government found it necessary to try to impose a centrally determined framework on what had hitherto been entirely local, often monastic, charitable initiatives. It placed responsibility for the poor upon each parish, with the requirement, under the Acts of Settlement, that the itinerant poor should be returned, if necessary, to their parishes of origin. The parishes were required to levy taxes on property known as 'rates' to provide for the relief of the poor.

The history of the poor-law between the sixteenth and twentieth centuries was one of attempts to make this work – for local initiative with broad guide-lines laid down centrally – despite social changes. As Britain became industrialized and urbanized, this strictly local system of administration came under strain. Population movements gradually rendered the Acts of Settlement obsolete. The tasks of the poor-law became more complex as parishes had to cope with, for example, trade recessions and outbreaks of infectious diseases, each affecting large numbers of people in the new towns and cities. By the middle of the nineteenth century developments in medicine offered a new challenge to the parish 'guardians' who had previously provided only the most rudimentary care to the sick.

The most significant nineteenth-century attempt to modernize the poor-law was the Poor-Law Amendment Act of 1834. This set up a national Poor-Law Commission to superintend the system, and formed the parishes into groups known as poor-law unions. This important step towards the development of a national system was only a limited success. However, its main contributions to the development of policy were the 'workhouse test' and the doctrine of 'less eligibility'. The aims of these were to curb indiscriminate 'outdoor' relief (that is, outside institutions). If the poor were not sufficiently desperate to enter the workhouse, they could not be really in need. The system was intended to ensure that those who received help were worse off ('less eligible') than the poorest people in work. In practice, many poor-law unions did not strictly enforce the workhouse test, and as the years passed, the elderly and the sick were increasingly given outdoor relief. Nevertheless, the elimination of the workhouse and the abolition of the means test adopted to confine relief-giving, became an important preoccupation of twentieth-century critics of the poor-law. The principle of less eligibility continues to influence decisions about relief today.

While the basic nineteenth-century response to poverty was to try to strengthen older institutions, some of the consequences of urbanization and industrialization posed problems for which entirely new responses were necessary. Measures were taken to curb the hours worked by women and children in factories, and to improve safety and working conditions. This significant development in state intervention in the economy seems to have come about as a result of a mixture of growing humanitarian concern and embryonic working-class pressure. The enforcement of this legislation was put into the hands of a central government inspectorate, the first of a number of such inspectorates to be set up in the nineteenth century and to operate, according to Roberts (1960), as an important source of pressure for further social reform.

The rapid spread of infection in areas where people were crowded together was, like the exploitation of child labour, not a new phenomenon. But in an increasingly urbanized society it took new forms which were more apparent to political opinion, and more threatening to life and industry; and there were very many more large populous areas devoid of the most elementary arrangements for disposing of waste or supplying pure water. Furthermore, it was only in the nineteenth century that scientific advance identified the main links between insanitary conditions and disease. In a few areas local government agencies took some steps to tackle this problem, but real progress did not come until central government gave local authorities powers to act effectively, and also required them to take such action.

Here, then, was an important area of government intervention, pushing local authorities to tackle some of the problems of their own areas. The local government system of the time had been given some shape by the Municipal Corporations Act of 1835, but it was not until the end of the century that it acquired a structure that would enable it to take on the range of functions it carries out today. In the nineteenth century, therefore, some reforms required local authorities to take action and to employ professional staff, such as the medical officers of health required by an Act of 1871. Others, however, set up *ad hoc* authorities to take on functions delegated by central government.

The evolution of state education during the nineteenth century provides a good example of a series of *ad hoc* responses. Religious societies had begun to become involved in the provision of inexpensive basic education for the children of the poor early in the century. By 1833 they had persuaded the government to provide a small grant towards this work. In 1839 the government set up an inspectorate to provide central supervision of the way the growing state aid was being spent. It was not until 1870, however, that the government moved forcefully into the provision of primary education. Motivated, it is widely believed, by a concern about the illiteracy of the growing electorate (the franchise had been considerably widened in 1867), but also undoubtedly by a recognition of a need for a better-educated work-force, Parliament provided that school boards, to set up state-financed schools, could be established where there was a clear educational need and the voluntary schools were insufficient in number. In 1880 a further Education Act made schooling compulsory for children between the ages of 5 and 10, and in the 1890s it was established that most elementary education should be free. During the last years of the century some of the school boards even became involved in secondary education, producing a confused pattern of educational growth that was to prompt government action at the beginning of the twentieth century.

Reference has already been made to the way in which developments in medicine began, in the late nineteenth century, to render inadequate the traditional poor-law approach to the care of the sick. Alongside the development of poor-law hospitals, many voluntary hospitals, assisted by charitable funds that enabled them to provide cheap or free services to the poor, were founded, or grew in strength from their earlier origins. The local authorities were also given powers to establish hospitals to fulfil their duties to contain infectious diseases and to care for the mentally ill. Medical care outside the hospitals grew in importance in the second half of the century, becoming more than the prerogative of the rich. This was partly a poor-law development, partly the extension of the services of the voluntary hospitals, and partly an aspect of the growth of insurance against misfortune widely invested in by the more prosperous of the working classes. In all, a very mixed package of health care measures was evolving. This complex mixture, dominated by a powerful medical profession firmly established during the nineteenth century, posed problems for subsequent attempts to rationalize the health services, and therefore influenced the shape that the National Health Service (NHS) eventually achieved.

At the end of the nineteenth century the verdict of the legal philosopher Dicey (1905) was that *laissez-faire* had given way to collectivism; that government had begun to assume a role in society that had taken Britain well on the way to becoming a socialist state. The factory legislation and the government intervention in the cause of health and safety implied important changes in the role of the state. The educational system at the primary (or, as it was known then, the elementary) level had received a crucial injection of public enterprise. The poor-law, on the other hand, had been changed but little. A need for new policies in that area was just beginning to become apparent at the end of the century, as scientific surveys (Booth, 1889–1903; Rowntree, 1901) and journalistic investigations charted the existence of severe problems of poverty caused by factors – in particular, sickness and old age – largely outside individual control.

It was stated earlier that the agencies set up during the nineteenth century to implement social policies were often *ad hoc* bodies. While local government was responsible for public health and for the rudimentary planning, housing and hospital functions required to help achieve more sanitary urban areas, education was made the responsibility of separately elected school boards. The poor-law came under yet another kind of authority, the boards of guardians, descendants of the former parish officials. However, legislation late in the century provided a new local government structure much better able to take on a wide range of functions. Local Government Acts in 1888 and 1894 set up a system of local authorities that was to remain almost unchanged until the 1970s. They gave a shape to local government, with a split between the highly urbanized areas and the rest of the country, that dominates local politics to this day. The less urbanized areas acquired a two-tier system of county government, accompanied by lower-tier urban and rural districts. In many urban areas county boroughs were set up as single all-purpose authorities. London acquired a special two-tier system of its own.

It is very convenient, for the presentation of historical accounts, when a specific date can be identified as a watershed. It adds further neatness when that date is the beginning of a century. While there is always an arbitrary aspect to the choice of such dates, particularly in social history, the dividing point between the nineteenth and twentieth centuries seems a particularly significant one. At this time the large working-class male element added to the electorate in 1885 was just beginning to influence political thinking. The Labour Representation Committee was set up in 1899 to try to get more working men elected to Parliament. This body was to turn itself into the Labour Party in 1906. The major political parties, the Conservatives and the Liberals, were increasingly aware of the need to compete for working-class support. For the Conservatives the formula was an interesting blend of imperialism and social reform (Semmel, 1961). The Liberals had a radical wing, temporarily disadvantaged by the conflict over home rule for Ireland and the jingoism of the Boer War, but ready to push the party towards acceptance of a package of new social measures.

Late in the nineteenth century Britain had begun to discover that an advanced industrial nation is vulnerable to alarming economic fluctuations, owing to the uncoordinated nature of much business decision-making and the international complications of the trade cycle. New competitors had also emerged, as other nations – particularly Germany, France and the United States – industrialized rapidly. The Empire still looked secure, but the competition for new trading outlets was increasing dramatically. At the same time as doubts were beginning to be felt about Britain's economic vulnerability, working people were increasingly organizing themselves into trade unions to try to secure, or guarantee, their share of the progress. The political price of economic failure was being raised. New initiatives to preserve the unity of the nation were required.

1900–1914

The period immediately before the First World War was dominated by a series of reforms adopted by the Liberal government after 1906. However, before those reforms are considered, two earlier events require comment. In 1902 the Conservatives passed an important Education Act. This passed the responsibility for state education from the school boards to the county and county borough councils, and devised a formula for the financial support of church schools that preserved a measure of voluntary control. The other important feature of this Act was that it legitimized expenditure on secondary and technical schools, and thereby stimulated the growth of this element of state education.

The other significant event was the Boer War. This rather inglorious episode in British imperial history had considerable significance for social policy. In general it led to a concern to examine what was wrong with *Great* Britain that she should have been unable to fight effectively against apparently fragile opposition. In particular, politicians, in this age when Britain's imperial success was believed to have been based upon racial superiority, sought to examine why so many volunteers to fight had been found to be unfit to do so.

An Interdepartmental Committee on Physical Deterioration was set up. It reported in 1904, urging the establishment of a school medical service and the provision of school meals within the public education system. Both these measures were adopted by the Liberals, and implemented soon after they came to power.

Before they lost office, the Conservatives had also responded to the growing evidence on the extent of poverty and the inadequacies of existing measures, by setting up a Royal Commission on the Poor Laws in 1905. The report of this body, which did not appear until 1909, contains a thorough discussion of British social policy at that time. There was both a majority and a minority report, and the latter provided a well-argued critique of the system. However, without waiting for the Royal Commission, the Liberal government decided to promote two pieces of legislation that significantly modified the role of the poor-law in the provision of social security: the Old Age Pensions Act of 1908 and the National Insurance Act of 1911.

These two pieces of legislation provide interesting contrasts in approaches to the provision of social security. The old-age pension was non-contributory, and based upon a simple test of means. It was an extension of the outdoor relief given by some boards of guardians, but its means test was a personal, not a family, one. The national insurance scheme, by contrast, was contributory but not means-tested. It provided cover against sickness and unemployment for some, initially limited, categories of workers. The contribution was to come jointly from the employee, the employer and the state. The sickness scheme provided not just cash benefits, but also medical treatment, from a 'panel' doctor who was remunerated on a 'capitation basis' in terms of the number of patients on his or her panel. The Friendly Societies and insurance companies, who were already involved in the provision of sickness cover for many working people, were allowed to participate as agents for the scheme and providers of additional benefits. The scheme protected only employees themselves, not any members of their families.

The National Insurance Act is most important for introducing the 'insurance principle' into British social security legislation. A number of European countries had adopted state or municipal insurance schemes during the last years of the nineteenth century. The British policy-makers were particularly aware of the German scheme. Heclo provides, in the following passage, an interesting account of the role played by Beveridge, one of the architects of the new scheme, in introducing insurance ideas:

In his first column for the *Morning Post,* February 16, 1906, he had dismissed contributory social insurance on the German pattern, as had all British investigating committees, with the standard view that it would require an 'un-British' amount of regulation of the individual. Beveridge, however, studied the German experiment more closely during the next year and concluded that the contributory insurance principle could not only reduce costs; it could also eliminate reliance on means tests. (Heclo, 1974, p. 81; see also Harris, 1977, on Beveridge's role)

The idea of social insurance had been adopted in the conservative society of Bismarck's Germany because it offered a low-cost mechanism to meet some social needs whilst committing workers, as contributors to their own benefits, to the social and economic *status quo*.

This adoption of the insurance principle had important consequences for the development of social policy. In various measures after 1911, governments extended benefits in ways that undermined the *true* insurance basis of the scheme. But the contributory principle remained an important political symbol, and from time to time attempts were made to return the scheme closer to its roots. It is always difficult to combine the hard-headed actuarial principles of insurance with a concern for effective, comprehensive social security; yet, as Beveridge recognized, when the only viable political alternative is means-testing, the contributory principle has a great appeal.

The 1911 National Insurance Act had implications for more than social security policy, in two ways. The provision of medical services under the sickness benefit scheme used a model for the state payment of general practitioners that has continued in the National Health Service to the present day. Abel-Smith (1976, ch. 2) has pointed out that before 1911, doctors were in conflict with the Friendly Societies about the conditions under which they were hired to care for members. Hence they were predisposed to secure contracts under the state scheme which preserved their freedom. This right to operate as independent contractors, rather than as salaried servants of the state, has been zealously preserved by general practitioners.

It is also important to recognize the National Insurance Act as the sort of response to the problem of unemployment that has remained dominant in Britain. The early years of the twentieth century saw a number of small experiments in combating unemployment by providing publicly subsidized work. Yet these did not achieve any scale, perhaps because of suspicions of their implications for state involvement in the economy. There was, however, one measure, adopted in 1908, the Labour Exchange Act, that came to assume importance. The National Insurance Act gave the newly set-up exchanges the role of administering the system of unemployment benefit. This was the activity with which they came to be most closely identified. The hallmark of the British response to defects in the working of the labour market became the provision of relief to the unemployed, not the creation of special work programmes or measures to facilitate movements of workers between jobs (see Harris, 1972).

The Liberal government could, of course, have developed its social security measures to redistribute incomes without either means tests or contributions. Neither then nor later have social security measures involved the wholesale redistribution of resources. However, both of the early schemes required quite large subventions from taxation. It is important, therefore, to bear in mind the significance of the budget that Lloyd George introduced in 1909 to finance both social welfare reforms and increased government expenditure on other matters such as defence, by increasing taxation and making it more income-related. This seems to have been the first occasion on which a British government's annual budget was presented, or perceived, as an instrument for the redistribution of income. This in itself is of note. Lloyd George, whose penchant for the rhetoric of class warfare gives a misleading impression of his readiness for the reality of such conflict, described the budget as follows: 'This is a war budget. It is for raising money to wage implacable warfare against poverty and squalidness.' The most controversial aspect of the budget was a group of measures to tax land. Lloyd George defended them by an aggressive verbal attack on the privileges of landowners:

> The ownership of land is not merely an enjoyment, it is a stewardship. It has been reckoned as such in the past, and if the landowners cease to discharge these functions, the time will come to reconsider the conditions under which land is held in this country. No country, however rich, can permanently afford to have quartered upon its revenue a class which declined to do the duty which it was called upon to perform. (Speech made in 1909)

Such was the populist rhetoric of the time. It did not usher in a revolution, but it helped to change the tenor of British politics. Inside Parliament the working-class interest was advanced by a comparatively cautious radical Liberal group, supported by an equally cautious small caucus of Labour MPs. Outside, Marxist socialism was beginning to be given attention by orators, and syndicalist trade unionists were beginning to flex their industrial muscles. Against all this, the land-owning interests – not, it should be noted, the industrialists – fought a rearguard action. The House of Lords threw out Lloyd George's budget. The consequence was the Parliament Act, with which the Lords eventually acquiesced after two general elections and the threat of mass creation of peers, which curbed the power of the Lords to block Commons legislation.

The events of 1909–11 have been given comparatively lengthy attention. The political balance in Britain tipped quite markedly at that time, with important implications for social policy. Such was the ferment of the times throughout Europe, and such was the rising volume of political controversy within Britain (bear in mind also the suffragette agitation and the conflict over the future of Ireland), that a more dramatic tipping of the balance than actually occurred in the next few years might have been expected. Certainly many new social policies were shortly to come, but these did little to disrupt the *status quo*; indeed, many must be seen as designed to preserve it.

1914–1939

It is important not to regard the development of social policy in Britain as simply involving two dramatic jumps forward in the periods 1906–11 and 1944–9. Between these a great deal happened to influence policies and to give them a character they often retain.

In the First World War Britain experienced conscription for the first time and the mobilization not only of the whole male work-force, but also of many women, hitherto not in employment, to assist the war effort. The war economy produced many domestic shortages. Initially the government was reluctant to impose controls and rationing, but its desire to curb wage rises and industrial unrest forced it to intervene. In general, then, the 'collectivist state' advanced considerably during this period. Civil servants learnt to carry out, and members of the public came to expect, government policies in areas of life never before influenced by state action. This was the general impact of war upon public policy. Its specific impact upon social policy was more limited. The imposition of controls upon private rents in 1915 was a rare, but significant, example of social policy innovation in this period.

However, during and at the end of the war the government made many promises for a better future. Even before the war ended, an Education Act was passed which recognized the case for state support for free education up to the age of 14. At the end of the war Lloyd George promised 'homes fit for heroes', and one of the first pieces of post-war legislation was a Housing Act that provided government subsidies to local authorities to build houses for the working classes. This Act, known as the Addison Act after its sponsor, the Minister of Health, while not the first legislation to allow local authority house building, was the first to subsidize it. It effectively initiated a pro-gramme of council house building that continued, albeit subject to regular modification as governments changed the subsidy arrange-ments, until the late 1970s. After the Addison Act both of the minority Labour governments, in power in 1924 and 1929–31, extended the local authority house-building programme by means of further subsidies. In the 1930s there was a shift in housing policy, with the government encouraging local authorities to put their emphasis in house provision upon clearing the slums. The strict rent control, introduced in the war to protect private tenants, was partly lifted during the inter-war period. But with this, as with council-house building, no real attempt was made until the 1980s to turn back the clock on processes that were ultimately totally to transform the character of Britain's housing market.

The evolution of relief policies for the unemployed in the inter-war years is an interesting story. Unemployment was a recurrent problem throughout this period. Immediately after the war the government mismanaged the discharge of servicemen back into civilian life, and unemployment rose rapidly. Then the economy picked up, and the problem abated. But this proved to be a temporary respite, and by 1921 registered unemployment was over 2 million. It remained over a million throughout the inter-war period, falling back a bit in the mid-1920s, but then rising steeply in 1930. By 1931 it was over 2 million again, and it did not fall below 2 million until 1936.

The 1911 National Insurance Act provided unemployment benefit only for workers in a limited number of trades which were not liable to extensive, prolonged unemployment. It also contained strict rules to protect the insurance fund. Benefits were dependent upon past contributions, and the duration of weekly payments to individuals was limited. The scheme was not designed to provide widespread relief in a period of mass unemployment. Gilbert, in his detailed study of social policy in this period, has shown that politicians were alarmed by the reports they received of unrest and agitation among the ranks of the unemployed (Gilbert, 1970). They were particularly conscious of the expectation by ex-soldiers that they would receive generous treatment from the government. Hence the government faced a dilemma. They resolved it by breaching the strict insurance principles and extending the scope of the unemployment benefit scheme.

It would be inappropriate here to set out all the convolutions in public policy on relief for the unemployed. What a whole succession of ministers and official committees had to try to resolve was the conflict between the demand for economy in government expenditure and the rising cost of an insurance benefit scheme no longer entirely restrained by insurance rules. Broadly, the compromise reached was extended but not unlimited insurance benefits, the operation of strict and quite unrealistic tests to ensure that people were 'genuinely seeking work' (a measure particularly aimed at unemployed females) (Deacon, 1976), the use of additional means-tested benefits known then as 'doles', and acceptance that the poor-law authorities would give extensive 'outdoor' relief to the unemployed. Eventually rationalization came, in 1934, when a unified national means-test scheme for benefits additional to insurance benefits was devised, to be administered by the Unemployment Assistance Board (UAB). This new organization was the forerunner of the National Assistance Board set up in 1948. The UAB provided a model that enabled central government to take over the functions of the poor-law agencies. It transferred responsibility for means-tested benefits for the unemployed to this national organization in 1934, added similar benefits to the elderly to its responsibilities in 1940, and added most other cash aid in 1941. By 1948, when it was finally killed, the poor-law was all but dead already.

The demise of the poor-law was also assisted by another piece of legislation in this period, the Local Government Act of 1929. This handed over responsibility for the poor-law from the boards of guardians to the local authorities. As far as the administration of relief was concerned, this made little difference; the public assistance committees of the local authorities could be regarded as broadly the guardians under another name. However, the hand-over of powers brought the institutions that had evolved from the old workhouses into the hands of authorities that could more effectively bring them up to date. This was particularly important for the hospitals, since a unified public service could now be provided. This was an important step towards a National Health Service, though in practice few authorities did much to modernize their facilities. Instead, the transformation of the hospital service awaited the special arrangements that were made to co-ordinate their activities with those of the voluntary hospitals during the Second World War.

While little attempt was made to alter the character of the patchwork of health services available in the inter-war period, all the parties that were to be involved in their transformation in the 1940s were beginning to examine the weaknesses of the existing provision and to formulate alternatives. In view of the importance of medical acquiescence in the system eventually adopted, it was probably necessary for many doctors to become aware of the need for change.

Education services similarly went through a phase of detailed examination of their weaknesses and future potential during the inter-war period. Here, however, the roles given to the local authorities by the Acts of 1902 and 1918 left scope for innovation where money allowed. The teaching profession grew in strength at this time, developing a formal system of training to replace the nineteenth-century pupil-teacher system. Education beyond the primary stage grew in various ways, and this part of the system was ready for rationalization by the end of the 1930s.

This section has described the inter-war period as a period of consolidation in social policy. But at least one really significant innovation occurred, the development of a public housing sector, and the inroads made into poor-law were of considerable significance for the future. One other element of this that deserves a brief mention was the adoption in 1925 of a contributory pension scheme to run alongside the non-contributory one.

This period is often thought of as one of failure in British politics, of failure to cope with the rise of Hitler and Mussolini abroad and failure to deal with unemployment at home. But it was also a period in which complete adult suffrage was achieved, and in which a political consensus was built up that enabled the Labour Party to establish itself alongside the older parties, so that an element of working-class power developed without turning into a revolutionary force. The key Conservative politicians of that age, Baldwin and Chamberlain, were very much men of the 'consensus', eager to promote cautious innovation in social policy. The key Labour politician, Ramsay MacDonald, was equally eager to occupy the middle ground. Some historians of the period regard this consensus politics as another of the failures of this age, urging that the compromises by the Left prevented radical change from occurring. Its significance for social policies, however, was that it created a platform for changes to occur in the 1940s, changes that secured very widespread social and political acceptance.

THE 1940s

The government was very much more ready to mobilize all the nation's resources in the Second World War than it had been in the First. Regulation and rationing were not adopted reluctantly, but as measures essential to the war effort. Politically, at least after Churchill replaced Chamberlain as Prime Minister in 1940, the nation was more united. The Labour Party regained its self-confidence, after being deserted by its leaders, who formed a national government and then heavily defeated Labour in a general election in 1931. It regarded attention to social policies as one of the conditions of its involvement in a coalition government. Although Churchill sometimes appeared to be unhappy about it, planning for the peace was widely accepted as a legitimate political task during the war. But before looking at the two most important examples of planning for peace, the Beveridge Report and the Butler Education Act of 1944, it is important to note a number of ways in which peacetime policy changes were foreshadowed by *ad hoc* wartime measures. In the last section reference was made to the way in which the Unemployment Assistance Board, which was renamed the Assistance Board in 1940, took over various functions from the public assistance committees in the early part of the war. Mention was also made of the integration of the hospital services during the war, under the Emergency Hospital Scheme. The evacuation of children called for the development of special services, foreshadowing developments in child care practice after the war. Rents were again strictly controlled, and empty houses were requisitioned. The wartime state had many of the characteristics of the welfare state, which is popularly regarded as having been created after the war.

The Beveridge Report was the report of a committee, chaired by one of the architects of the 1911 National Insurance Act, on *Social Insurance and Allied Services*, published in 1942. This recommended the adoption of a contributory social security system which improved on the existing system by protecting all citizens against sickness, unemployment and old age. The new system should, it was argued, include family allowances, maternity benefits and provision for widows. The contribution principles should be insurance ones, involving the employee, the employer and the state, as before; but the coverage of the scheme should be universal, and therefore involve a national pooling of risks. There was, in the arrangements for dependants and widows, inevitably built into the scheme certain assumptions about the male bread-winner and his relationship to the family unit, which have left a difficult legacy for attempts to balance the interests of men and women in our own age.

Beveridge argued that other social policies were necessary to underpin his insurance scheme. Support for children would be necessary through a universal 'family allowance' scheme. A system of means-tested assistance would be necessary as a 'safety net' for the minority whose needs were not adequately covered by the scheme. The maintenance of full employment would be essential to enable social insurance to work properly. A universal health service should take over the provision for medical care in the old insurance scheme, and effectively underpin the new one.

Beveridge's insurance scheme was broadly put into legislation. Family allowances were provided by one of the last measures of the coalition government. Most of the rest was enacted by the post-war Labour government, though there was a crucial departure from the insurance principle in that the qualifying period for a full pension was very short. This deviation from Beveridge's plan made the scheme expensive to general taxation, and probably tended to prevent the adoption of benefit levels sufficient to provide subsistence incomes to those with no other resources and to inhibit subsequent increases to keep up with the cost of living.

The Education Act passed in 1944 and often identified by the name of the minister responsible, R. A. Butler, provided the framework for the education system until 1988. The Butler Act provided for universal free state secondary education, but did not specify the form it should take or rule on whether or not there should be selective schools.

At the end of the war the coalition broke up. In the ensuing general election both parties promised substantial social policy reforms, but the electorate swung strongly towards the Labour Party, rejecting the old war-leader Churchill in favour of Labour's clearer commitment to a vision of the welfare state. The social security reforms embodied by the Labour Party in the National Insurance Act of 1946 and the National Assistance Act of 1948 have already been mentioned. With the adoption of these measures came the abolition of the poor-law, its income-maintenance responsibilities going to the National Assistance Board and its responsibilities for residential care and other welfare services going to local authority welfare departments.

In 1946 the creation of the National Health Service provided another crucial innovation in social policy. General practitioner and hospital services were provided free for everyone, in a complex structure designed to unify the hospital sector, while leaving general practitioners as independent contractors, and other community services in the control of the local authorities. This structure was achieved after hard bargaining between the minister, Aneurin Bevan, and the doctors, who were deeply suspicious of state medicine (see Eckstein, 1960; Pater, 1981). The scheme was funded out of general taxation, though an element of payment for the health service remained in the national insurance contribution, creating a confusing illusion that this was what paid for the service. The notion of a totally free service did not last for long. Very soon, Chancellors of the Exchequer, exploiting concern that demand for services was much greater than expected, secured first small payments for spectacles and dental treatment, and then prescription charges, as ways of raising revenue.

Among these widely publicized social policy reforms came another measure, with much less impact upon the general public, but nevertheless with important implications: the Children Act of 1948. The origins of this reform of services for deprived children seem to have been in a child care scandal, the O'Neill case, which led to the setting up of the Curtis Committee to investigate contemporary practice (Packman,

1975, ch. 1). The Children Act consolidated the existing child care legislation, and created departments in which professional social work practice would develop in child care, and in due course in work with families.

The Labour government of 1945–51 did not alter the system of subsidizing local authority housing developed in the inter-war period, but it did, by the Housing Act of 1949, substantially extend the subsidies available. The Act formally removed the limitation confining local authority provision to housing for the 'working classes'. The government's concern throughout the late 1940s was to stimulate building, to make up for the deficiencies in housing stock arising from bomb damage and the wartime standstill in house building. However, post-war shortages of materials made it difficult to accelerate new building. The Labour government laid its emphasis upon local authority housing, rather than on private building for sale. It also involved itself, as no government ever had before, in an attempt to secure effective land-use planning and to curb land speculation. The Town and Country Planning Act of 1947 provided a grand design for this purpose, though one of limited success, which was subsequently dismantled by the Conservatives. Another crucial planning innovation, with major implications for the provision of public housing, was the New Towns Act of 1946. This provided jobs and houses in new communities for people from overcrowded cities and run-down industrial areas.

Government involvement in the planning of the use of national resources, which had been one of the necessities of wartime, was continued by the Labour government as a matter of principle. This in itself was important in enlarging the involvement of government with many aspects of life in Britain. There was a commitment to the maintenance of full employment, with the Keynesian doctrine (Keynes, 1936) that budgetary management could achieve this now a matter of economic orthodoxy. In the 1940s such economic management was slightly inflationary, but this was broadly seen as a reasonable price to pay for full employment and economic growth. In retrospect it is hard to judge the extent to which the success of this policy (and, for all the worries it caused at the time, it was a success by comparison with the economic management disasters of either the 1920s and 1930s or the 1960s and 1970s) was due to good management, and the extent to which it was due to external and internal economic factors outside government control, in particular the post-war recovery and the stimulus provided by the continuing military activity of the 'cold war' (see Cairncross, 1985).

The 1940s were, in both war and peace, crucial years for the building of the system of social policy that Britain has today. But it has been shown that few of the innovations of this period were without precedent in the policies of earlier years, and that much of the crucial thinking about the form which these new institutions should take had been done in the inter-war period. Continuity is also evident in the behaviour of the two major political parties. The Butler Education Act and the Family Allowances Act were both measures of the Conservative-dominated wartime coalition. Preliminary work had also been done during the war on ideas for the social security scheme, and plans had begun to be drafted for a health service.

Political continuity is also apparent in the fact that the Conservatives did comparatively little, on returning to power in 1951, to dismantle the welfare state. The Labour Party policies that they did contest, and partly reverse, were its nationalization policies, not its social welfare ones. Otherwise, they shifted the house-building emphasis from public to private building, but by no means eliminated a substantial public element from their enlarged building programme; they were marginally more ready to increase health service charges; and they were, perhaps, rather slow to raise social security benefits. In the later 1950s they encouraged education services to flourish; and some local authorities began to innovate in this policy area in ways that in due course came to be regarded as radical and politically contentious.

SINCE THE 1940s

The presentation of policies in this section will be sketchy, because they are generally covered more fully in the appropriate detailed chapter later in the book. The aim here is to give the flavour of the key developments in this period as part of the history of social policy.

Broadly, the period 1951–95 can be divided into four:

1951–64, a period of comparatively little social policy innovation, which may be regarded as a time of consolidation or stagnation, according to one's political viewpoint;

1964–74, a period of fairly intense policy change stimulated by both political parties, in which considerable difficulties were experienced in translating aspirations into practice;

1974–9, a period in which rapid inflation, rising unemployment and government by the Labour Party without a parliamentary majority administered a severe shock to the political and social system, and to all who believed that there was still a need for developments in social policy;

1979–95, when much more explicitly anti-welfare state Conservative administrations reinforced that shock by deliberately treating inflation as more deserving of its attention than unemployment, attacking public services which were seen as inhibiting economic recovery and seeking ways to 'privatize' public services.

Bearing these points in mind, this section will look at developments in each of the main policy areas over the whole period. The many changes since 1979 could have been made the subject of a separate section. However, that would have detached them from the discussion of related policy changes occurring immediately before. Instead, therefore, a separate section will sum up the recent period, with reference to the dramatic economic and political changes which occurred. These have been seen by some as creating a 'crisis' for social policy and the demise of the British welfare state.

Housing

The period 1951–64 was a boom period for house building, both private and public. It was during this time that two kinds of tenure began to dominate in Britain: owner occupation and local authority tenancy. The decline in the size of the privately rented sector was rapid, and towards the later part of this period it was accelerated by slum clearance. In 1957 the government, believing that the private rental market could be revived if rent controls were removed, passed a Rent Act that allowed some decontrol. The main impact of this measure was that many landlords used the freedom to evict that was allowed under decontrol to sell previously let properties for owner occupation. In the 1960s the Labour government legislated to restore security of tenure and to allow rent levels to rise only to levels that fell short of market prices.

When Labour returned to power, they were committed to reversing the emphasis upon building for owner occupation within the building boom; but they also wanted to produce even more houses per annum. The use of restraints upon building investment as an economic regulator to prevent excess domestic demand made it difficult for them to achieve their targets. By the end of the 1970s, the additions to the housing stock had been so considerable that arguments were increasingly heard that Britain had enough houses. What complicated this debate was the question of whether there were enough houses of the right kind in the right places. Certainly some of the earlier building activity may have been misplaced effort. In particular, many local authorities produced poor-quality, industrially built high-rise flats which were hard to let (Dunleavy, 1981).

Another of Labour's policy commitments was to try again, like their predecessors in 1946, to do something to rationalize planning and curb the activities of land speculators. While the central problem here was unrestrained inner-city office and commercial development, the concern about this issue also had implications for owner-occupied housing.

Politicians of both parties became, by the late 1960s, increasingly concerned to stimulate owner occupation. Tax relief was used to assist borrowing. In the 1980s changes to financial markets led to growth in the availability of finance for buyers. The growth of house prices fed a belief that there was little risk in mortgage borrowing. Then, at the end of that decade and in the early 1990s, the combination of a new recession and government efforts to combat inflation (including a reduction in tax relief on mortgages) led to a fall in house prices. Many buyers, particularly those who lost jobs, found themselves in 'negative equity' situations in which their houses had fallen in value and their mortgage repayments were hard to meet.

When they came to power in 1970, the Conservatives decided that public expenditure on local authority housing needed to be curbed. Their Housing Finance Act of 1972 set out to adapt the 'fair rent' principle, which Labour had applied to private rents in the 1960s, to the local authority sector. They linked this with a national rent rebate scheme, rationalizing the variety of local schemes that had been set up over the previous decade, to offset the costs to poorer tenants. This Act was designed to reduce the general subsidy to council tenants; it was linked to changes in the system of national subsidies to local authorities designated to phase out indiscriminate help of this kind in due course. Labour opposed this measure, and limited its impact; but, on returning to power in 1979, the Conservatives, by reducing new expenditure on public housing, modifying the subsidy formula and encouraging rents to rise, set out to eliminate most subsidies to public housing other than means-tested benefits (housing benefit) for individual occupiers. Measures at the end of the 1980s prevented local government subsidy of council housing, and accelerated the rate at which central subsidies were withdrawn.

In addition, legislation enacted in 1980 to give local authority and housing association tenants a 'right to buy' has also made extensive inroads into the system of public housing. An Act passed in 1988 sought further to dismantle the system of local authority-owned public housing. It aimed to replace it by a mixture of housing associations, tenant co-ownership schemes and private landlords. In practice, the government faced difficulties in implementing this legislation. Tenants and local authorities were often resistant to change, and private capital was not particularly eager to move in. At the time of writing, a new initiative to encourage the voluntary transfer of local authority houses to housing associations is being considered by Parliament.

Social Security

The Conservatives did little to change the social security system in the period 1951–64. Towards the end of the period, the two parties began to produce competing plans to superimpose an earnings-related pensions scheme on top of the inadequate flat-rate system. In 1959 the Conservatives introduced a very limited graduated pension scheme. In 1964 the Labour Party came to power committed to a much more comprehensive scheme. However, they failed to complete the preparation of this before they lost office in 1970. The Conservatives then took the idea up in a slightly more limited way; but Labour returned to power, and put their own scheme on the statute-book in 1975. This scheme provided for a mixed scheme of public and private pensions, with many of the better-paid, more secure groups of workers able to 'contract out' into private schemes so long as they were at least as good as the 'state earnings-related pensions' (SERPS). Conservative legislation in 1986 extended the scope for contracting out, allowing schemes, which do not necessarily compete favourably with the state scheme, and also reducing the benefits available under SERPS. This encouraged a rapid growth of private pensions schemes, including some which were very poorly protected. The collapse of some of these led in the early 1990s to further regulatory legislation.

In the early 1960s a number of academic studies were published showing that the welfare state had by no means abolished poverty (Cole and Utting, 1962; Lynes, 1962; Abel-Smith and Townsend, 1965). This 'rediscovery of poverty' would seem to be a function of an academic and political interest that had emerged, concerned to look at the adequacy of social policies. Indeed, it can be said to be a consequence, but also a cause, of the growth of the academic subject with which this book is concerned. It was not, at that time at least, a consequence of any particular social or economic change between the late 1940s and the early 1960s, except inasmuch as increased affluence for many highlighted the poverty of those left behind (Townsend, 1954; see also Townsend (ed.), 1970; Townsend, 1979; Holman, 1978). The emphasis upon the weaknesses of existing social security policies for the relief of poverty led to a reappraisal of those policies. The Labour government of 1964–70 made a number of changes, therefore. Some of the changes raised some people's incomes, and there were a number of increases in benefit rates. Inflation was increasing, however, and public resources were, as ever, limited and in great demand for a wide range of policy objectives.

The main social security policy changes in this period were the introduction in 1965 of earnings-related supplements to sickness and unemployment benefits and of a redundancy payments scheme. Also, in 1966 'national assistance' was replaced by 'supplementary benefits'. This reform was designed to remove the stigma of assistance by making rights to these means-tested benefits much clearer, particularly for pensioners.

One particular focus of attention in the debate about poverty was family poverty, and particularly the problems faced by the low wage-earner. The principle, adopted in 1834, that wages should not be subsidized had been carried forward in social security legislation, but the margin between the income of those in work and those out of work sometimes made the principle of less eligibility appear under threat. The Child Poverty Action Group (CPAG), a pressure group set up in the 1960s, urged governments to deal with this problem by increasing family allowances. These had fallen in value, in real terms, since little effort had been made to update them properly. However, the conventional political view at that time was that family allowances were an unpopular, indiscriminate hand-out. CPAG sought to persuade the government that family allowances could be increased at the expense of child tax allowances. This approach was gradually accepted, though not before inflation had reduced the tax threshold so low that most poor wage-earners were also benefitting from the tax allowances. In the 1970s the Conservatives floated an alternative approach, a form of negative income tax called 'tax credits' (HMSO, 1972), and implemented a means-tested benefit for poor wage-earners, 'family income supplement'. Labour, on return to power in 1974, decided to press on with the development of a new family allowance scheme, called 'child benefit', designed to replace the older allowance, extend it to the first child in each family, and offset it against the abolition of tax allowances (see McCarthy, 1986, for a discussion of these developments). But it did not abolish family income supplement.

On first returning to power in 1979, the Conservatives set out to make piecemeal adjustments to the social security system. They reduced the value of contributory benefits by altering the procedure for inflation-related increases and by extending the taxation of benefits. They eliminated earnings-related additions to sickness and unemployment benefits. They then shifted the responsibility for provision of sickness absence for the first 28 weeks from the national insurance scheme to a statutory sick pay scheme to be run by employers. They attempted also to rationalize the burgeoning supplementary benefit scheme by developing a stronger rule-based structure, and introduced a housing benefit scheme.

However, in 1983 they decided that more radical reform of social security was necessary. It was an element in public expenditure which they were finding very hard to control, not surprisingly in the face of an ageing population, rapidly rising unemployment and government measures designed to shift the subsidy of housing to the social security scheme. Proclaiming themselves to be engaged in the most radical review of social security since Beveridge, they set up a number of ministerially dominated committees to explore options for reform. The eventual outcome was the 1986 Social Security Act. This legislation modified SERPS (in the way outlined above), replaced supplementary benefits by 'income support' and family income supplement by 'family credit'. These two new schemes operate with much simpler rule structures than had supplementary benefits. Housing benefit was altered to bring it into line with these other two benefits. Some anomalies which had been arising as a result of the previous piecemeal evolution of means-tested benefit were eliminated. The maternity grant and the death grant, two universal benefits initiated in the 1940s but not properly updated in line with inflation, were abolished, to be replaced by means-test-related benefits for the very poor. The system of single payments available to help people on supplementary benefits with specific needs was replaced by a much more limited system, known as the 'social fund', under which all that most people could get were loans.

Alongside these major structural changes, the Conservatives substantially weakened the benefits designed to protect the unemployed, making support for under-18s conditional upon undergoing training, and sharply reducing the help available to other young unemployed people. Penalties for refusing to undergo training and for leaving jobs were made very severe.

This last was an issue to which they returned with further legislation in 1995 to rename unemployment benefit 'job seeker's allowance', to emphasize the behaviour required, and make it means-tested for all after the first six months. At about the same time the Conservatives changed invalidity benefit to incapacity benefit, aiming to force all but the severely handicapped below pension age to become job-seekers.

Another feature of Conservative social security policy in the 1990s has been efforts to reduce state support to single-parent families. A complex piece of legislation designed to secure increased contributions from 'absent' parents, the Child Support Act of 1991, ran into implementation difficulties, and was revised in 1995.

In many respects the Beveridge design for social security had been undermined before 1979 by failures to update insurance benefits adequately, by rising unemployment and by the need to provide means-tested benefits for the increasing number of single-parent families. The policy changes of the 1980s continued that process, ensuring that means-tested benefits were increasingly of key importance for the relief of poverty. In particular, the 1986 Act extended and rationalized means tests, but it did not take social security in the radical new direction that 'negative income tax' or 'social dividend' advocates were suggesting (for further discussion see Hill, 1990, ch. 9).

Education

In the period 1951–64, of all the policy areas with which this book is concerned, it was probably education that saw the most innovation. This was, however, very much localized and piecemeal within the general structure laid down by the Butler Act. That had, as I have stressed, laid the foundation for the creation of a sound secondary education system. Initially the orthodox view was that such a system should be selective and tripartite, with children routed at the age of '11-plus' into grammar, technical or secondary modern schools according to their aptitudes and abilities. The concept of a separate form of technical education did not become established (Sanderson, 1991). Then, as time passed, even the notion of a bipartite system was increasingly questioned, and an alternative, non-selective, comprehensive model was championed. Various local authorities began to introduce comprehensive schools in the 1950s, motivated sometimes by political and educational ideology, but sometimes, particularly in rural areas, by a recognition that such schools were a more realistic response to local needs. It was not until the 1960s that battle-lines began to be drawn up, with Labour in favour of comprehensivization and the Conservatives against; and even then, the Conservatives in central government were not hard-line opponents of this policy in the way that, by the end of the decade, Labour had become hard-line advocates. Nevertheless, Labour legislation requiring local authorities to introduce comprehensivization schemes, enacted in 1976, was repealed by the Conservatives in 1980.

In a variety of other ways the Conservative governments of the period 1951–64 rapidly increased the resources available to state education. In many respects, this was a necessary response to the child population 'bulge' created by the 'baby boom' of the immediate post-war years. This in itself created a need for new schools and teachers, and therefore provided a platform for educational innovation. But clearly, governments were ready to encourage innovatory thinking.

Advisory groups were created to look at various educational issues. These produced a memorable series of reports: on early leaving (Central Advisory Council for Education, 1954), on education between the ages of 15 and 18 (*idem*, 1959), on the education of less academic children (*idem*, 1963), on higher education (Robins Committee, 1963) and on primary education (Central Advisory Council for Education, 1967). The crucial policy changes influenced by all this committee activity were the rapid expansion of higher education in the 1960s, the raising of the school-leaving age to 16 in 1973 (after delays in implementing a change first announced in 1964), and a distinct shift away from streaming and selectivity at all stages before the teenage years. But it was the change in amounts of public money spent on education that was most important.

By the mid-1970s the 'bulge' had nearly worked its way through the system, and this, together with disillusion with innovation in education, brought to an end the role of the education service as an expenditure growth-leader among the public services. Controversy grew about some of the bolder experiments in egalitarian education, and it was increasingly alleged that basic education, the 'three Rs', was being neglected. Some people put some of the responsibility for the growing youth unemployment on educational inadequacies, giving support to the Department of Employment's bid to control low-level post-school education. Once the Conservatives came to power in 1979, the unrest began to be translated into policy. The completion of the com-prehensivization programme was arrested, and new opportunities were created for state-financed places at private schools. The 1980 Education Act, which extended parental choice of schools, was seen as creating pressures for the raising of academic standards, and had the effect of increasing the tendency towards social segregation.

The 1988 Education Act was much more fundamental, largely replacing the 1944 Act as the framework law for state education in England and Wales. This Act requires that there should be a 'national curriculum' of 'core' subjects (English, maths and science) and 'foundation subjects' (see p. 169). It requires children to be tested regularly, starting at the age of 7, to assess the extent to which attainment targets have been achieved, and information about test outcomes is published. This legislation also weakens local government control over education by strengthening the autonomy of individual school managements, and by enabling schools to apply to become directly funded by central government (grant-maintained schools). This legislation, supplemented by further legislation, also extends central control over higher and further education, and has removed the last vestiges of local authority responsibility for these sectors.

Conservative policy on higher education went through various phases in the period 1979–95. The government's general objectives have been to tighten control and keep costs down, whilst recognizing the high demand for places. The old polytechnic sector has been assimilated into the university sector (or perhaps, in light of the attack upon the latter, it is more appropriate to put it the other way round). Student grants have been cut in real terms, and a loans scheme has been introduced to make up the shortfall.

Health

In the 1950s the principal government concern about the health service was with difficulties in controlling costs. No substantial changes resulted from this preoccupation. The relationship of the doctors to the government was, and remains, a sensitive area. A great deal of attention was given to their terms of service and remuneration.

The only major item of legislation in the health field between 1951 and 1970 was the Mental Health Act of 1959, which altered the procedures for the compulsory admission and retention of the mentally ill in hospital, abolishing the old 'certification' procedure. At that time, the treatment of mental illness was advancing rapidly, with the advent of psychotropic drugs, and this probably contributed more than the legislative change to reducing both the use of compulsory procedures and the incidence of long stays in hospital. A further Mental Health Act in 1983 continued the liberalization of the treatment of the mentally ill.

In the 1960s, as part of the wholesale review of the institutions of central and local government, proposals were introduced for the reorganization of the National Health Service. Two green papers were produced, suggesting different ways to do this (HMSO, 1967 and 1968a). Eventually the change was effected by the Conservatives in 1974. This change created a new structure, with the former local authority community health services integrated with the rest of the service. Lay participation in the running of the service was reduced; in its place, community health councils were created to represent the public. The new structure, with its three tiers of regions, areas and districts, was criticized as over-elaborate almost as soon as it was created. Discontent over the operation of the new service was one of the factors that led the Labour government to set up a Royal Commission on the National Health Service in 1976. This reported in 1979 (HMSO, 1979) recommending the removal of a tier; the new Conservative government responded, by eliminating areas, but enlarging some districts, in 1982.

Two important stimuli to the search for the right structure for the

NHS throughout this period were concern about effective policy control in the face of professional domination and anxiety about the extent of inequalities in health between social classes and between regions. These two concerns were brought together during the 1970s with the development of a system for the allocation of resources between regions and districts based upon health indices. They, particularly the former, also fuelled a concern to strengthen management. In a report of 1983, a hierarchy of general managers was advocated for the NHS, weakening the influence of the nominated regional and district 'authorities'. This proposal was enacted.

Despite these changes, the rising costs of the NHS, due largely to the ageing of the population and advances in medicine, led the Conservatives to explore further structural changes. Their 'right wing' urged them to privatize the system. Whilst being unprepared to go this far, the government, in the National Health Service and Community Care Act of 1990, encouraged hospitals to become quasi-independent 'National Health Service Trusts', and general medical practices to become 'budget-holders'. Both these measures were designed to bring about increases in efficiency, accompanied by general arrangements for a managerial split between 'purchasers' and 'providers'. The overall aim was to create an 'internal market' system within the NHS, in which hospitals would be in competition with each other. Nearly all hospitals and many community health services have changed to trust status. General practitioners have been slower to seek budget-holder status. About 40 per cent had done so by 1995. These developments made another alteration in the structure of the system necessary: the elimination of 'regions' (except as administrative outposts of the centre) and an amalgamation of the authorities which managed the family practitioner services with the district health authorities, which took place in 1996.

Personal social services

The development of the personal social services between the 1940s and the 1970s is a story of steady consolidation and one important structural change. At the end of the 1940s local authorities organized these services within two or three departments. Children's services were the responsibility of one department, required by statute. Children's departments built up a body of social work expertise, and gradually extended their activities, from work relating to acute child care problems to work designed to prevent child neglect and abuse and work with delinquent children. Two Children and Young Persons Acts, in 1963 and 1969, legitimized and encouraged these changes in emphasis.

The other local authority welfare services, or personal social services, were organized by welfare departments and by health departments (or by departments that combined these two functions). A social work career was developed in connection with this work, but not so effectively as in the children's departments. A government report in 1959 made recommendations that influenced developments in the training of social work staff of this kind. But the activities of these departments were growing in other ways, too. Their legacy from the poor-law was a stock of homes, for the elderly and disabled, that were ex-workhouses. A central task, therefore, was to phase out these institutions and replace them by smaller, more welcoming, civilized homes, and to seek to develop ways of caring for people within the community. Developments in day care, the home help service and other domiciliary services were the currency of growth in these departments. In 1970 the Chronically Sick and Disabled Persons Act placed obligations upon the local authorities to identify and help disabled people. But progress in this area of policy should not necessarily be measured by statutes. Earlier, permissive legislation had already enabled some authorities to innovate in services for disabled people.

The important structural change for all these local authority services was an Act passed in 1970, on the recommendations of the Seebohm Committee (HMSO, 1968b), which created integrated 'social services' departments in local authorities in England and Wales. In Scotland the Social Work (Scotland) Act of 1968 had already created integrated 'social work departments', including probation officers, who remained in a separate service independent of local government in England and Wales. The structural change in England and Wales was accompanied by a change in central government organization, whereby the Home Office's responsibility for children's services was handed over to the Department of Health and Social Security, which was already responsible for other welfare services. These changes represent another example of the statutory creation of a 'platform for growth'. This duly occurred, but by the 1980s had been checked by constraints upon local government spending.

With that check came renewed questioning about the balance between services provided by the social services departments and the many forms of family, neighbourhood and commercially purchased care that they supplemented. Within social work the quest continued for the best way to organize a service that would be responsive to community need (Barclay, 1982). Outside social work, doubts were increasingly raised about the adequacies of that profession, particularly in the face of a growing number of child abuse 'scandals'. Child protection legislation was consolidated and updated in the Children Act of 1989.

A related problem, exacerbated by the ageing of the population, has concerned the balance between community and residential care. This is a complex issue, because it is not only about forms of care, but also about who should bear the costs of care. The community care debate is about both care *in* the community and care *by* the community. In the 1980s a strange piece of government carelessness brought the whole issue to a head. The social security minister relaxed the rules under which means-tested benefits could be used to subsidize private residential care. The result was an explosive growth of this sector, making demands upon the social security budget that were hard to control. A whole range of anomalies developed in the relationship between residential and community care (Audit Commission, 1986). The Conservative government's eventual response to this problem was to try to develop a version of the health service's purchaser–provider split, in which local authorities would be purchasers, and the various forms of community care would be provided by a range of organizations among which private and voluntary enterprises would be dominant. The 1990 Act, which developed similar ideas for the NHS, authorized this, and was brought into full force in April 1993.

The local government system

During the period 1964–95 the local government structure, within which many of the social services are based, came under review. In 1972 the Local Government Act made the first major change in the local government system of England and Wales, apart from restructuring in London, which took place in 1963, since the nineteenth century. This reform created a new two-tier system of local government. In the metropolitan areas the model, like the earlier one adopted in London, was of lower-tier authorities responsible for most functions and top-tier counties responsible primarily for structural planning. Outside the metropolitan areas the division of social policy functions was more even, with the counties acquiring responsibility for education and social services, and the districts made responsible for housing. Similar changes followed in Scotland soon afterwards. Then, in 1986 the government abolished the metropolitan counties. Their functions were either devolved to the districts or given to single-purpose joint boards. In 1991 the government decided to have another look at the structure of local government. It set up a Commission for England, which recommended a series of *ad hoc* changes, mainly involving increasing the number of single-tier authorities in urban areas. Many of its proposals have provoked controversy (at the time of writing the government is enacting some of its less controversial proposals). These particularly entail creating new, single, all-purpose authorities. In Scotland and Wales there has been a wholesale restructuring to create single-tier authorities everywhere.

An accompanying central government preoccupation about local government in this period was the fact that it was spending more and more money (not surprisingly in light of central government's expectations of it in areas like education, personal social services and housing). In the period up to the mid-1970s, central government steadily increased its grant contributions to local expenditure. It also struggled, rather fruitlessly, to find ways to wholly or partly replace the system of local taxation, the rates assessed on property. In the later years of the 1974–9 Labour government the central contribution to local expenditure began to be cut. After 1979 the Thatcher government continued this process much more zealously, developing a formula which deliberately penalized those authorities they deemed to be overspenders. Then, in addition, they decided that they must limit the powers of local authorities to go on increasing local rates. They developed a power which enabled them to 'rate cap' a group of authorities whom they deemed to be high spenders. Finally, they decided to abolish rates and replace them by a poll tax known as the 'community charge'. This measure proved to be enormously unpopular, and contributed to Margaret Thatcher's political downfall (see Butler et al., 1994). Her successor as Prime Minister, John Major, rushed legislation through Parliament to try to get rid of the stigma of the poll tax. He sharply increased the central subsidy to local finance, and enacted a modified version of the old domestic rating system known as the 'council tax'.

What is clear from this flurry of activity concerning local government and its finance is that central control over the resources available at the local level has become very strong, and is likely to remain so. Any measure which extends local taxation powers is likely to be unpopular and difficult to enact.

Conclusions

This section has described policy developments in a period in which the Conservatives and Labour alternated in power. Thirteen years of Conservative rule was followed by nearly seven years of Labour rule. Then there was an episode of nearly four years of Conservative government. After that, Labour 'enjoyed' a period of four years in government, in which their continuance in office depended upon the support of the Liberals. Then, in 1979 the Conservatives won a clear majority. They won a second term of office in 1983, and a third term in 1987. Margaret Thatcher lost the leadership of the Conservatives in late 1991. In April 1992 her successor, John Major, led the Conservatives in another successful election campaign, but one in which there was a marked fall in their majority. As this book goes to press, that majority is systematically disappearing – as a result of by-election losses and defections.

THE EMERGENCE OF A CRISIS FOR BRITISH SOCIAL POLICY?

In the period between 1951 and 1975, levels of controversy over social policies were, arguably, not particularly high. Conservative ideologists had much to say about the case for bringing market conditions more effectively to bear upon the distribution of social services, but only in the housing field did Conservative governments take steps that represented major responses to this viewpoint. Labour disappointed many of its supporters, who closely identified the party with the advancement of the welfare state. A succession of economic crises limited the money available for new social policies. Yet both parties considerably advanced public expenditure, particularly on social policies, to the point where some economists argued that this kind of expenditure had become an inflationary force, limiting the scope for new wealth-creating private investment. This is a view that both parties have taken very seriously. The most staggering growth was in public employment and in social security transfer payments, two forms of growth that politicians find very hard to limit.

It is tempting to attribute the change in the climate for social policy in Britain to the election of Margaret Thatcher in 1979. But changes had been gradually taking place before that date, and those changes were rooted as much in economic factors as in ideological ones. It was a Labour minister, Anthony Crosland, speaking in 1975, who warned local government that as far as public spending increases were concerned, the 'party is over'.

In the 1950s Keynesian economic management techniques, involving manipulation of levels of government expenditure and taxation, were employed to try to retain full employment without inflation. Critics of policies of that period such as Samuel Brittan (1971) have suggested that Chancellors of the Exchequer found it difficult to time their uses of the economic 'brake' or 'accelerator' properly, and that the 'stop–go' pattern that emerged provided a poor economic environment for investment decisions, and thus inhibited British growth. The particular motivation for some fairly panicky use of the 'brake' was a concern with Britain's tendency to run into balance-of-payments problems, importing more than it was exporting. However, during this period, a rate of growth was achieved that was good by later standards; full employment was maintained; and inflation, while ever present, was never so high as to cause alarm.

In the 1960s, despite an increasing commitment to economic planning, the cyclical pattern got worse. Inflation increased; balance-of-payments crises forced strong restraints to be applied to public expenditure and private incomes on a number of occasions; and, at the depressed point of the cycle, quite marked increases in unemployment occurred. In the mid-1970s Britain faced a more severe crisis, in which very high inflation, a balance-of-payments problem and continuing high unemployment occurred all at the same time. Measures to cope with the first two by traditional means worsened the third. At a time when governments seemed to have learnt a great deal about economic management, they found it increasingly difficult to put it into practice. In fact, the rise in economic management problems can be correlated with the dramatic increase in the number of economists in the civil service!

Different schools of economists have preached different solutions to these problems. On the Right the 'monetarist' school of thought became increasingly influential, arguing that governments must control the money supply and let economic forces bring the system under control (Friedman, 1962, 1977; for an overview of this theory see Bosanquet, 1983). This viewpoint was put partly into practice in the 1970s, but politicians were reluctant to let bankruptcies and redundancies occur on a scale sufficient to really test the monetarist hypothesis. More influential, and more in conformity with Keynesian orthodoxy, were those economists who argued that income restraint was necessary to bring unemployment and inflation into balance, and to prevent Britain's balance of payments getting out of hand as rising wages led us to import goods we could ill afford, while making it more difficult to sell things. In their view, what was happening was that wage bargaining was no longer being restrained by the social and political forces that had hitherto limited rises to figures that would not disrupt the economy. Incomes policies were seen as crucial to help solve our problems; yet, over and over again, governments found that political pressures made these very difficult to sustain for any length of time. The whole picture was complicated, moreover, by changes in the pattern of trade in the world, and particularly by rises in prices of primary commodities, especially oil.

After 1979 the 'monetarist' theory was more boldly put into practice. The government treated the money supply, and particularly the public sector borrowing rate, as the key phenomena to keep under control. It was prepared to let unemployment rise rapidly in the cause of the war against inflation. It abandoned incomes policy in the private sector, seeking only to keep pay increases to public employees tightly under control. Initially it found that the removal of pay controls and its own taxation adjustments produced severely inflationary effects. It was subsequently successful in bringing inflation under control, but achieved that at the expense of a rapid increase in unemployment. Numbers registered of those out of work rose from just over a million in 1979 to over 3 million in 1983.

Later in the 1980s the government abandoned any rigorous attempt to keep the money supply under control, concentrating attention instead upon the foreign exchange value of the pound. But it continued its tight control of public borrowing. By the 1990s, with the economy depressed and the 1992 election approaching, even the latter monetarist nostrum was abandoned by the Conservatives.

Changes to the official method of counting makes comparison of data on unemployment difficult after the end of 1982. Significant numbers of the unemployed – in particular, people registering for work but not receiving benefit – were excluded from the count. There was a real fall in unemployment in the second half of the 1980s, but not as large as the official figures suggested. Moreover, many of the jobs created at this time were part-time or temporary. Then, at the end of the decade, a new recession developed. In 1993, according to the official count, unemployment in the United Kingdom was close to 3 million. Since this estimate includes only unemployed people registering for benefits, the real figure will have been anything up to a million higher. By the end of 1995 the official figure had improved a little, to about 2.25 million.

In chapter 9, one of the issues which will be examined will be whether social policy measures can help to cope with unemployment, or whether it is primarily an economic problem. Doubts are increasingly raised as to whether specific national policy interventions can counter a developing global trend towards fewer job opportunities. There is evidence that the character of demand for labour is changing, and that new investment is essentially capital-intensive, and therefore unable to absorb much labour. Analysis of the issue is complicated by questions about the changing composition of the labour force, which large numbers of married women have joined since the war, and about the extent to which the unemployed lack the skills and capacity now required by industry (Gilbert, 1989).

Early in this chapter it was pointed out that at the beginning of the century British governments adopted an approach to the relief of unemployment that largely ruled out the creation of specific employment opportunities. In the early 1970s interest was awakened in Britain in the case for the development of 'active labour market policies' of the kind adopted in Sweden (Mukherjee, 1972). These involved such things as assisting labour mobility, expanding training when unemployment rises, and creating special work projects for the unemployed. Their appeal was that they were measures to alleviate unemployment, in a largely fully employed economy, without creating inflation.

Their adoption in Britain occurred at a time of high unemployment. Accordingly, instead of serving the economic function for which they were originally advocated, they have been modified to serve the political function of reducing the number of unemployed whilst minimizing intervention in the economy as a whole. There has been a particular concentration on measures for young people, to the extent that many who leave school at 16 can expect up to two years in government schemes which combine work experience with training. Indeed, at the end of the 1980s the government adopted a strategy for employment policy which largely abandoned other job-creation measures but strongly emphasized training (Department of Employment, 1988a, b).

These reflections upon some of the problematic relationships today between economic and social policies have ended with some specific details on employment policy (left over from the previous section). The main concern of this section has been to emphasize how the problems for social policy in the recent past need to be put in an economic context.

On the other hand, there is no doubt that Conservative governments since the rise of Margaret Thatcher have been hostile to state social policy. This hostility has been rooted in a commitment to curbing public services and a lack of concern about inequality. Paradoxically, while the Conservatives have been very committed to public expenditure restraint and have stopped the growth of public employment, they too have found social policy expenditure hard to curb.

Public sector housing expenditure has experienced severe cuts. Education expenditure has remained more or less static in real terms. Health and personal social services expenditure trends are harder to interpret. The figures indicate growth in real terms, but needs and specific health care costs have also risen, so there has been some decline in volume terms. Nevertheless, social policy expenditure as a whole has grown, driven upwards by the considerable growth in its major component, the social security budget (see Hills (ed.), 1990, for a detailed analysis of these trends).

Demographic and economic changes have had a strong impact upon these trends. As was shown in the last section, there have been many detailed changes to social policy, many of which were initiated in the hope of reducing expenditure. Their long-run legacy may be, more than anything else, a new institutional map of social policy – the purchaser–provider split, a reduced role for local government, greater participation by private providers and so on (see further discussion in the next two chapters).

The first edition of this book was completed in the week the Conservatives came to power in 1979. This fifth edition is likely to be published sometime in the run-up to a general election in early 1997. Since, at the time of writing, the opinion polls suggest that the next government is very likely to be a Labour one, I have once again to face the possibility that what I say may date quickly.

However, the Labour Party is very fearful of being seen as the party of high taxation. It is, accordingly, reluctant to pledge itself to make social policy innovations which will cost money. Its recent statements about education and health policy also suggest a cautious approach to institutional change. Change may therefore come quite slowly after the next election. There is, perhaps, a 'new consensus' which will give social policy a lower priority, even for a party of the Left, than it had in the 1945–79 period.

SUGGESTIONS FOR FURTHER READING

Such is the wealth of historical literature that it has been difficult to decide what to note in this chapter. References have been confined to some of the more significant primary sources and to secondary sources that readers may find particularly interesting or readable. Some of the major historical works upon which I have depended have not been listed.

Derek Fraser's *The Evolution of the British Welfare State* (1984) is a good general historical textbook, but is stronger on the nineteenth than the twentieth century. Pat Thane's *The Foundations of the Welfare State* (1982) deals with the period from 1870 onward. The inter-war period is well covered by Gilbert (1970). A number of recent books deal with the 1945–51 Labour government. Amongst these, Morgan's *Labour in Power 1945–51* (1984) is recommended, also Hennessy's *Never Again* (1992).

Morgan has also written an account of the whole period 1945–89 (1990), but it gives comparatively little attention to social policy. However, four books which deal specifically with social policy are my *The Welfare State in Britain* (Hill, 1993b), Rodney Lowe's *The Welfare State in Britain since 1945* (1993), Nicholas Deakin's *The Politics of Welfare* (1994) and Howard Glennerster's *British Social Policy since 1945* (1995).

The impact of the Thatcher and Major governments upon social policy has provoked various accounts, each rapidly dated by further developments. The most up to date is the collection edited by Savage et al. (1994).

THE MAKING OF SOCIAL POLICY

INTRODUCTION

This chapter deals with the social policy-making system, and introduces the key institutions involved in the process in Britain. The next chapter looks at the implementation of social policy. The two chapters must be considered together; dividing the policy processes between 'making' and 'implementation' is, in various respects, difficult. It is hard to identify a dividing line at which making can be said to be completed and implementation to start. There is also a considerable amount of feedback from implementation which influences further policy-making, and many policies are so skeletal that their real impact depends upon the way they are interpreted at the implementation stage.

The starting-point here is the ideal to which the British system of government is presumed to correspond, in which policy-making is seen as the responsibility of our representatives in Parliament, who answer to the people at a general election for their stewardship of the public interest. The chapter will first look at the features of the system that correspond to this model, and at the institutions that are reputedly responsible for the policy-making process. It will also look at the implications of the presence of lower-tier organs of government, at local levels, and at the way in which representative government seems to be expected to work within them.

Having done this, the discussion will then turn to consider the various ways in which the model of representative government is modified – or perhaps even undermined – in practice. It will consider how the people's will is translated into political action. It will look at the part played by pressure groups in the system, and will examine the case that has been made for regarding democracy as significantly undermined by 'political elites'. The relationship between government and Parliament will be scrutinized, together with its parallels in local government. Attention will be given to the role played by the machinery of government, by the civil service and by local government officers, in the policy-making process, and some general points will be made about what we mean by that 'process'. These later issues will lead naturally into the examination of the implementation process in the next chapter.

THE REPRESENTATIVE GOVERNMENT MODEL

When the systems of government in Britain, the United States, most of Western Europe and much of the Commonwealth are claimed to be democratic, that claim rests upon a view that a form of representation of the people prevails in their governmental systems. Clearly, these systems do not involve direct democracy, since in complex societies large numbers of decisions are taken by small numbers of representatives. Some countries seek to involve the people more directly, from time to time, by the use of plebiscites.

There is a further sense in which representative government is indirect. A distinction is often made between representatives and delegates. Delegates are regarded as mandated by those who elect them to support specific policies and to return to explain their subsequent decisions. British politicians have persistently rejected the view that they should be regarded as delegates, arguing instead that their duty is to make judgements for themselves in terms of their understanding of their constituents' best interests, while recognizing that they may, of course, be rejected at the next election if they become seriously out of touch with the people they represent. In this sense they claim to be concerned with the interests of all their constituents, not just those who voted for them. This doctrine was first expounded by Edmund Burke in the late eighteenth century. Today, of course, the importance of political parties makes it difficult for Members of Parliament to claim to represent all their constituents; but, equally, it makes it difficult for them to assume the role of delegates. The presence in Parliament, and in the local councils, of party groups exerts an influence in favour of party programmes, and away from a direct relationship between Member and constituency. The modern modification of representative democracy is therefore to see the public as being allowed to choose from time to time between two or more broad political programmes, and being able to reject a party that has failed to carry out its promises (Schumpeter, 1950).

According to the theory on which this model of democracy is based, social policies may be expected to be determined by the commitments of the political parties, and proposals for policy changes will be set out in election manifestos. The growth of the welfare state will be clearly relatable to the growth of democracy, with the people *choosing* to see their society change in this way. There are weaknesses in this view of the policy-making process, which will be explored later in the chapter. But first there is a need to identify more explicitly the institutions of government to which such an analysis must relate. Those who have previously done courses on the British constitution may wish to skip the next two sections.

THE CENTRAL GOVERNMENT SYSTEM

The curious feature of the British constitution is that Britain has democratized institutions that were created in an undemocratic age. Most countries have systems of government that are relatively modern creations, either designed after cataclysmic political events which required setting up entirely new institutions, or set up to meet the needs of newly created or newly independent states. The governments of France and Germany, for example, fall into the first of these categories, and those of the United States and the Commonwealth countries into the second. The British pride themselves on having developed a system of government that has been a model for the rest of the world. The truth is, however, that while many constitutional ideas certainly *have* been borrowed from Britain, the British system contains features that no one designing a system of government today would conceivably want to adopt.

The monarchy and the House of Lords are the two most significant British 'anomalies'. Formally, neither has much influence on the policy-making process. Monarchs have relinquished their rights to interfere; the House of Lords has been largely stripped of its rights by successive Acts of Parliament since 1911. Here we do not need to go into the residual rights and responsibilities of the two.

The House of Commons is elected from over 600 constituencies (an exact number has not been given, since regular constituency boundary changes alter it), each of which returns the candidate who gains a simple majority of votes at each election. After a general election the monarch has the formal responsibility of asking the leader of the majority party to form a government. On most occasions the monarch's duty is clear, but situations in which there is no party with a clear majority may complicate the task. Broadly, the expectation is that the monarch will not have to take a decision that will then prove to be a violation of the democratic process, because it will be up to whoever agrees to form a government in these circumstances to prove that he or she has adequate parliamentary support. In other words, the position of a minority government can be made untenable if all the other parties combine against it. There are, however, ambiguities in such a situation, as the lives of minority governments may be perpetuated more by a reluctance to force them to resign than by any positive commitment to their support.

The newly appointed Prime Minister will then form a government, giving a hundred or more governmental offices to his or her supporters. Again, the normal assumption is that these will be members of his or her own party, but exceptionally a coalition may be formed in which government offices go to members of other parties. All those given office will normally be, or will be expected to become, members of either the Commons or the Lords. Most will be members of the Commons (known as 'Members of Parliament' or 'MPs'). The choice of members of the government rests significantly upon the preferences of the Prime Minister. But he or she cannot disregard interests and factions within his or her own party, and will obviously give some attention to the competence of those appointed.

The most important Prime Ministerial appointments will be those to the Cabinet. The normal practice is to appoint a Cabinet of fifteen to twenty-five members. It will include heads of the main departments of government, together with some members who do not have departmental responsibilities, who may be given political or co-ordinating roles. The Cabinet, chaired by the Prime Minister, is the key decision-making body within the government. New policy departures of any significance and new legislation will need Cabinet approval, and conflicts of interests between departments will have to be fought out in the Cabinet or its committees. Each Cabinet sets up a number of committees to do more detailed work. Some of these will draw on the help of non-Cabinet ministers.

The government departments to which attention must be given in the discussion of social policy in England (the different situation in the other component countries of the United Kingdom is outlined later) are the Treasury, the Department of Health, the Department of Social Security, the Department of the Environment, and the Department for Education and Employment. Two other departments, the Cabinet Office and the Home Office, also play a small part. Readers must be warned that it has been the practice of governments in recent years to alter the departmental structure from time to time, ostensibly in an effort to find the best possible framework for policy co-ordination, but – it may be suggested – with less elevated political motives in mind too. Accordingly, it may be the case that by the time you read this book, departments may have new names, and policy responsibilities may have moved from one department to another. For example, in 1995 the Departments for Education and Employment were combined.

The Prime Minister is technically the First Lord of the Treasury. This archaic title serves to remind us that, while today we regard the Chancellor of the Exchequer as the senior Treasury minister, the Prime Minister is, above all, bound to be involved in major decisions on expenditure, taxation and the management of the economy. The importance of this aspect of policy is so great that there are often other Treasury ministers in the Cabinet, such as the Chief Secretary to the Treasury and the Paymaster-General. These may be expected to play important roles in relation to decisions on public expenditure.

Each of the departments listed above has its senior minister, the secretary of state, in the Cabinet. Again, the Prime Minister may choose to have other ministers from specific departments as Cabinet members. Each department head has the support of several junior ministers, known as ministers of state or under-secretaries, who may take on particular responsibilities for specific policy areas.

The role of the minister who is also a Cabinet member involves a quite considerable conflict between being a member of the central policy co-ordinating team within the government and being responsible for protecting and advancing the interests of a department. In his *Diaries of a Cabinet Minister* (1975–7) the late Richard Crossman gave considerable attention to this problem. It is personally difficult for any individual to give whole-hearted attention both to departmental issues and to the main political strategy problems arising outside his or her own responsibilities. There is likewise a crucial problem for a rational approach to government in which strategic questions may not be best resolved by bargaining between a group of individuals all of whom have conflicting, 'tunnel vision' images dictated by departmental needs and priorities. Clearly, members of the Cabinet without departmental responsibilities are expected to help to resolve this problem, but they often suffer from a sense of being outsiders without the detailed departmental briefs possessed by their colleagues (see ibid., vol. 2). The creation of a group of special civil servants, including individuals recruited from outside the public service for their expertise or political connections, has been seen as a further device to strengthen strategic thinking in government. There would seem, however, to be a continuing and inevitable conflict here.

As far as departmental duties are concerned, a minister's work will fall into roughly four categories:

1 He or she may be responsible for putting forward new legislation. Clearly, this is something the ambitious politician will want to do. He or she will hope to secure a job that involves the initiation of policies from the party's programme.

2 He or she will have a large amount of day-to-day administration to oversee. Much of this will involve the formulation of new policies that do not require legislation, or the determination of responses to new crises within the department. It is in this kind of work that the distinction between policy-making and implementation becomes so unclear. In many respects any issue that a department regards as requiring a ministerial decision is likely to be describable as a 'policy issue'.

3 He or she will have to deal with questions from MPs about the policies and activities of the department. While this may be seen primarily as a defensive kind of action, involving much routine work by civil servants who are required to produce the information required for parliamentary answers, it may also provide opportunities for publicizing new policy initiatives. Indeed, many questions are planted by friendly MPs, from the back-benches on the minister's own side, to enable activities to be advertised.

4 The minister has a wide public relations role beyond Parliament. This will involve a programme of speeches, meetings and visits relating the department's activities to the world outside.

Several references have already been made to the support of ministers by civil servants. It is self-evident that civil servants have an important role to play in implementing policy. What also needs to be emphasized is that civil servants are heavily involved in making policy. Until recent changes in the structure of the civil service, designed to reduce barriers between the various grades and to stress the importance of many of the managerial roles played in connection with policy implementation, it was possible to draw a fairly clear distinction between the 'administrative class', containing the 'higher' civil servants responsible for policy, and the rest of the civil service. Now, the policy-making group is a little more difficult to define. Each major department has at its headquarters a group of a hundred or so civil servants, up to the top position of 'permanent secretary', who are concerned with decisions of a 'policy' kind, many of which require ministerial approval. The theory of representative government clearly requires that they be called the *servants* of the minister, ostensibly providing information and evidence on policy alternatives, but not taking policy decisions.

The British system of government involves more than a network of departments headed by ministers. Responsibility for various specific public services is hived off to a range of special agencies, though in each case ultimate responsibility for policy lies with one of the central departments. Again, these subordinate bodies might be described as being concerned with implementation, not with policy-making. But, while this is broadly true, many implement within only general guide-lines and therefore have an important, if subordinate, policy-making role. Students of social policy will come across a number of important examples of bodies of this kind, some with a nation-wide remit, others with local or regional responsibilities. They have grown in numbers and importance in recent years, as a result of what has come to be called the 'next steps initiative', which aims to delegate most routine governmental tasks to separate 'agencies'. In social policy the most significant of these agencies are those concerned with social security and unemployment, particularly the Benefits Agency and the Employment Services Agency (see next chapter for a further discussion of agencies).

The discussion in this section has moved from the consideration of the composition of Parliament and the nature of the relationship of government to Parliament to a more detailed account of the organizations concerned with policy-making. There is a need, however, to look a little more at the role of Parliament. It has been shown that about 100 of the 600 Members elected to Parliament become involved in specific government jobs. What role do the rest play in policy-making?

Primary policy-making involves the promulgation of Acts of Parliament. The overwhelming majority of these are promoted by government, and thus the initial 'Bills' are prepared by civil servants within the various departments. Bills then go through four stages in each House: a 'first reading', which simply involves the formal presentation of the Bill; a 'second reading', at which there is likely to be a large-scale debate on the basic principles of the Bill; a 'committee stage', when the legislation is examined in detail (normally by a small 'standing committee', not by the whole House); and a 'report stage' and 'third reading', at which the Bill that emerges from the committee is approved, but may be re-amended to undo some of the actions of the committee. Clearly, Members without ministerial office may participate in all these stages, and opposition Members will take particular care to scrutinize and attack government action. The leading opposition party organizes a 'shadow cabinet' to provide for a considered, specialized response to the activities of the government.

Back-bench MPs may be able to promote new policies through 'private Members' bills'. These cannot have direct financial implications for the government, and they have little chance of becoming law without government support. Occasionally governments assist private Members with their Bills, particularly by allowing extra parliamentary time. Some significant social policy measures have become law in this way. The Abortion Act of 1967, for example, was promoted by a Liberal MP, David Steel, and became law because many key ministers were sympathetic. In this case the Bill concerned an issue of conscience on which many felt it would be inappropriate for Parliament to divide along party lines. The abolition of capital punishment and reform of the law on homosexuality came about in a similar way. In the 1970s the Labour government supported a private Members' Bill which took over an item which would have been included in its own programme if there had been sufficient parliamentary time. This curious reversal of roles may have owed something to the agreement of the Liberals to support a government without a clear majority; the legislation was the Housing (Homeless Persons) Act of 1977 promoted by a Liberal, Stephen Ross.

In addition to Acts of Parliament, both Houses have to deal with a great deal of what is known as 'subordinate' or 'delegated' legislation. Many Acts allow governments to promote subsequent changes and new regulations. It is important to recognize that many policy changes pass through Parliament in this way. It would be an extravagant use of parliamentary time to require new legislation for all detailed changes of this kind. Controversy arises, however, over the extent of the use of delegated legislation, since some Acts convey very wide scope for this kind of ministerial action. To promote subordinate legislation, the government has to publish a 'statutory instrument' which is open to scrutiny by MPs. Some of these require parliamentary approval; others may be annulled if a negative resolution is passed by either House within 40 days of their initial publication. Hence back-benchers may intervene to prevent subordinate legislation. A joint committee of the Commons and the Lords has been set up to scrutinize statutory instruments, and therefore to facilitate parliamentary review of subordinate legislation. They have, however, a mammoth task, and can give detailed attention to only a limited number of the statutory instruments that are put before Parliament.

Readers will find a good example of legislation for which statutory instruments are important in the 1986 Social Security Act. They will look in vain in the Act for detailed information on, for example, the housing benefit scheme or the social fund, this being contained in subsequent regulations. In particular, actual benefit rates are not included in such legislation, but are set out in regulations which are regularly updated and amended.

Reference has already been made to parliamentary questions as providing an opportunity for back-bench scrutiny of government actions. Members put down initial questions in advance. Many questions are answered in writing, but those that receive oral answers may be followed up by supplementary questions. In addition to the powers to ask questions, various parliamentary procedures provide scope for MPs to promote short debates on topics that concern them.

The main opposition party is extended more specific facilities of this kind, so there are days allocated for debates on topics of its choice.

One peculiar characteristic of the British Parliament that distinguishes it from many legislatures in other countries, and particularly from the United States Congress, is the slight use made of specialized committees. This is also a difference between the central government system and the local government system in Britain. The committees that consider Bills are in no way specialized; they consider new legislation in rotation, regardless of subject, and do not do any separate investigatory work.

There is also, however, a system of rather more specialized select committees. Perhaps the most important of these is the Public Accounts Committee, concerned to look at the way in which public money has been spent. Then there are select committees on the work of the Parliamentary Commissioner for Administration (the 'Ombudsman'), on statutory instruments and on European legislation. In 1979 a system of 14 committees was set up, each of which was to concern itself with the work of specific (or in some cases two specific) government departments. In the field of social policy the social services committee has conducted a number of influential investigations of issues. *Ad hoc* committees may also be set up to investigate specific subjects. But such is the power of the executive in our system that it is doubtful whether these committees can do other than play a rather superior pressure group role. They investigate specific topics, with the aid of specialist advisers, and have issued some influential reports. But, as stressed above, they have no role with regard to legislation.

This account of the institutions of British central government has shown that elected representatives have a wide range of parliamentary duties. If they belong to the party that wins power, they may well take on a government office of some kind. If they do not achieve office, they are still in a special relationship to government, in which, while some advantages may accrue from being a member of the ruling party and having many colleagues and friends in office, there may also be disadvantages, in that party allegiance implies a duty to support the government. Some of the scope for criticism of policy that comes to opposition Members is denied to government supporters. On the other hand, opposition, in a Parliament organized strictly on party lines, implies a situation in which it is very hard to secure majority support for your ideas.

REGIONAL AND LOCAL GOVERNMENT

The term 'regional government' is used here to cover two phenomena:

the government of Northern Ireland, Scotland and Wales, and the organization of the government of specific services on a regional basis.

Northern Ireland

Northern Ireland had a devolved system of government between 1922 and 1972. The Government of Ireland Act of 1920 conferred a considerable measure of self-government upon Northern Ireland. All social policy legislation was the responsibility of the Northern Ireland government, and revenue was raised partly by local taxes and partly by the United Kingdom taxation system. In practice, legislation at Stormont, the Northern Ireland Parliament, tended to follow legislation at Westminster quite closely, but often a few years behind. The people of the province were represented both at Stormont and at Westminster. The British government possessed reserve powers, so that it could interfere in the government if it so wished. Until the 'troubles' of the late 1960s it studiously refused to do so. However, in 1972 the Northern Ireland (Temporary Provisions) Act suspended Stormont, and imposed direct rule from Westminster. In 1974 an attempt to begin to restore self-government through a new Northern Ireland Executive, elected by proportional representation to try to provide for the involvement of the Catholic minority in government, was brought to an end after a strike by Protestant workers. Government of Northern Ireland is through a secretary of state for Northern Ireland at Westminster who heads a Northern Ireland Office. Within Northern Ireland itself the former separate departments operate, but all are technically under the jurisdiction of the Northern Ireland Office. The various junior ministers in the Northern Ireland Office share the 'ministerial' responsibilities for these departments. Naturally, the Northern Ireland departments operate on the basis of legislation passed before the demise of Stormont. This is supplemented by special legislation from Westminster where appropriate. A crucial part of the 'peace process', going on at the time of writing, involves a search for new governmental arrangements which can win the support of Catholics and Protestants.

Scotland

Scotland's affairs are conducted from Westminster by way of a secretary of state for Scotland and a separate Scottish Office, which is split into several departments. Much Scottish legislation is already separate. Those social services that come under local government – housing, personal social services and education – have their control devolved to the Scottish Office, and are regulated by separate legislation. The health service in Scotland has a slightly different structure from that in England and some separate legislation, but here the centralizing tendency for control from London has been very strong. The social security system is, on the other hand, a Great Britain-wide one. Within Parliament there is a convention that only Scottish MPs participate in debates on Scottish matters. Since the 1987 general election, the ranks of Scottish Conservative MPs have been reduced to a very small number. This has brought the arrangements for Scottish legislation under strain, and has increased the pressure for political devolution.

Wales

Devolution to Wales is not so extensive. Whilst there is a separate Welsh Office, most legislation deals jointly with England and Wales. In many respects the Welsh Office is little more than an integrated 'regional office' bringing together, in a way not found in the English regions, concerns about health, personal social services, education and housing.

Acts were passed in 1978 allowing for devolution of most of these administrative powers to elected assemblies in Scotland and Wales. These were subject to acceptance by the people of those countries, who were consulted by referenda early in 1979. The people of Wales conclusively rejected the proposals. In Scotland there was a majority in favour of devolution, but it fell short of the 40 per cent of the electorate required by the statute. This issue is likely to arise again if Labour comes to power.

The Channel Islands and the Isle of Man have substantially more independent systems of government, and do not send MPs to Westminster. In view of their small size, however, it does not seem appropriate to say anything more about them here.

In the context both of the discussion of devolution to Scotland and Wales and of the consideration of the reorganization of local government, some attention has been given to the case for regional government in England. While it is hard to predict whether or not a real system of regional government will be developed, it is important to note that most government departments with responsibilities for local services have systems of regional offices. These regional structures appear to have comparatively little significance for policy-making.

Local government in England is organized into two distinctive systems. In the metropolitan areas of London, West Midlands, South

Yorkshire, Greater Manchester, Merseyside, and Tyne and Wear there is a one-tier system of districts responsible for personal social services, education and housing. In April 1996 and 1997, a number of further one-tier authorities are being brought into operation. These are mostly in urbanized areas, with enlarged districts taking over powers from counties. In some cases – Avon and Cleveland, for example – county authorities have disappeared altogether.

In the rest of England there are county authorities, which are responsible for education and personal social services, and also a lower tier of districts, which include housing amongst their responsibilities. Planning responsibilities are shared between the two tiers.

There is also a third tier of parish councils, with minimal powers. Whilst many of these are old parishes, others are towns that previously had significant powers of their own, some retaining mayors and calling themselves town councils. None of these third-tier authorities has significant social policy responsibilities, so they will not be examined further here.

The local government system of Scotland has been totally restructured; throughout the country there is, since April 1996, a one-tier system of local government. There is a similar but slightly more complicated situation in Wales, with most powers being in a single-tier authority, known either as a county or a county borough; but there is also a system of community councils resembling the parish councils in England.

Local government in Northern Ireland has been stripped of almost all its significant powers. It had previously been notorious in some areas for the manipulation of electoral boundaries and for the practice of religious discrimination. Health services and personal social services now come together under four appointed boards. Education is the responsibility of three separate education and libraries boards. Public housing is the concern of the Northern Ireland Housing Executive.

The health service, outside Northern Ireland, has its own separate system of single-tier authorities, originally designed with some regard for local government boundaries.

National legislation defines the powers of local authorities, and may set limits to those powers. It also imposes upon local government a range of duties. The relationship between central and local government in Britain is a complex one. Local government is not autonomous; but neither is it merely local administration. Some statutes impose fairly clear tasks for local authorities. But many give powers, and indicate ways in which those powers should be used, without undermining the scope for local initiative. Other Acts of Parliament merely grant powers to local authorities, which they may choose whether or not to use.

Exceptionally, a local authority may itself promote a 'private' Act to secure powers to undertake new ventures. Local authorities are therefore able to make or elaborate policies, and are not merely implementing agencies.

However, the relationship between central and local government involves both partnership and conflict. Central government seeks to impose its will not merely through legislation, but also through the communication of large amounts of guidance. This may be embodied in circulars, regularly sent from central departments to local authorities, or through less formal communications from ministers, administrators and professional advisers. Central intervention is justified in terms of national political commitments, to ensure that central policies have an impact upon all localities. There is an inherent conflict between the demands of local autonomy and the principle of 'territorial justice', which requires that citizens in different geographical areas secure comparable treatment.

Central government also justifies its interventions in local government in terms of its concern with national economic management. It is its financial control over local government that tends to weaken its claim that the central–local relationship is a partnership. The problem is compounded by the lack of a satisfactory way for local government to raise its own revenue.

Local authorities have three major sources of income: local taxes, payments for the provision of services and government grants. The first of these was, until the mid-1980s, a system of rates upon property, both domestic and business. Then the government replaced domestic rates by a tax on individuals, the community charge or poll tax, and centralized control over business rates. The poll tax was met by a popular reaction which contributed to the end of Margaret Thatcher's career as Prime Minister (see Butler et al., 1994). After her fall, her successor sharply increased the central government grant to soften the impact of the poll tax, financing this out of an increase in value added tax. He then, in 1993, replaced the poll tax by the council tax. The latter is a simplified form of the former domestic rates, with the number of adult occupants of a property partly taken into account.

All these changes to local taxation involved a sharp reduction in the independence of local government. Even before the poll tax, the Conservative government had given itself powers to prevent local authorities from raising local taxation over centrally prescribed limits. It has continued this 'capping' practice. At the same time, the centralization of the commercial rating system had the effect of bringing three-quarters of local revenue under direct central control; and the panic reaction to reduce the impact of the poll tax, after

Margaret Thatcher's fall, had the effect of pushing the centrally controlled proportion up to around 80 per cent of local government revenue (Central Statistical Office, 1995b, p. 24). Given the inflexibility of property-based taxation systems, by contrast with income tax or value added tax, it is unlikely that any future government will dare to reverse this situation.

Central government also maintains control over local authority borrowing. The trend, in recent years, has been away from a system of strict, item by item, controls to broad limitations upon total borrowing. The system is currently a complex combination of these two approaches to control.

Policy-making in local government is the responsibility of elected members. These represent districts, or wards, within each authority, in much the same way as MPs represent constituencies. Today a great deal of local politics is arranged along party lines, and most councillors represent the political parties that are also found at Westminster.

Local authority members each belong to a number of committees. Most business is transacted in these committees, so the meetings of the full councils are largely rubber-stamping affairs, affording opportunities for making political points. The committee structures are primarily related to the various functional responsibilities of the authority. Many local authorities operate 'policy committees', which aim to co-ordinate the activities of the authority as a whole. In most authorities the parties are represented on the committees in proportion to their distribution on the whole council. Generally the majority party will assume the chairmanship of each of the committees.

The politicization of local government has intensified the conflict between central and local government. This was particularly sharp in the early 1980s between radical Labour authorities and the central Conservative administration. In 1996 the potential gulf between central and local government is bigger than ever, with most local authorities controlled by Labour or the Liberals. However, the powerful central controls over finance have severely limited the scope for local resistance.

THE UNITED KINGDOM IN EUROPE

There is one aspect of the political and administrative system which needs to be mentioned at the end of this discussion, even though its impact upon social policy is slight. The United Kingdom's membership of the European Union has had an impact upon its constitution and upon its policy-making process. There are areas of the law which are now determined by the institutions of the European Economic

Community, where the role of the United Kingdom Parliament is limited to one of administering implementation.

It is mainly economic activity which is subject to this European dominance. The origins of the European Community lie in the aspiration to build a supra-national trading area. Other European legislation has since followed from that aspiration:

1 The presence of different regulatory systems in different countries to deal with production standards, consumer protection, environmental control and terms of employment will have an influence upon competition. Countries with lower standards may have competitive advantages over those with higher ones, which the latter will want to see eliminated.
2 Economic co-operation between nations is enhanced if they enjoy broadly similar opportunities for employment and standards of living.
3 The concept of a single market embraces a single labour market, in which workers can move freely across boundaries in search of work. They will want to carry social rights with them if they do so.

Hence, the evolution of the Community has led it to develop 'social policy' alongside economic and environmental policy. But that policy has been principally concerned with the rights of employees and with efforts to stimulate employment through investment and training. The principal social policy interventions have been limited efforts to harmonize rules relating to employment and the provision of funds to help create work and aid training programmes (see Gold (ed.) 1993). The European Social Fund (not to be confused with the social fund in social security – see ch. 5), which sounds like a major social policy instrument, is in fact a vehicle for the subsidization of training (and to a lesser extent work creation). Compared with agricultural support, Social Fund expenditure is low, and countries receiving this money are required to add matching contributions to schemes which it supports. There is, additionally, a rather larger Regional Fund, which certainly has 'social effects', since it is used to try to stimulate economic development in regions suffering from underdevelopment or economic decline.

Social policy has figured in arguments about the scope of the role of the European Union, in which British Conservative governments have, during the 1980s and 1990s, been advocates of a limited, cautious approach. Britain secured agreement that it need not accept the 'social chapter' in the Maastricht Treaty of 1992. Whilst a new government may reverse this decision, it is important to recognize that the aspirations of that 'chapter' – towards a greater harmonization of social conditions and of social protection legislation – will not be easy to realize. At whatever speed the European Union may be moving towards greater unification, social policy is likely to be a weak element. The areas where change has occurred, and will continue to occur, concern the elimination of discrimination in the labour market.

However, the presence in Brussels of a directorate which aspires to advance European social policy – which sets out goals for policy, which encourages social policy experiments (the European poverty programmes), and which publishes data on social conditions and social security systems – provides a source of pressure upon national governments, and helps to keep social policy issues on the agenda (see Commission of the European Communities, 1993).

THE VOICE OF THE PEOPLE?

It has already been noted that in the British system of government MPs and councillors are elected in individual constituencies on the basis of a procedure in which the candidate with a simple majority is the winner. It is generally the case that the voter has to choose among two to four candidates, each of whom is the representative of a specific political party. In this way electoral choice is peculiarly structured. Voters have to make their decisions on the basis of assessments of particular people, with their own special policy commitments, in relation to the more general political biases and policy commitments of their parties. The parties' intentions are of more importance than individuals' commitments. However, what the parties offer are broad packages of policies, within which voters may like some items while disliking others.

Hence the individual voter's starting-point in trying to influence policy through the electoral process is a situation of very limited choice in which it is general policy biases or even more general considerations, often described as 'party images', that must govern his or her selection of an MP. Moreover, his or her vote will be taken together with large numbers of other votes, perhaps motivated by very different policy preferences. Hence, one person's voting choice may be influenced by a party's commitment to raise pensions, which leads him or her to support it despite its commitment to other policies – say, increasing educational expenditure – with which he or she disagrees. But others who vote for the same party may be motivated by directly opposite considerations – a strong commitment to education, say, but no concern about pensions. Furthermore, the candidate for this party in one constituency may stress a commitment to education, while colleagues in other constituencies may make the pensions increase the central plank in their programme.

The above example was chosen to illustrate the basic underlying problem with using choices between representatives as a means of settling policy priorities. The reality is that party platforms are considerably more complex, with choices between desirable ends deliberately obscured. No party presents the electorate with explicit choices between widely desired ends; they generally seek to convince it that they can bring a little more of everything that is wanted, probably at less cost. Voters are forced to discriminate between the parties in terms of their general ideologies, value biases and images.

Furthermore, most voters do not really make electoral *choices*. Many vote for the same party every time they vote, and probably give little attention to the personalities or policies of specific candidates. Voters behave in ways that, as far as the collective pattern of choices is concerned, political scientists are to a large extent able to predict from their occupations, social origins and personalities. Only a minority of the electorate changes sides between elections. Indeed, many of the changes that alter the balance of power in Parliament are no more than changes between voting and non-voting, or vice versa. Research findings suggest, moreover, that the people most likely to change their voting behaviour – the floating voters – are generally the least informed within the electorate, and are thus not people who can be said to be making careful choices between policies. It is suggested, instead, that political *images* are particularly significant – the personalities of the leaders, their projections of competence and of their capacities to deal with the nation's problems. An important consideration at a general election is the success or failure of the government in power in coping with the economic situation. In this sense a verdict may be given on its policies, but only in a very general way.

Clearly, therefore, voters are not normally provided with opportunities to make clear choices about social policies or between social policy options. There are certainly general characteristics of the parties' approaches to social policies that may help people to decide between them; and at particular elections, stands for or against social policy may be particularly clear. But at other times it may be very difficult to single out policy issues that divide the parties. In 1970 the Child Poverty Action Group attacked the Labour government's failure to deal effectively with family poverty, and secured a pledge from the Conservatives that family allowances would be increased. The Conservatives did not increase these allowances; but it is doubtful whether many voters were influenced to change their allegiances on the basis of this issue. Those who studied the parties' platforms carefully would have had to balance the Labour Party's generally stronger commitment to universal social security policies against the Conservatives' specific pledge. It may be suggested that what the Child Poverty Action Group expected, and wanted, was a new Labour government returned to power, chastened by criticism of its family policies, and not a Conservative government (see McCarthy, 1986).

Another characteristic of social policies is that, while some involve broad responses to popular needs and wishes, many are specific measures to assist quite small disadvantaged groups in the population. Policies to assist disabled people, for example, may be viewed as generally desirable, and in that sense may have electoral appeal; but the number of people they benefit directly or indirectly is small. Disabled people may be a relatively 'popular' minority group; but what about policies to help the long-term unemployed, rehabilitate criminals or provide facilities for vagrant alcoholics, for example? If there were a direct relationship between the pursuit of electoral popularity and the determination of social policies, surely minority causes would receive much less attention than they do now, and unpopular minority causes would receive no attention at all (or even more punitive responses). Opinion polls suggest that a variety of social reforms carried out in Britain – the abolition of capital punishment and the liberalization of the law relating to homosexuality, for example – were enacted in the face of popular opposition.

Other survey evidence suggests, moreover, that, whilst there are strong public commitments to pensions and the health service, other social policies which favour those most in need of help from the welfare state, such as the unemployed and single parents, have little popular support (Taylor-Gooby, 1985; Edgell and Duke, 1991).

Further, it is important to add to this examination of the impact of 'the voice of the people' upon social policy determination the observation that our 'first past the post' electoral system can convey a very ambiguous message. After the 1987 election, Margaret Thatcher had a large majority in Parliament, and thus claimed to have a very clear mandate. But her opponents were able to point to the fact that a majority of the electorate had voted against her. This opposing vote was, of course, split, largely speaking, between the Labour Party and the Liberal/SDP Alliance. Moreover, more than a quarter of the electorate did not vote, and the disadvantaged would have been disproportionately represented amongst the non-voters. It can also be shown, as has already been suggested with reference to Scotland, that in our very centralized political system, government support was nevertheless very low in some regions. The 1992 election continued this pattern, albeit with a much lower parliamentary majority for the Conservatives. However, the introduction of some kind of proportional representation system would not necessarily solve this 'political arithmetic' problem, for policy priorities would then be influenced by the way in which negotiations between potential coalition parties developed.

Pressure groups

Much of the detailed analysis of the role of pressure groups in the policy-making process has been carried out in the United States. There the political system has several characteristics that particularly facilitate the mobilization of small groups of people to influence decisions. First, power within the system is very fragmented – between the President and the two houses of Congress, between the federal government and the states, and between the state government and local government. Second, in that vast, diverse country, political choices are much more dictated by local interests than they are in Britain. Hence the relationship between a member of Congress and his or her local electorate is much less affected by national party considerations. Third, at federal level the parties are accordingly much less unified by political ideologies. Political actors are therefore readily influenced by small groups, which can effectively threaten to have an electoral impact.

In Britain pressure groups are probably just as much in evidence as they are in the United States. A number of studies (Finer, 1958; Wootton, 1970; Roberts, 1970; Jordan and Richardson, 1987) have dispelled the notion that they are of no importance in the British system. But there is a need to beware of the assumption that they have as direct an impact upon the political system as they do in the United States. Their importance in the politics of that country has led political scientists to propound a modification of the theory of representative government in which the weakness of the individual voter, discussed on pages 63–6, is seen as compensated for by his or her membership of interest groups (Dahl, 1961). Democracy is thus seen as 'pluralist' in character, with politicians engaged in continuing processes of compromise with multiple groups. Such a theory is then seen as explaining the deference of politicians to the interests of minorities; and a new – and perhaps superior – version of democratic theory is presented which has as its hallmark the achievement of a political consensus in which minority interests are protected.

This theory has, however, come under fire in the United States. It has been pointed out that there are biases in the system that make it much easier for some interests to be heard than others, and much easier for modifications to the *status quo* to be vetoed than to be supported (Schattschneider, 1960; Bachrach, 1969).

These general points about the plurality of pressure groups are worthy of our attention, since they suggest important questions about the way the British system operates. The contrasts made above between the political systems on the two sides of the Atlantic suggest that it may be much more difficult for British pressure groups to identify points at which the political system is particularly open to influence. In individual constituencies grievances with the established political parties have to be very deeply felt, and very widely shared, to upset national electoral swings. Direct interventions in elections motivated by local issues are rare, except in the areas where nationalist parties can have an impact. Outside Scotland and Wales politicians have often been able to be singularly insensitive to local issues. And the current three or more party system further distorts the picture.

There are similar problems for a national pressure group trying to persuade political parties that disregard of its case carries electoral dangers. Furthermore, any interest group able to threaten in this way probably already has a special relationship with a major political party, and is acknowledged as important in that sense. Many of the most powerful British pressure groups tend to have an established relationship with one or other political party. The trade unions are, of course, the clearest example of this phenomenon. They played a key role in the original establishment of the Labour Party. Although the modern party is trying to distance itself from them, they still provide a significant proportion of its funds. Correspondingly, the other side of industry is an important paymaster for the Conservative Party. It is unlikely that the major elements in either of these groups will actually change sides, but the parties may feel threatened if they are lukewarm in their support.

It is important to look more closely at the ways in which specific groups enjoy an institutionalized relationship with the political system. In particular, it is necessary to go beyond the examples of close relationships to political parties to recognize that the positions some groups enjoy in relation to the political system owe nothing to particular party allegiances. Indeed, there are groups whose very power in Britain might be jeopardized if they were seen as identified with specific political parties.

Political elites

The power of some pressure groups can only be explained in terms of what may be called an 'insider' status within the policy-making system.

This implies a further deviation from democratic theory, a system within which some individuals and groups have special status. A number of political scientists and sociologists have suggested that societies possess a political 'elite' (see Bottomore, 1966; and specifically on Britain, Urry and Wakeford (eds), 1973, and Stanworth and Giddens, 1974), that decision-makers are drawn from a narrow spectrum within a society. Traditional Marxist analyses of the social structure suggest that the political system is dominated by representatives of the bourgeoisie, the capitalist class. Modern updates of this theory have pointed out the relevance of patterns of domination based upon race and gender as well (Williams, 1989). But other political theories, notably those of Pareto and Mosca, suggest that there is a ruling elite that is not necessarily characterized by the possession of economic resources.

Modern interpretations of elite theories seek to show either that key policy offices are held by people from a narrow spectrum of social origins, or that a limited number of people, characterized by close links with one another, dominate decision-making roles. For Britain it has been shown that Cabinet ministers, senior civil servants, members of key advisory bodies, and the heads of prestigious organizations tend to be drawn from a relatively narrow social class group, characterized by education at public schools and Oxbridge and by having had parents in a similarly narrow range of upper-middle-class occupations. The picture is not simple, however, and there is some evidence that the backgrounds of top decision-makers have changed in recent years to embrace a slightly wider range of social origins. While certainly it seems plausible to suggest that if there are people from similar social or educational backgrounds in a number of key roles, the relationships between those people will facilitate the sharing of ideas and opinions, the processes involved cannot necessarily be explained as simply as this.

What is more important in explaining the place of some pressure groups in Britain in relation to the structure of power is to examine the sense in which the policy-making process is perceived as involving assumptions that some interests should be consulted. Such assumptions rest upon several foundations. One is that expertise conveys the ability to help with public decision-making. This is the technocratic view, that experts' opinions carry a greater weight than other people's. It is the basis upon which academics sometimes secure a measure of influence in government. Similarly, some pressure groups secure attention because of their expert knowledge. In the educational and medical fields such 'heavyweight' pressure groups abound. It has been suggested that there are a number of 'policy networks' or 'policy communities' in various specialized policy areas, in which regular consultations occur between policy-makers and representatives of pressure groups (including groups representing employees, particularly professional ones) who have been granted partial insider roles (see Smith, 1993).

Another foundation upon which pressure groups may secure influence is their association with traditional elite groups. Voluntary organizations believe that they benefit by royal sponsorship and by the acquisition of prestigious figures as vice-presidents and supporters. Such sponsorship is not always easily earned. It is clearly helpful to have a cause that readily attracts the sympathy of influential people. It may also be important to behave in ways that are deemed respectable. This is a curious feature of this kind of pressure group activity; to some extent, the power of groups depends upon their ability to forswear the more direct weapons in the pressure group armoury, to avoid mounting vociferous opinion-forming campaigns or threatening forms of direct action. The supposition here is based upon a belief that there is an underlining elitist approach to government in Britain. A fairly narrow range of people are responsible for key decisions; some of these attain such positions through democratic representational procedures, but they co-opt others to their ranks. These other people may be individuals of shared social backgrounds, but the process of co-optation may be more haphazard. Individuals from pressure groups, or at least representing specific interests, secure entry into the ranks of those who exercise power by virtue not only of expertise but also of personal qualities, such as persistence and charm, which enable them to persuade others that they have something to contribute to public decision-making. They also generally have to establish that they understand some of the unspoken rules relating to public participation: that they won't embarrass their sponsors by the use of direct tactics or indiscreet communications to the press or unseemly behaviour in committee situations. In so doing, they join the ranks of those who have been called upon over and over again to sit on public committees and advisory bodies.

This argument, then, is that political influence may be secured in Britain without the aid of independent power. The system co-opts others to join its ranks, and pays attention to some citizens very much more readily than others. In this day and age, people are rightly cynical about propositions regarding the power of ideas. They look around for other explanations and ulterior motives. But in the study of social policy, the importance of individuals should not be wholly underestimated. There are examples of people who, through the strength of their commitments and the power of their attention to detail, have secured a place in the policy-making process. In the first half of this century, William Beveridge (Harris, 1977) was such an individual. In the 1980s, experienced businessmen were turned to as advisers, and one (Sir Roy Griffiths) had an important influence on the organization of the health service and on community care policy. There are many lesser examples around, of people whose influence upon policy-making owes nothing either to any notion of representative government or to the cruder theories about pressure group activity.

A great deal of pressure group activity is, of course, concerned with 'good causes'. Again, a theory of the policy-making process needs to find room for good causes as well as for 'good people'. There are important questions that should not be brushed aside about the place of altruism in policy-making. It is not naïve to argue that politicians – or, if you prefer, some politicians – have commitments to ideals. It is certainly important to recognize that many politicians want to be seen to be supporters of good causes. Hence, pressure groups for the disabled, the old, neglected children and so on will exert influence out of proportion to their naked power. For them the skilful use of mass media may be important, and key contacts with those in positions of power will be a great help. In this sense they aim to be co-opted into policy communities.

No account of social policy-making should disregard the potential influence of these good causes, however much scope there may be for controversy about their real power in situations where interests are in conflict. Indeed, one of the frustrating phenomena that many pressure groups of this kind experience is continuing assertions by politicians that they do matter, accompanied by minimal concrete action. It is very hard to predict the political circumstances that will favour interests of this kind; but, manifestly, many have secured benefits without the use of any perceptible political 'muscle'. It is perhaps useful here to bear in mind the distinction often made in the study of pressure groups between 'interest' groups and 'cause' groups, though in the tactical struggle for influence, each may seek to co-opt the support of the other. Interests seek to be recognized as 'good causes', and causes try to enlist the backing of more powerful 'interests'.

It was suggested earlier that pressure groups provide a crucial qualification to the notion of a simple relationship between electors and elected. Some writers have suggested that they solve the problem of the powerlessness of the individual in relation to the political machine (Dahl, 1961; Beer, 1965). While there are many circumstances in which this is true, it seems important to acknowledge that the political system contains biases that make it much easier for some groups to secure influence than others. In addition, in Britain there is the peculiar phenomenon of the exercise of influence by groups that, according to the crude calculations of political arithmetic, do not seem to have a power base at all. This must lead us to look at the shortcomings of the 'how many divisions has the Pope' approach to the estimation of political influence. It implies, however, a recognition that the minority who occupy powerful positions in British society are able to make choices, based neither upon notions of democracy nor upon calculations about who has power, but about whom they will listen to or consult.

MINISTERIAL POWER: THE ROLE OF OFFICIALS AND THE INFLUENCE OF OUTSIDE GROUPS AND POLICY COMMUNITIES

In *The Sociology of Public Administration* (Hill, 1972) I developed a typology of government styles, to try to elucidate different characteristics of politician/official relationships in different political situations. I identified three types of political system: 'ideological politics', 'administrative politics' and 'bargaining politics'.

A system of 'ideological politics' relates most clearly to the model of 'representative government'. It is one in which the traditional distinction between politics and administration is most easily made. Political parties compete to win elections by submitting distinct programmes from which the electorate can choose. Politicians instruct administrators to frame policies compatible with their mandates and commitments. The Thatcher governments stood out as examples of this phenomenon.

'Administrative politics' describes a contrasting system in which full-time officials are much more clearly dominant. The 'politics' are organizational rather than public, and many of the key conflicts are between departments. Ministers in central government, while formally possessing the key decision-making powers, in fact find themselves involved primarily in expounding views and defending policies generated within their departments. Politicians of the majority party without ministerial office find themselves frustratingly shut out from a decision-making process into which they are given few insights. In British local government the committee system provides scope for the wider use of elected representatives in an administrator-dominated context, though here such involvement may further undermine representative government, since it depends primarily upon personal characteristics.

The concept of 'bargaining politics' was derived from examination of accounts of local politics in the United States. Partly as a result of exposure to the American literature and partly because of a desire to adopt a tough-minded approach towards power, British social and political scientists have been on the look-out for signs of a similar system in Britain. In such a system political outcomes are seen to depend upon inputs of resources of power. Those who hold elected positions are not 'representatives' so much as 'brokers' who bring together coalitions of interests. Their desire for re-election forces them to adopt strategies in which they are highly sensitive to pressure groups. Some reservations about this view have already been suggested, but it was acknowledged that elements of bargaining are by no means absent from the British scene. Bargaining politics implies a clear role for politicians, which may suggest that officials occupy subordinate positions. While this is true inasmuch as political futures are at stake, it has been argued that in Britain deals with quite explicit electoral implications are rare. Bargaining may therefore be more concerned with the maintenance of specific policies or particular organizational arrangements. If so, it may be that officials have more to lose, or have more explicit commitments, than politicians. Key conflicts concern relationships between departments and the outside world; ministers are expected to help defend departmental interests.

It is not suggested that the individual types fit any specific political system. British central government must be noted as a context in which conflicts often appear to be of an ideological nature and the representative model is treated as of some importance. Yet a key theme in discussions of relationships between ministers and their departments has been the extent to which politicians start out with apparent policy commitments, but become socialized into roles determined by the permanent administrators, and particularly by the need for 'policy maintenance' within their department (this was cleverly satirized in the television series *Yes Minister*). Furthermore, a theme related to the ministerial discovery that cherished policy innovations are not administratively feasible is the recognition that vested interests and pressure groups carry a political 'clout' that had not been realized when policies were planned outside government. Policy-making outcomes may be determined by the interaction of three forces: political input (ideological politics), organizational considerations within departments (administrative politics), and external pressures (bargaining politics). Marsh and Rhodes's *Implementing Thatcherite Policies* (1992a) offers a good account of the way in which ideological politics was muted in practice in the 1980s. Conversely, Campbell and Wilson (1995) show how the model of civil service domination outlined by Crossman has been partly undermined by the tendency of the Thatcher and Major governments to advance civil servants who have been prepared to offer them uncritical assistance in the pursuit of ideological goals.

Beyond these generalizations, a more detailed study of the factors that influence the way in which policy is made needs to take various considerations into account. First, what are the kinds of policies involved? This raises the question so far evaded in this book: What is policy? Writers on policy analysis are agreed that a policy is more than a decision. Friend and his colleagues suggest that 'policy is essentially a *stance* which, once articulated, contributes to the context within which a succession of future decisions will be made' (Friend et al., 1974, p. 40). Jenkins (1978) similarly stresses the notion of interrelated decisions concerned with the selection of goals and the adoption of a course of action. Smith suggests that 'the concept of policy denotes . . . deliberate choice of action or inaction, rather than the effects of interrelating forces'. He emphasizes 'inaction', and reminds us that 'attention should not focus exclusively on decisions which produce change, but must also be sensitive to those which resist change and are difficult to observe because they are not represented in the policy-making process by legislative enactment' (Smith, 1976, p. 13; see also Marsh and Rhodes, 1992a).

Policies are thus not easy to define. It is doubtful whether much can be gained by trying to achieve any greater precision than that suggested in the definitions above. It is more fruitful to look in a concrete way at the relevance of policies for the activity of a minister and his or her department. On appointment to office, a new minister will take over responsibility for many departmental policies. The overwhelming majority of these will be just existing ways of doing things. A good many will be enshrined in Acts of Parliament, but will be accompanied by organizational arrangements, systems of administration and working conventions which will also help to define policy. There is a distinction to be made between policy and the arrangements made for its implementation. This will be explored further in the next chapter; here it must be stressed that these arrangements will in many cases have a quite fundamental impact upon the character of the policy, and may thus be deemed to be part of that policy.

It is this existence of policies that determines much everyday practice in a department, and therefore provides the most crucial group of constraints for a new minister. Existing policies keep most people occupied most of the time. Innovations depend upon finding opportunities for staff to work on developing new policies. They may also depend upon getting people within a department to work to change old policies, which have hitherto been regarded as quite satisfactory. Clearly, an innovating minister has to find ways to get a vast operational organization to change its ways.

What is perhaps more significant is that a new minister will also find that his or her department is developing new policies. These are not necessarily merely the left-over business from a previous administration. Many of them will derive from weaknesses in existing policies that have been recognized within the department, and that administrators are striving to correct. Some, moreover, will have their roots in changes in the world in which existing policies operate, changes that are making those policies unsuccessful or irrelevant. This group of policies or 'would-be policies' is important. The new minister may find that his or her own, or the party's, policy aspirations mesh with the policy issues upon which the department is working. In such circumstances he or she may find it comparatively easy to become, or to be seen as, an innovator. But he or she may have to face the fact that his or her own view of the department's policy needs are regarded as irrelevant to the main problem being tackled within it, or even that his or her own commitments lead in quite opposite directions to those being taken by those concerned with policy innovation in the department. Popular discussions of the success or failure of ministers are often carried on in terms of their personalities and their experience. Of course, it is often possible to distinguish 'strong' and 'weak' ministers; but it must not be forgotten that the comparatively temporary incumbent of the top post in a large organization may be just lucky or unlucky – in arriving when key advisers are likely to agree that exciting innovations are necessary, or, conversely, in finding that the consolidation of existing policies, or the confronting of unpleasant realities, is more important than the policy changes he or she cherishes.

There are various kinds of policy initiatives. Some policies may be enacted by the passing of a law. Reform of regulatory law, for example, may have only slight administrative implications. A second category of policies with only indirect consequences for the minister's own department are those whose enactment and implementation depend upon another agency. Legislation giving powers, and even sometimes duties, to local government falls in this category. The Chronically Sick and Disabled Persons Act of 1970 is a classic example. While it seems to involve the development of a national policy for the disabled, in practice its dependence upon local government makes it a gesture in which central government involvement is comparatively slight. This measure arose as the result of an initiative by a private Member, Alf Morris. A later piece of legislation on this issue, the Disabled Persons Act of 1986, seems to have similar characteristics. Individuals and voluntary organizations are likely to have to work hard to make local government implement it. Clearly, it is easier for a minister to accept this sort of legislation than to develop a policy that effectively changes the direction of a great deal of work going on *within* the department. In the above case the policy-making may be more 'symbolic' than real; ministers may hope to derive kudos without really enacting innovations.

Once a minister seeks to enact policies that require the expenditure of 'new money', he or she becomes engaged in what is inevitably a more difficult political exercise. Formally, the approval of the Treasury is required, probably together with the support of the Cabinet in one of its priority-setting exercises, where the minister is involved in competition with colleagues who have alternative expenditure aspirations. What this implies for the minister's relationship with civil servants is altogether more complex. The specific expenditure commitment will be by no means the only one which the department might undertake. Hence there will be an intra-organizational battle regarding the case for that particular innovation. What the outside world sees as a minister promoting a particular project is probably the end of a long process in which different groups of civil servants within the department have argued about the case for that venture as opposed to other ventures. A minister who says 'I want to do X' will have to face civil servants who argue 'But we need money for X, Y' and so on. The political negotiations between a minister and the Treasury ministers will be matched by much more elaborate negotiations among civil servants. A case that is comparatively weak when argued within the department will come up against further problems in this tough forum, and a minister who successfully overrides objections within his or her own department may well lose in this wider battle. Students of government have raised questions, moreover, about the extent to which civil servants will fight effectively for their minister against the Treasury, in view of the prestige and power of the latter within the civil service as a whole (see Heclo and Wildavsky, 1981).

In differentiating among different kinds of policies, and in interpreting their implications for ministerial power, it must be recognized that some policies have implications for more than one department. A new approach to assistance with housing costs, for example, may have to be considered both by the Department of Social Security, with its concern for social security policy, and the Department of Environment, with its responsibility for housing policy. In addition, local government is likely to be involved. This adds a form of complexity that greatly enhances the significance of negotiations among civil servants and the related tendency to maintenance of the *status quo*. Such policies place strains upon the unity of the political group involved. Two key aspects of government emphasized in the Crossman diaries are the difficulties facing a minister with departmental responsibilities who tries to take an overall view of government policies, and the related tendency for ministers to take narrowly departmental views which sabotage inter-departmental co-operation.

This discussion has distinguished between policies that ministers can enact with relatively slight implications for their own departments and those that require elaborate departmental involvement. It has implied that where ideological commitments are involved, a distinction may be made between relatively easy gestures and hard administrative battles. Yet it may also be the case that some difficult aspects of bargaining politics are involved where policy success depends upon the responses of other organizations.

The Thatcher government found some of its ideas for tax and social security reform affected by the reservations of small business about new tasks for government. The power of doctors in health policy provides similar examples. In this case the problem comes, if not exactly within a secretary of state's own department, at least from within a public agency. Also important for the analysis of social policy is the interplay between central government and those other organs of government, particularly local government, which have a crucial role to play in the implementation of policy, but are also themselves in certain respects policy-makers.

A new minister with an overall responsibility for the health and personal social services within the Department of Health, or for education, or for housing policy (together with local government in general) within the Department of the Environment, will find an 'established' relationship between the department and local government or the health service with certain key characteristics. There will be a body of enacted legislation, a pattern of grants from central government, a range of procedures relating to the sanctioning of new initiatives, including the taking up of loans for new capital expenditure, perhaps a pattern of inspection or policy review, and a variety of policy expectations enshrined in circulars and related messages from the centre. In a few cases the obligations of the local authorities will be quite clear. In a rather larger number of situations the authorities will have quite explicit duties, but will not have been given detailed guidance on how to carry them out. In yet other important cases the local authorities will regard themselves as the key policy-makers; the central requirements will have been specified in such general terms that the decisions that really dictate the quality of the service given to the public are made locally. Then there will be situations in which central government has made it very clear that the policy initiative rests with the local agency, by *permitting* activities if they so wish. Finally, there will be a few situations in which local authorities are almost entirely the innovators, in which they have sought to promote local Acts through Parliament or in which they have interpreted general powers given to them in quite novel ways.

The new minister who wants to introduce changes into this pattern has a variety of options open, but each may involve complications wherever there is resistance to new ideas. New policies are expressed as much in ministerial statements, White Papers and circulars to the local authorities as in new statutes. In each case the minister may be able to back up a recommendation with indirect weapons: by control over loans and other powers to permit or limit activities, by co-operation or lack of it in situations in which joint central–local action is necessary. In the National Health Service, control over funding facilitates policy change from the centre.

Local authorities often fight hard to try to protect their independence. They may be unresponsive to ministerial suggestions, and they may make their opposition very clear through the local authority associations. The threat of non-co-operation from local authorities may make a minister think again. The most publicized cases of such non-co-operation have occurred where authorities have stood out against a minister on a highly political issue. It may be suspected that issues on which there is widespread local resistance, but where a party political split is not clearly in evidence, rarely hit the news headlines because they are quietly negotiated in private discussions between the minister, or civil servants, and the local authority associations. The public conflicts of recent years have involved confrontations between different political ideologies: the resistance from the Clay Cross Urban District to the Conservative Housing Finance Act, the rejection by Merthyr County Borough of the Conservatives' withdrawal of free milk for schoolchildren, the resistance of a number of Conservative education authorities to the Labour commitment to the introduction of comprehensive secondary education, the resistance of Labour local authorities to the Conservative government's legislation on the sale of council houses, and the forms of 'creative accounting' developed in the mid-1980s by some local authorities to evade expenditure restraints. The evidence suggests that a determined central government, generally backed by the courts, has, at least since 1979, been able to impose its will in most central–local battles. The new financial controls, described above (pp. 60–1), have surely strengthened this domination.

Although the local authorities are themselves policy-makers, as has been suggested, the force of influence for policy change is not just one-way. Just as a new minister encounters groups of civil servants within the department with policy concerns that conflict with his or her own, so too does he or she encounter local authorities keen to take new initiatives. They will be eager to protect their own autonomy, but may also seek to convince a minister that their local initiatives should be enshrined in national policy.

Hence, as sources of local initiatives, local government may be as important as central government. The example of comprehensive education is again interesting. Before the 1964–70 Labour government made it Department of Education and Science policy, a number of local authorities had already set up comprehensive schools. It is significant that, while in some areas – such as London – this development was motivated by a political commitment, in other places – for example, rural Devon – it was educational administrators who had convinced councils, of a broadly Conservative persuasion, that the development of such schools was the most appropriate policy. It is equally interesting to note that the trend towards comprehensivization continued after the Thatcher government repealed the legislation which had been forcing the pace in the late 1970s.

In this section the discussion has ranged over many of the influences upon policy. Using the notion that is particularly associated with representative government, of a new minister with explicit policy commitments, attention has been paid to the pressures that frustrate such commitments or replace them by commitments derived from other sources. It has been stressed that there are strong forces in favour of the maintenance of existing policy, and that many new initiatives are in fact derived from concerns not so much to innovate as to correct the imperfections of existing policies.

Hence, it is interesting that, whereas the historical account of social policy tended to stress a variety of significant contributions to policy, building constructively on the past – the 1911 National Insurance Act, the 1944 Education Act, the 1946 National Health Service Act – perhaps a key element in writings on the policy process during the 1960s and 1970s was the absence of rational forward planning, but in its place a phenomenon that has been called 'disjointed incrementalism' (Braybrooke and Lindblom, 1963). Then, during the 1980s and 1990s, Britain entered another major period of change.

Braybrooke and Lindblom, the theorists who drew attention to the significance of incrementalism, were particularly concerned to attack that portrayal of the policy process which perceived it as, or able to become, a rational appraisal of all the alternative consequences of alternative policies followed by the choice of the best available. If incrementalism is perceived in these terms, there is little difficulty in understanding its applicability to social policy. As the historical chapter 2 showed, the development of social policy has been very much a process of piling new initiatives on top of older policies, without ever clearing the ground to facilitate a fresh start. Then, as this piling-up process has proceeded, it has created new interests, which future developments have had to take into account. Since political values have often been at stake in conflicts over social policy, the very character of the ideological issues has precluded a cool appraisal of all the policy options.

If the choices are between understanding policy-making as a pure exercise in rational decision-making, as the putting into practice of ideologies, or as a quite incoherent process of bargaining and muddling-through, then it is sensible to reject each alternative. It is a compromise among all three, with perhaps the first least apparent and the third most in evidence.

SUGGESTIONS FOR FURTHER READING

Like the previous chapter, this one has drawn upon a vast literature, this time largely from the discipline of political science. References have largely been chosen to include some of the classic works that expounded particular theoretical viewpoints, together with textbooks that most clearly interpret theories and issues for British audiences. The following suggestions for further reading are primarily in the latter category.

For those who require a basic textbook on British government, Hanson and Walles's *Governing Britain* (latest edition, 1990) and Jones et al. (1991) are recommended. For more advanced accounts, written from a strong political science perspective, books by Dearlove and Saunders (2nd edition, 1991) and Jordan and Richardson (1987) are worth consulting, the former offering a comparatively radical account of events, the latter a more conservative one. Smith (1993) explores the issues about 'policy networks' and 'policy communities.

An account of the local government system is provided by Tony Byrne (6th edition, 1994). While it is not appropriate to recommend wide reading on the European Union here, the book edited by Gold, *The Social Dimension* (1993), is a good source on social policy.

Reference has been made in the text to Marsh and Rhodes's *Implementing Thatcherite Policies* (1992a); whilst its title suggests that it is appropriate reading for the next chapter, on implementation, its focus on issues regarding the translation of ideology into policies make it relevant for the policy-making process as a whole. Chris Ham's and my *The Policy Process in the Modern Capitalist State* (1993) explores many of the theoretical issues regarding policy-making.

CHAPTER 4

IMPLEMENTATION

INTRODUCTION

Why devote a chapter in a book on social policy to the study of policy implementation? What is the significance of this issue for our subject? There are several reasons why it is important. First, the discussion of policy-making in the latter part of the last chapter suggested that many new initiatives stem from the recognition that older policies are failing to meet desired goals. This may be because these goals have changed, but it may equally be because the social world for which the original policies were designed has changed. This is an implementation problem. It may also be because there were weaknesses in the older policies, many of which became apparent only when policies were implemented. So it is important to scrutinize the implementation process with some care.

Second, concern with the ineffectiveness of policies is now recognized as requiring the asking not only of questions about the character of policy but also about what is wrong with the implementation process and the organizations responsible for implementation. It may be that the policies are at fault, or it may be that corrective action is most appropriately applied to the implementing agencies. This is the central concern for what we may call the 'top down' approach to the study of implementation: Why don't those who are expected to carry out policies do what is required of them?

Third, and finally, while it is true that the impact of all policies must be subjected to careful scrutiny, it is particularly important to give attention to what it feels like to be on the receiving end of social policy. This may be described as a concern with 'impact', rather than with 'implementation'. It is this concern that has led students of social policy to give increasing attention in recent years to the activities of that group of public servants who may be called 'street-level bureaucrats' (Lipsky,

1980), and to ask questions about what actually happens in the exchanges between these people and the public.

STRUCTURES FOR POLICY IMPLEMENTATION

This section provides a brief account of the main groups of people responsible for social policy implementation in the United Kingdom. An examination of the wide range of people involved, of the many different roles they play, and of their varying involvement in or distance from the policy-making process will help to stress the importance of giving attention to implementation and to introduce the more theoretical discussion that follows. Since the organizational arrangements vary within the constituent countries of the United Kingdom, the comments below should be taken to apply only to England, except where there is an observation to the contrary. However, in the cases of social security and employment there is a single system for Britain, and the system in Northern Ireland is in most respects a copy of that.

Social security benefits are calculated and paid to the public by a very large number of civil servants based in regional and local offices throughout the country. These people now come under one of a number of public 'agencies', carrying out functions delegated to them by the Department of Social Security, to whom they are ultimately answerable.

The Benefits Agency deals with payment of both contributory and means-tested benefits. The former are determined by a largely computerized central system. The calculation of means-tested benefits is also increasingly concentrated in a small number of offices, leaving the local offices in touch with the public to take in applications and to deal with queries. A minority of Benefits Agency staff, social fund officers, are concerned with the highly discretionary 'social fund', with regard to which determinations are still made at the local level. There is a separate agency which collects national insurance contributions.

A social security agency which has been the subject of considerable controversy is the Child Support Agency set up to administer legislation enacted in 1991 to strengthen the system for securing contributions to child support from absent parents (mainly fathers). The Child Support Agency was set targets for sums to be collected which were not achievable with its resources in the face of widespread public resistance. Its first chief executive resigned in 1994, after considerable criticism, much of which might more properly have been directed at the secretary of state who appointed her.

There is only one other large group of people defined in Britain as civil servants that is concerned with the implementation of the social policies discussed in this book, and that is those involved in the employment services. These come under the Department for Education and Employment, and again are organized into an agency (the Employment Services Agency). This also services local training and enterprise councils, whose membership is drawn from employers.

Otherwise, field-level social policy implementation is the responsibility of National Health Service and local authority officials, who, since they are not employees of central government departments, are not regarded as civil servants. However, in order to relate to local implementation systems, a number of central government departments have regional offices. Examples relevant to social policy implementation are the Department of the Environment's system of regional offices which handle many aspects of relationships with local authorities, and the Department of Health's regional social work inspectors who help the department to relate to local authority social services departments.

The implementation of health policy in England and Wales is devolved in a complex way. At national level there is a National Health Service Executive. This is staffed by civil servants from the Department of Health, and may in many respects be regarded as an extension of that department with direct accountability to the secretary of state. That Executive has a regional 'arm', which has replaced the former regional health authorities. At the local level there are health authorities, which, from April 1996, have combined the responsibilities for the provision of all services at the local level, including family practitioner services. These are quasi-autonomous organizations with directors (executive and non-executive) appointed by the secretary of state, but with their own employees.

The health authorities in England and Wales (their equivalents are health boards in Scotland, answerable to the Secretary of State for Scotland) may be *direct* providers of services, but in practice most local provision will be 'purchased' from other organizations. As far as primary health care services (general practice, dentistry, ophthalmic services) are concerned, there are contractual arrangements with professional providers on lines much like those established when the NHS was set up in 1948. Some general medical practitioners have, since 1990, become fund-holders, with power to purchase hospital and community services for their patients.

As regards most hospital services and many community health services, the providers are trusts set up under the terms of the National Health Service and Community Care Act of 1990. These trusts are not as autonomous as their names, and some of the rhetoric of those who devised the system, suggest. They have been set up with secretary of state approval and with directors appointed by that minister.

There are purchasing contracts between health authorities and private providers, but these are of limited importance for the system as a whole. Clearly, the establishment of trusts could be a first step towards a much wider system of publicly funded private provision for health. Re-election of the Conservatives in 1997 might lead to such a development. By contrast, Labour has already made clear its wish to keep trusts under close control.

While recent developments in health administration have made the managerial links in the chain, peopled largely by lay managers, of increasing importance, health remains an area of social policy in which professionals – particularly doctors – have extensive degrees of autonomy. It is often difficult to make a distinction between policy-making and policy implementation with reference to a service operated by professionals. Day-to-day service provision decisions may actually determine, or pre-empt, priorities. In this sense they can be described as policy decisions. The purchaser–provider split is seen as limiting the scope for this to happen. Observers of health services are divided about the extent to which professional power has been curbed.

Responsibility for the implementation of education policy is divided between local authorities and a series of arrangements for direct links between the central ministries (Education and Employment in England, the Scottish and Welsh Offices) and the schools and colleges.

As suggested in the last chapter, there has been a considerable amount of conflict in recent years about the autonomy of local authorities as policy-makers. To some extent the implementation issues in the local authority education service concern the relationship between the authorities and the schools. While the chain image is not entirely appropriate, since varying responsibilities and degrees of autonomy are involved, and individuals in the chain may be bypassed, it is important to acknowledge that implementation may depend upon the following series of links: education committee, chief education officer and his or her administrative staff, local authority inspectors and advisers, school governing bodies, head teachers, departmental heads within schools, and class teachers. Examination of policy implementation in the education service raises a number of interesting questions about local authority autonomy, the role of school management and the place of professional discretion.

The 1986 Education Act has strengthened the powers of the governing bodies of local authority schools, laying down rules to determine their budgets and giving them autonomous responsibilities. But it also enables schools to apply to the secretary of state to become grant-maintained schools, directly accountable to him or her, rather than under local authority control. By the end of 1994 about 1,000 of the 30,000 schools in England and Wales had achieved this status (Ranson, in Jackson and Lavender, 1995, p. 199). There is a special funding council for these schools. Whilst the government has seen this as a form of decentralization, increasing the feasibility of parent power, the weakening of local political control through the provision of a centralized administrative framework can equally be seen as increasing centralization (see Glennerster et al., 1991). The latter impression is further reinforced by the development of the national curriculum.

Higher education in Britain has required special forms of organization designed to take into account the fact that many colleges serve more than the local authority area in which they are based. For the university sector a special intermediary body has long existed. However, the 1986 Education Act replaced the comparatively independent University Grants Committee by more directly government-controlled university funding councils. At the same time it took the polytechnics out of local authority control, setting up a special funding council for them. Subsequently, the Further and Higher Education Act of 1992 renamed the polytechnics 'universities' and brought them under the same funding councils as the universities; it then brought the remaining local authority colleges of higher and further education under ministerial control through another funding council.

The personal social services in Britain are the responsibility, inasmuch as they are under public rather than voluntary control, of social services departments (social work departments in Scotland) within local authorities. Since 1993 local authorities have been required to operate, in respect of their community care services, but not their child care services, a purchaser–provider system rather like that applying in the NHS. Providers may be sections within the local authority department required to operate with some degree of managerial and, particularly, accounting autonomy. But they may also be voluntary or profit-making organizations. They may also be health service trusts.

The government has been concerned that providers from outside the local authority should have a good chance of competing for personal social services contracts. In the area of the provision of residential care, which was already heavily privatized, local authority direct provision is rapidly disappearing.

Many directors and senior staff in social services departments are professionally qualified social workers, but only a relatively small proportion of the staff is engaged in social work. Other key workers include home helps, residential care staff and occupational therapists. Policy implementation is often influenced by the character of co-operation between these different occupational groups.

Whereas for education there is a major department of state, the

Department for Education and Employment, which is responsible for national policy and the relationship between the centre and the local authorities, the personal social services constitute only a small proportion of the policy concerns of the Department of Health. One implementation problem here is that the central department responsible for local government is the Department of the Environment. This department, together with the Treasury, deals with the main financial and legal links with local government, but has no responsibility for education or social services. This exacerbates a tension at the local level between the demands of an integrated, corporate approach to local government and the separable service interests of these two large, heavy-spending departments of education and social services. The statement in the last paragraph applies only to England. In Scotland and Wales the integration of service responsibilities with financial responsibilities in a single department seems to facilitate co-ordination.

Local authority housing in Britain is the responsibility of the unitary or lower-tier local authorities. In Northern Ireland protests about discrimination by local authorities led to the creation of a province-wide Housing Executive; and in Scotland there is an important, nation-wide 'public' housing association to supplement the work of the local authorities. There is also in England and Wales a housing corporation, responsible for the provision of funds for housing associations. A feature of recent government policy has been a quest for new ways to manage and finance housing. This is increasing the importance of bodies like housing associations, financed by public money or by a combination of public and private money.

The implementation of housing policy is fragmented, not only because of the mixture of kinds of housing authorities, but also because this is an area of social policy in which many significant decisions are made by private agencies. Since there are three main types of housing tenure – renting from a local authority or housing association ('social housing'), owner occupation and renting from a private landlord – and the government intervenes, or has intervened, to try to influence the quality and cost of each type, policy implementation is often a very complex matter. In studying it, attention must to be given not only to the relationship between government and the local authorities, but also to government attempts to influence the behaviour of building societies and landlords. There are also some other public–private interactions of some significance for housing policy. For example, there have been government efforts to influence the price of land and to curb land speculation, government interventions in the money market, and government manipulation of the costs and benefits of various statuses in the housing market by means of taxation and social security policy.

Support for the housing costs of low-income tenants comes from housing benefit. In Britain, policy responsibility for this lies with the Department of Social Security, but local authorities administer the scheme. They receive direct reimbursement of most of their costs, except in respect of a few rather difficult issues (such as the treatment of some high rents) where they are given discretion at their own expense.

Finally, it is misleading to suggest that the relationships between government and the various private sectors are of no concern to local housing authorities. The latter increasingly seek to influence housing opportunities of all kinds in their areas, and to give advice to those they do not house themselves. Moreover, the housing authorities, of course, have a significant interest in land prices, and have planning responsibilities to relate housing activities to other kinds of developments in their areas. Housing policy implementation thus has many dimensions.

THE RELATIONSHIP BETWEEN POLICY AND ITS IMPLEMENTATION

In the previous chapter it was suggested that policies are complex phenomena which are hard to define with any precision. This obviously makes for difficulties in distinguishing policy-making and implementation and for identifying implementation issues and problems. The distinction between policy-making and implementation seems to need to rest upon the identification of decision points at which a policy is deemed to be made and ready for implementation, like a commodity that is manufactured and ready for selling. The difficulty with this analogy, however, is that policy-making and implementation merge. The policy-making process is like the design of a building for a specific occupant by an architect; the implementation process affects policy design quite early on, and will continue to influence some details of it even after implementation has begun, just as modifications are made to buildings after occupancy. Or, to take another analogy, Glennerster has compared an implementation process he studied, the introduction of general practitioner fund-holding, with a geographical exploration process, filling in details of unknown territory from a known starting-point like the head of a river (Glennerster et al., 1994, p. 30).

Policies have characteristics that must affect the nature of the implementation process. Many policies will be complex, setting out to achieve objectives x, x_1, x_2 ... under conditions y, y_1, y_2. ... These complexities may very well influence the implementation process. Some policies will involve vague, ambiguous specifications of objectives and conditions. These will tend to become more specific during the implementation process.

Constraints are not merely contained within new policies themselves. While it is possible, in the abstract, to treat policies in isolation from other policies, in practice any new policy will be adopted in a context in which there are already many other policies. Some of these other policies will supply precedents for the new policy, others will supply conditions, and some may be in conflict with it. The process of inaugurating new policies will continue after the adoption of the policy, and will then further affect implementation.

A further general constraint that must not be overlooked is, of course, that the scarcity and control of public finance frequently sets limits to policy development. In some cases these limits are quite explicitly set by central government. Perhaps they arise because the government does not recognize the true costs of their new policies, or perhaps because of a resistance to making a particular policy effective which comes from within the central government machine. In other cases the split between central government as a policy initiator and local government in the role of implementer produces a situation in which central intentions appear to be thwarted by local scarcities. In the area of community care, local authorities have received some additional funds to enable them to meets costs which were previously met by central government from the social security budget. At the same time they are subject to centrally imposed limits on their capacity to raise local revenues. Many consider that their resources fall far short of their responsibilities under the new legislation. There is a certain political duplicity here in legislation which expects local agencies to provide benefits that the centre makes them unlikely to be able to afford.

Policy goals are often specified, as has been pointed out, in general or unclear terms. We can identify a number of different reasons for this lack of clarity. First, it may be simply that policy-makers are far from clear about what they really want. The lack of clarity may be so total that it is comparatively meaningless to seek to identify a policy or to study its implementation. Some 'policies' of this kind derive from political aspirations to demonstrate a popularly desirable commitment. It was suggested in the last chapter that some so-called 'policies' may be merely symbolic. This is true of some aspects of the legislation which appears to give rights to disabled people.

Second, it is important to take account of the extent to which a lack of clarity about policy stems from a lack of potential consensus. Policies emerge that are not merely compromises, but also remain obscure on key points of implementation. Where this occurs, there is likely to be a lack of consensus among the implementers, too. Hence wide variations in practice may emerge, together with a range of conflicts surrounding the implementation process. The 1977 Housing (Homeless

Persons) Act provides examples of implementation problems – concerning the definition of priority groups, the extent of the duty to provide help and advice, and the identification of the responsible authority – that would appear to have emerged from the conflict during the legislation process.

This source of implementation problems is closely related to another of some importance. Sometimes political ambivalence about a policy is reflected not so much in the policy itself as in the constraints that are set upon the implementation process. The simplest form of constraint here, of course, is the failure to provide the means, in money and staff, to enable a policy to be implemented properly.

Another example of a quite deliberately imposed implementation problem is the adoption of administrative procedures that are explicitly designed to affect the impact of a policy. Thus Deacon (1976) has shown how 'the genuinely seeking work test' was manipulated in the 1920s to make it difficult for unemployed people to establish their claim to benefit. He describes the test as imposed as a quite explicit deterrent, without reference to the actual availability of work. The modern parallel to this is the conditions under which the job seekers' allowance is paid.

While acknowledging that many policies are made complex and ambiguous by the conflicts within the policy-making process, it is important to recognize that it is intrinsically difficult to specify some policy goals in terms that will render the implementation process quite clear and unambiguous. This is one important source of discretion for implementers. Jowell (1973) has drawn attention to cases where the concern of policy is with 'standards' that are not susceptible to precise factual definition. He argues that standards may be rendered more precise by 'criteria', facts that are to be taken into account, but that 'the feature of standards that distinguishes them from rules is their flexibility and susceptibility to change over time'. Questions about adequate levels of safety on the roads or in factories, or about purity in food, are of this kind. So are many of the issues about need in social policy. Discretionary judgement is likely to be required by policy, alongside the more precise rules that it is possible to promulgate.

If a policy is a complex, ambiguous phenomenon, with aspects that go 'too far' for some people and 'not far enough' for others, it is important to acknowledge that the dissension that attends its 'birth' will continue to affect its implementation. It may therefore provide opportunities for some implementing agencies to develop new initiatives that were perhaps not envisaged originally. However, policies often contain 'footholds' for those who are opposed to their general thrust, or who wish to divert them to serve their own ends. Bardach

(1977) has developed an extensive analysis of the various 'implementation games' that may be played by those who perceive ways in which policies may be delayed, altered or deflected. While some policies contain few features that their opponents can interfere with – laying down, for example, a clear duty to provide a particular service or benefit – others, such as the Department of Health commitment to the development of community care for the mentally ill, depend heavily upon the commitments of implementers, and are relatively easily diverted in other directions or even rendered ineffective.

It is important to raise questions about the ways in which policies are expressed and the evidence required to establish the extent of implementation. Policies may be conveyed to local implementers in a range of ways, from, at one extreme, the explicit imposition of duties and responsibilities to, at the other end of the continuum, the very loose granting of powers which may or may not be used. We can contrast, for example, the comparatively strict ways in which regulations under the 1986 Social Security Act instruct local authorities in the administration of housing benefit with the powers given (originally in the 1963 Children and Young Persons Act, now in the 1989 Children Act) to local authorities to make money payments in exceptional circumstances to prevent children being taken into care, where no attempt has been made to prescribe how this should be done.

In this discussion it has been hard to draw a line between issues that are essentially *characteristics of policy* that affect implementation and points that are really observations about the characteristics of either the relationships between central policy-makers and local implementers or of the organization of the implementing agencies. While it is helpful to make a distinction between policies on the one hand and the implementation process on the other, this must raise problems at the margin. Policies are formulated with the implementation process in mind, and often it is more realistic to see policies as *products* of implementation rather than as 'top-down' inputs into the process.

THE CENTRE–PERIPHERY RELATIONSHIP

It is possible to some extent to distinguish between those implementation issues that arise essentially from the 'distance' between what we may describe as 'centre' and 'periphery' and those that are facets of other aspects of relationships within complex organizations. The latter, which will be discussed in the next section, are of course considerably complicated by the problem of 'distance', particularly when two or more separate organizations are involved.

In British public administration the centre is generally involved in the policy-making process. But where implementation is delegated to other organizations, the centre generally maintains an interest in the implementation process. Equally, the periphery has an interest in policy-making, and can be expected to contribute to a feedback process from implementation to policy elaboration. However, there are several different kinds of centre–periphery relationships that significantly influence the implementation process. The simplest model is clearly that in which the centre and the periphery are parts of the same organization. The most complex occurs where policy implementation depends upon co-operation between separate autonomous organizations, particularly where responsibility at the periphery is (a) delegated to several organizations with separate territories, and (b) dependent upon co-ordinated action between two or more local organizations. Health and personal social services collaboration tends to fall in this category.

Recognition that there may be issues to consider about 'levels' emphasizes the importance of this dimension for the study of implementation where separate organizations are involved. It is clearly important to identify not merely the issue of the relationship between different levels of elected government, but also the existence of a variety of organizations whose relationships to either central or local government, or both, is often ambiguous: the health authorities, the urban development corporations, the funding councils for higher education and the universities, the new town corporations and so on.

The new agencies set up to administer central services – like the Benefits Agency – seem, *prima facie*, to have clearer mandates. They are governed by framework agreements which appear to make their implementation responsibilities explicit. Yet the intrinsic difficulties in making a clear distinction between policy-making and implementation mean that anything they may do to alter the service they provide to the public may raise political concerns (see Ling in Clarke et al., 1994). Furthermore, as the case of the Child Support Agency, discussed above, has indicated, when something goes wrong, there will be argument about whether an agency has failed to fulfil its mandate or whether the mandate itself was flawed. In fact, as this example shows, their apparent separation enables the agency's executive staff to be offered up as sacrifices for ministerial mistakes.

In some situations it is important to bear in mind the wide range of inter-agency linkages that may be necessary. Pressman and Wildavsky (1973) have made a tentative attempt to draw attention to what may loosely be described as the mathematics of implementation, the way in which the mere quantity of agreements necessary may, even when all parties are committed to a policy, undermine or delay effective action.

Hence it is necessary to give attention to the following issues about centre–periphery relations:

1 A relationship is likely to involve two or more organizations at either the centre or the periphery or both. Effective implementation may depend upon co-operation not merely between the two levels, but also between different organizations at the same level.
2 A centre–periphery relationship may be mediated through one or more intermediary or regional bodies.
3 Relationships between agencies, in practice, involve a number of different issues, and the symmetry that it is possible to depict in an abstract model will not be the same for each issue.

In reality, any organization is involved in a web of relationships, which vary in character and intensity according to the issue. Hence, local authorities have to deal with a number of different central government departments, but the extent to which this is the case varies from issue to issue. Equally, some activities require considerable co-operation between peripheral agencies, while others require very little. However, it may be misleading to lose sight of the overall pattern, since the outcome of one relationship affects responses to another. Relationships are ongoing; each has a history that conditions reactions to new issues. Equally, each organization develops its own sense of its task, mission and role in relation to others. These too affect its response to anything new.

One issue deserving of attention, if only because of the importance it assumes in the American implementation literature, is the 'special' agency set up to concern itself with policy-making and implementation in a specifically limited policy field. Schon (1971) has described government agencies as 'memorials to old problems'. It has long been recognized in the United States that there are difficulties in getting old agencies to implement new policies. Crucial innovation strategies have therefore involved the creation of new agencies for this purpose. However, students of this process have pointed out that these new organizations then face problems about their relationships to older agencies (see Selznick, 1949; Moynihan, 1969). While a new organization may possess a strong commitment to a new policy, and may have powers that enable it to bring together the resources for its implementation that were not possessed by any single previous organization, it still has to relate to a world in which other agencies have a great deal of power to influence its success.

One of the crucial issues, to which the creation of *ad hoc* agencies in the United States is a response, is the problem, at all levels but particularly at local level, of 'overlapping governments'. There are so many ways in which different government agencies can veto or neutralize other agencies' initiatives that a new agency, with more precisely defined policies, is seen as offering, perhaps in desperation, a new way to 'get something done'. While it would be foolish to suggest that this kind of problem does not exist in Britain, it is important to recognize that ours is a simpler system, in which individual agencies have more clearly defined powers and more definite boundaries to their responsibilities and sphere of influence. There are, therefore, fewer examples of agencies set up explicitly to circumvent problems of this kind. Moreover, when they do occur, they generally operate in territories (in both a spatial and a policy sense) in which intervention by others is limited.

The new towns are examples of successful British innovations of this kind. What is interesting about them is that, while the development corporations acquired powers that gave them a great deal of autonomy within their own territories, there is today a variety of questions to be raised about the extent to which their 'success' was secured at the expense of other policies to which they 'ought' to have related. While the new towns often built up relatively successful, prosperous new communities, they did little to relieve the problems of the least privileged in the old communities from which they drew; hence, while they have helped to solve some inner-city problems, by providing for 'overspill', they have exacerbated others.

While the use of the new town device is now being discontinued, British governments continue to experiment with approaches to urban renewal which bypass existing agencies. The urban development corporations are more recent such devices, spawned by a central government which sees local authorities as likely obstacles to local economic development.

Three motives can perhaps be identified for the creation of special agencies in Britain, although there are of course dangers in taking ostensible motives as real ones: to create an effective separate, accountable 'management system', to reduce political 'interference', and to provide for the direct representation of special interests. In Britain today the last of these is clearly the dominant motive, organizations like the training and education councils (TECs) having been designed to ensure that private employers control the local implementation of training policy.

The removal of some aspects of the elaboration of policy from direct political influence, particularly when there are powerful special interests within the quasi-autonomous body, introduces complications that make it particularly difficult to distinguish policy-making from implementation. Special agencies may be seen alternatively as implementers that affect the character of policy or as independent creators of policy forever in a relationship of tension with the centre. It is this tension which can then sometimes be seen as leading to central efforts to curb the independence of agencies whose freedom was initially provided by government. The arena of quasi-autonomous agencies is a turbulent one, requiring regular revision of textbooks like this one!

THE ORGANIZATIONAL CHARACTERISTICS OF IMPLEMENTING AGENCIES

In the study of agencies concerned with policy implementation, two significant bodies of literature can be drawn upon. These are:

studies by organizational sociologists that suggest limitations upon the formal control of subordinates by means of rules (see, for example, Crozier, 1964; Argyris, 1960);

behavioural studies of law enforcement, which have emphasized the significance of bargaining and discretion in the activities of the police and other rule-enforcers (Bottomley, 1973; Gunningham, 1974).

Both suggest that there are finite limits upon the prescription of subordinates' behaviour. Very detailed rule-making is a difficult, time-consuming activity. If it has to be backed up by close supervision and control, a point may be reached at which such activities are self-defeating. If the subordinate has to be so elaborately controlled, the supervisor might just as well undertake the task him or herself. Conformity to rules requires compliance, upon a willingness to work within a regulated framework, which Etzioni (1961) has suggested rests either upon acceptance of a 'utilitarian' financial bargain or upon a 'normative' commitment. A key point about the former is that it also invokes in practice some measure of 'tolerance' on both sides, some concept of 'trust' (Fox, 1974). This implies limits to the things a supervisor can require a subordinate to do, and involves acceptance by a superior of limited deviations by a subordinate from the activities that are expected.

It is interesting to note how much manufacturing industry has moved away from what has been described as the 'Fordist' model of routine mass-production work. Managerial gurus like Peters and Waterman (1982) extol the virtues of flexible forms of organization, engaging the commitment of employees and enabling them to innovate and cope with organizational change. This approach has been seen as relevant to government too (see Pollitt, 1990; Butcher, 1995). Such thinking seems to have influenced such innovations as the creation of agencies and the purchaser–provider split. Yet public administration may demand the performance of tasks, particularly the more mechanical ones, in a consistent way in the interest of equity. The Citizens' Charter movement in Britain, which John Major sees as his big contribution to the country, leads the public to expect speedy, consistent services from public bodies. The administration of means-tested benefits in Britain has evolved from one permeated by discretionary powers to (with the exception of the social fund) a largely formula-driven system. Yet its own internal auditing system has found massive error rates in many areas of benefit decision-making. This may be largely because of staffing levels, such that pressure to process large numbers of claims quickly leads to mistakes. But there must be concerns about the extent to which a group of officials – entering the job with increasingly high educational qualifications – are required to work in a traditional 'Fordist' manner.

In many other areas of social policy there will be a strong element of discretion in many tasks. Earlier in this chapter three sources of discretion were identified, arising from:

deliberate recognition of local autonomy,

political difficulties in resolving key policy dilemmas,

logical problems in prescribing standards.

This discussion has added two more:

inherent limits to the regulation of tasks,

human motivation problems which follow from trying to regulate them.

In practice, prescriptions for policy implementation convey discretionary powers to field-level staff for reasons that are combinations of these 'sources' of discretion.

An alternative way of looking at the phenomenon of discretion is to see the field official as a 'street-level bureaucrat' (Lipsky, 1980). His or her job is characterized by inadequate resources for the task, variable and often low public support for the role, and by ambiguous and often unrealizable expectations of performance. The official's concerns are with the actual impact of specific policies upon their relationships with specific individuals; these may lead to a disregard of or failure to understand the wider policy issues that concern those higher up in the agency. The street-level role is necessarily uncertain. A modicum of professional (or semi-professional, see below) training defines the role as putting into practice a set of ideals inculcated in that training. Yet the street-level bureaucrat is also the representative of a government agency, one that is itself subject to conflicting pressures. In day-to-day contact with clients and with the community at large, he or she becomes to some degree locked into the support of individuals and groups that may be antipathetic to the employing agency. In such a situation of role confusion and role strain, a person at the end of the line is not disposed to react to new policy initiatives from above as if he or she were a mere functionary. New policies are but factors in a whole web of demands that have to be managed.

There are 'two faces' to street-level bureaucracy. It may be seen as the effective adaptation of policy to the needs of the public or as the manipulation of positions of power to distort policy towards stigmatization, discrimination and petty tyranny. Which it does will vary according to the policy at stake and the values and commitments of the field-workers; but it will also depend upon the scope accorded by the organizational control system, for this phenomenon is not necessarily independent of 'biases' built into the policy delivery system. Workers may more easily manipulate their 'system' in favour of, or against, some clients in situations where their agency grants them licence to deploy such commitments.

Consideration of discretion and of the roles of street-level bureaucrats must also involve looking at the implications of professionalism for implementation. For Etzioni (1961) the compliance of professionals with their organizations rests upon normative commitments. But policy-makers may be said to have to 'pay for' a lessening of day-to-day control problems with concessions in the implementation process; professionalism tends to involve participation in the determination of policy outcomes. In the health service, for example, doctors have been able to secure a very full involvement in policy-making within the service as one of the prices for participation. Three interrelated points may be made about professionalism:

it may entail a level of expertise that makes lay scrutiny difficult;

professionals may be, for whatever reason, accorded a legitimate autonomy;

professionals may acquire amounts of power and influence that enable them to determine their own activities.

These sources of professional freedom clearly have a differential impact, depending upon (a) the profession involved, (b) the organizational setting in which professionals work, and (c) the policies that they are required to implement. The importance of the level of expertise for professional power has led some writers to make a distinction between professions and semi-professions (Etzioni, 1969), with doctors and lawyers in the former category, social workers and teachers in the latter.

The issues around expertise are complex, however. They interact significantly with the phenomenon of 'determinacy' – the extent to which the professional response can be pre-programmed. The more complex professional tasks are a mixture of activities which can be routinized, together with situations in which professionals must have the capacity to respond to the unexpected. For example, much doctoring is routine – either patients present clear symptoms for which there is a predictable response, or there are logical testing procedures which must be gone through to reach a diagnosis – but a good doctor must to be able to spot the exceptional condition and respond to the unexpected reaction to treatment. Should health care systems lay down 'protocols', and monitor to ensure that standard procedures are followed? Or should they allow doctors to exercise their discretion, so that they are able to respond flexibly to the unexpected rather than as Fordist workers practising 'cookbook' medicine? This is, of course, not an either/or matter; the task is to find the ideal path between the extreme positions.

The second point above, regarding autonomy, has been the subject of controversy about the impact upon professional activities of organizational, and particularly public, employment. The conclusion would seem to be dictated by some of the considerations in the last paragraph. That is, it depends on the profession and upon the organization. On the third point, once again, a good deal depends on the nature of the policy involved.

In a large number of situations it is expected that professional judgement will have a considerable influence upon the implementation process. Clearly explicit in many policies is such an expectation. This applies to many decisions made in face-to-face relationships between professionals and their clients. Many of the issues involved are increasingly the subject of controversy, involving arguments about 'rights' versus 'discretion'. Within these arguments disputes arise about the significance of expertise and about the scope for effective limitation of discretionary power. Effective resolution would also pose many difficult policy questions – about moral rights to choose (for example, with reference to abortion) and the best way to allocate scarce resources (for example, with regard to kidney machines) – which are at present partly masked by professional discretion.

There are also some important questions here, which are very hard to resolve, about how to link together professional autonomy in dealing with an individual relationship with a client and a policy-based concern (or 'public concern') about how professionals allocate their services as a whole. Professionals have been found to be reluctant to face up to priority questions, tending to prefer to deal with each patient or client as an individual in need, without any reference to a collective ethic which requires some degree of priority ranking. A consequence of this may be lengthening waiting lists. The political response has been to treat waiting lists as crucial indices of services to the public (enshrined in charters and published). But this does not solve the problem of competing priorities. It either forces a watering down of the service offered to all, or, more likely, forces attention to be paid to certain issues (like the rapidity with which patients secure a certain routine operation) at the expense of others where the quantitative indices are not available or cannot be so easily interpreted.

A further important complication for the study of implementation introduced by the involvement of professionals is that some activities depend upon the co-operation of two or more professional groups. Studies of attempts to co-ordinate the efforts of various professions concerned to protect children from injury by their parents have suggested that particular professional practices, activities and terminology may intensify communication problems. There are also, clearly, some key problems regarding the boundaries between the various professional 'territories'.

It is important to recognize the extent to which professional involvement with policies implies not merely scope to influence implementation, but also an impact upon policy itself. Within the health service the very direct influence of doctors has been subjected to considerable attention by policy analysts (Ham, 1992; Klein, 1995; Harrison et al. 1990). What have perhaps been accorded less attention are the ways in which policy and implementation involve feedback from implementation as policies are found to be inadequate to meet the demands of 'good professional practice'.

Packman (1975) has examined the way in which social workers in children's departments gradually found that good child care practice required not merely the control and care powers possessed under the 1948 Children Act, but also preventive work to keep children out of 'care'. They innovated as far as possible under the 1948 Act, but eventually secured a further Act, in 1963, which legitimated 'preventative' work. A similar concern to extend social work practice, to enable integrated work with whole families, led, as Hall (1976) has shown, to further legislation in 1970 bringing all local authority social work within one department. The process that Packman described is still going on. Whilst the Children Act of 1989 was influenced by ideological concerns about the role of the state in relation to the rights and duties of parents, it must also be seen as a product of a continuing concern within social work about how to carry out preventative child care work, fed by a succession of enquiries into child abuse scandals (involving under-reaction in some cases, over-reaction in others).

The discussion in this section has developed the key points about inter-organizational practice by means of consideration of the rules–discretion dichotomy. But to end it, three issues must be raised, which have been implicit rather than explicit within the argument so far: the relevance of the lack of clarity within much policy, the significance of value conflict, and the importance of rewards.

The first of these points does not require much further emphasis at this stage. A lack of clarity in policy has already been identified as one explanation for discretion. But equally, when the relationship within a system of rules between means and ends is far from evident, then implementers may be more disposed to break, and their supervisors may be disinclined to enforce, rules.

A lack of clarity about policy goals and conflict about values, as already suggested, often go hand in hand. Burton Clark (1956) has written of 'precarious values'. Policies may have among their goals objectives that lack support in the community. Implementers will be aware of the controversial character of the policies, and may not themselves subscribe to the goals entailed. The official who is required to secure the delivery of benefits or services to one-parent families, but is also expected to prevent abuse, may well take the latter duty more seriously than the former, letting his or her conception of morality and stereotypes regarding the social behaviour of the claimants influence behaviour (Marsden, 1973).

But the implications of Clark's analysis go further than this. Clark sees the problem of precarious values as affecting not merely day-to-day behaviour, but also the way in which a whole organization may conceive its tasks. In particular, an organization that is given a task that is controversial and unpopular in many quarters, such as one charged to promote racial equality or to provide help to a stigmatized group such as vagrant alcoholics, may find that it is given an unclear mandate and is placed in a position in which it finds it hard to acquire 'legitimacy' for its activities. This may lead to the adoption of 'safe', uncontroversial activities, organizational security being put before any movement towards potentially disruptive goals.

The problem of precarious values may also be related to the problem of rewards. We return here to Etzioni's analysis of the distinction between utilitarian and normative rewards. Clearly the official placed in a position of 'role strain' between the demands of superiors and the expectations of the public, or of 'value conflict' between his or her own ideals and those embodied in policy, will be influenced by rewards of both kinds. Benefits now and hopes of advancement may curb an inclination to deviate from the requirements of superiors; a feeling that some parts of the job are 'worth doing' may be even more influential. But the substitution of 'unofficial' or 'official' goals may be a product of recognition that more 'worthwhile' activities may thereby be undertaken. The motivation of field-level staff is an important issue even within the most integrated organization. Where, however, 'control' is attenuated by a gap between those concerned with policy and the implementing agency, it may assume crucial significance.

It is appropriate to return here to the issue raised earlier about output statistics and performance indicators. In British social policy in the 1990s the form that hostility to traditional bureaucratic modes of delivery has taken is the creation of apparently separate organizations controlled either by means of output targets (perhaps specified in a contract, as in health, or by budgetary sanctions, as in higher education, or by performance-based employee reward systems, as in social security) or by an expectation that the public will draw their own conclusions and withdraw support (as in schools) (Butcher, 1995). Some have spoken of these as quasi-market systems (Le Grand, 1990), but they are very far from real markets, and are very susceptible to political manipulation. The connection here with the points made above about precarious values and normative rewards is that these controls encourage a very utilitarian short-termism on the part of public officials.

THE SOCIAL, POLITICAL AND ECONOMIC ENVIRONMENT

Policies are evolved in a wider environment, in which problems emerge that are deemed to require political solutions, and pressures occur for new political responses. Implementing agencies continuously interact with their environments. Much has already been said that has a bearing upon the underlying significance of the environment.

Whatever the relationship between state and society, policies may be interpreted as responses to perceived social needs. Government is concerned with 'doing things to', 'taking things from', or 'providing things for' groups of people. Putting policies into practice involves interactions between the agencies of government and their environment. Those who do that are, of course, themselves a part of the social environment in which they operate.

However, in looking at social policy, we must also question whether the distinction between the policy system and its environment can be easily made. In chapter 1 it was established that it is misleading to see any simple equation between the activities of the social policy system and the enhancement of social welfare. But just as the policy determinants of welfare are multiple, and sometimes unexpected, so individuals' welfare is influenced by phenomena that have nothing to do with the activity of the state. As pointed out, the determinants of an individual's welfare can be broadly classified as depending upon the person's own capacity to care for him or herself, combined with (a) market activities and relationships, (b) the behaviour of 'significant others' as providers of 'informal care', amongst whom family members are likely to be the most important, and (c) the role played by the state. To study welfare requires attention to all the 'determinants'. Changes in the way in which welfare is provided are particularly likely to involve shifts in the roles played by these determinants and in the relationships between them. In other words, the process of interaction between policy system and environment is a very active one, and those interactions occur across an ambiguous, shifting boundary. To give a concrete example, personal social services care is only one element in individual care systems in which family, neighbour and purchased care are likely also to play a part. A shift in the availability of, or character of, any one of these ingredients is likely to have an impact on the others. Day-to-day policy implementation in the state-provided sector involves the management, or mismanagement, of its relationships to the other elements.

Accordingly, studies of social policy have conceived of the system as a 'mixed economy of welfare' (Webb, 1985). Furthermore, 'social divisions of welfare' have been identified, recognizing not merely that there are different sources of welfare for individuals, but also that individuals differ in the access they have to different welfare systems. Titmuss (1958), who originated the notion of social divisions of welfare, identified, alongside mainstream 'public welfare':

'fiscal welfare', the system of relief from taxation (of which the relief for mortgage interest payments and pension contributions are among the most important examples);

'occupational welfare' (the range of fringe benefits available to some employees).

Titmuss, together with others who developed his work, such as Sinfield (1978) and Townsend (1979), argued that these other welfare systems may provide large benefits additional to, or quite separate from, the benefits provided by the more central institutions of the welfare state. They may operate in a direction quite contrary to any egalitarian tendencies in the mainstream policies. The social divisions theme has been taken up in another way by some recent feminist writers who have been concerned to show not merely that many welfare provisions discriminate against women, but also that services by females within the family and neighbourhood form crucial separate welfare systems, enhanced in importance when other systems fail or are withdrawn (Rose, 1981; Land and Rose, 1985). Bryson (1992) suggests that we may speak of 'men's welfare states' and 'women's welfare states' as being very differently, and unequally, constituted, because of differences in access to benefits, dependent upon economic status and dominant expectations of family roles.

These points have been emphasized in this chapter because the implementation of many contemporary policy initiatives – privatization, the limitation of social expenditure, the extension of community care – involve changing the balance between the various ingredients in the mixed economy of welfare. Where government withdraws or reduces its direct contribution to welfare, it may still make an indirect contribution if the social security system subsidizes private provision; or it may have to acquire a new range of regulatory concerns about the quality of private services; or it may face increased problems in the other areas of concern, because of the new pressures placed upon individuals and families.

Relationships between the public and the organizations delivering public policies may be studied with a view to ascertaining whether implementation proceeds in terms of the even-handed justice that Max Weber (1947) suggested is, or should be, characteristic of bureaucratic administration. Clearly, questions about bias in the behaviour of public officials, the mechanisms by which scarce benefits or services are rationed, the roles played by 'gatekeepers' and the problems of securing effective 'take-up' of some benefits are issues of concern for the implementation of policies (see Foster, 1983). In the study of these matters, many of the issues around the motivation of implementers – about role strain, precarious values and the exercise of discretion – concern the interaction between the nature of policy, the implementation system and the characteristics of the public. Policy delivery is not easily made an 'even-handed' process; class, gender and race differences influence access to professional services; some social security applicants are less well informed and more easily deterred than others; and street-level bureaucrats who may be regarded as highly responsive to local needs in a white neighbourhood may be seen very differently in a black one. Here the 'environment' affects the way the policy is received. This chapter has portrayed the implementation process as a complex one, in many respects inextricably bound up with the policy-making process. It has suggested that in the study of social policy it is important not only to pay attention to implementation problems that arise directly from the characteristics of policy, but also to recognize that there is a complicated interrelationship between these and a range of inter- and intra-organizational factors. Finally, all these complications interact with a complex environment.

An approach to the examination of social policy has been introduced here that has not been given much explicit attention in relation to the study of specific policies. One justification for this lengthy examination of policy implementation is that, while we all experience the effects of the implementation process, and many of us participate in various ways in it, very few of us are involved in policy-making. Yet it is this policy-making, often particularly that which occurs at the highest level, that receives most attention. It is hoped that in reading the detailed discussions of particular areas of policy contained in the next section of this book, readers will bear in mind the importance of the implementation process for the actual impact of social policies upon the public.

SUGGESTIONS FOR FURTHER READING

Tony Butcher's *Delivering Welfare* (1995) offers an excellent overview of the organizational arrangements for social policy delivery in Britain, with a strong emphasis upon contemporary developments.

I have contributed to further discussions of the theoretical issues raised in this chapter in chapters 6–9 of my book with Chris Ham (Ham and Hill, 1993); contributions to parts 6-8 of my edited collection, *The Policy Process* (Hill, 1993a) are also very relevant. Susan Barrett and Colin Fudge's *Policy and Action* (1981) is also an important source. So too, in a more grounded way, is Marsh and Rhodes's book on implementation cited at the end of the last chapter (1992a).

A large literature is emerging on new approaches to the management of policy delivery and its implications for professionalism. The following are recommended: Clarke, et al.'s *Managing Social Policy* (1994), Hudson's *Making Sense of Markets in Health and Social Care* (1994) and Glennerster et al.'s 1991 article cited in the text. A rather older book on professionalism is Paul Wilding's *Professional Power and Social Welfare* (1982).

INTRODUCTION TO CHAPTERS 5-10

SPECIFIC AREAS OF SOCIAL POLICY

Each of the chapters in this part of the book will contain the following:

1 an account of the policies involved, dealing with their scope and coverage in Britain at the present time and examining their organization;
2 a consideration of the particular characteristics of the British system, with a view to giving some insight into the reasons why it takes the form it does and the general consequences of that form for the service provided for the public;
3 a more detailed examination of a selection of specific issues of contemporary importance: particular policy problems and interesting current policy innovations;
4 an examination of some of the new directions suggested for policy, and solutions to policy problems, which will be related to the factors that will influence their chances of adoption and implementation.

Readers should note that some of the sections on specific sub-topics may be relevant to more than one chapter. Hence, issues about the relationship between personal social services and both income maintenance and health services are discussed in the personal social services chapter, and the discussion of the education of ethnic minorities in the education chapter makes many points relevant to other policies.

CHAPTER 5

SOCIAL SECURITY

INTRODUCTION

The term 'social security' is used here to cover all the British state systems of 'income support'. These fall into three categories:

contributory benefits,

non-contributory benefits which are not means-tested but are contingent upon the individual being in some specific category (a child or disabled),

means-tested benefits.

The Beveridge plan for contributory benefits (Beveridge, 1942) envisaged that these should provide the main source of protection against old age, sickness, unemployment and widowhood. The legislation of the 1940s, picking up the main pieces from earlier contributory social security schemes, attempted to provide this coverage. The main contributory benefits date from that time, but the system of contributions, the nature of the benefits and the character of the alternative benefits available to back up the contributory system have all changed a great deal since then.

The Department of Social Security is responsible for the main social security benefits, using a group of agencies. The main agency for the delivery of benefits, the Benefits Agency, operates through a network of local offices. There are centralized, or concentrated, computer systems for main benefits. There are other agencies, including the Contributions Agency to deal with the collection of national insurance contributions and the Child Support Agency to collect contributions towards the maintenance of children in families dependent upon 'income support' from absent parents. Housing benefit is administered by the unitary, or lower-tier, local authorities, under either housing or finance departments. The Department of Social Security lays down a strong rule structure for the whole system, including housing benefit. The only part of the system for which there now remains extensive local discretion is the social fund (see pp. 110–11).

CONTRIBUTORY BENEFITS

All employees, together with the self-employed, are required to pay national insurance contributions. These are calculated as a percentage of earnings, but there is a low income threshold below which they are not required, a structure of lower rates before the full rate is reached, and an income level above which additional income is not taken into account. Normally employees' contributions are deducted by employers, who also have to pay employers' contributions on a similar basis for those they employ. These contributions should not be confused with income tax deductions.

The original national insurance scheme set up in the 1940s specified a clear relationship between contributions and a wide range of benefit entitlements. This is no longer the case. The link between contributions and benefit entitlements has been steadily eroded since 1979, so that it is now more appropriate to see contributions as simply a tax. The limited remaining contributory benefit entitlements are discussed in this section.

There is a flat-rate pension to which insurance contributors are entitled on reaching the age of 60 if they are women, 65 if they are men (the female qualifying age will be increased to 65 by a phasing-in process in the period 2010–20). The actual pension rate depends on the length of working life.

Since 1977 there has also been in operation a state earnings-related pension scheme that provides earnings-related pensions; benefits from this scheme will begin to reach a significant level in the late 1990s. Individual employees must contribute either to this scheme or to officially approved private schemes. Those who 'contract out' will secure only the flat-rate retirement pension from the state (though benefits from a limited interim scheme which operated between 1961 and 1975 provide small additions for some people).

The employee who is unable to work on account of sickness is initially dependent, since the enactment of the Social Security and Housing Benefits Act of 1982, upon his or her employer for support. The latter is, with some exceptions, required to provide sick pay at least up to minimum levels prescribed by Parliament for 28 weeks. This is, of course, not a contributory benefit *per se*, but this scheme replaced the former national insurance one, and small (formerly all) employers obtain some rebate of their insurance contributions in respect of sick employees.

Those who become sick when not in employment may get a contributory benefit if they were insurance contributors for a period until shortly before, a benefit that is now called 'short-term incapacity benefit'.

After the first six months of sickness, anyone still unfit for work moves on to a higher rate of short-term incapacity benefit, which continues until they have been sick for a year. During this period the individual must establish that they are unfit to return to their normal occupation.

After a year of sickness, people may move on to long-term incapacity benefit. The rate of payment is a little higher than that of the short-term benefit. However, the qualification rules for this benefit are much stricter. Claimants must prove that they are unfit to do *any* work. There is what the government has described as an 'objective' test, carried out by a doctor employed by the Benefits Agency, which individuals have to pass to obtain this benefit.

This new, strict approach to long-term incapacity benefit was introduced in 1995. One consequence of continued high levels of unemployment is that people with disabilities, particularly if they are middle-aged, have increasing difficulties in getting back into the workforce. Many countries (see Kohli et al., 1991) have devised premature retirement schemes for this group. In Britain the official stance until 1995 was to tolerate – and indeed to some extent to encourage (in order to keep down the numbers counted as unemployed) – claims for invalidity benefit (the predecessor of incapacity benefit) as a 'pathway' to premature retirement (ibid., pp. 234–5). This new measure put a stop to that, except for a group already over 58 and getting invalidity benefit at the time of the introduction of the scheme.

In addition to the benefits described above, there are special, in general more generous provisions, applying to those whose incapacity for work arises from an industrial accident or a prescribed industrial disease. These will not be considered in detail here.

There is a system of statutory maternity pay, like statutory sick pay, payable for 18 weeks. This is backed up by a reduced state maternity allowance for women with recent work records who do not qualify for pay from their employers.

Another contributory benefit to which entitlement has been severely eroded is that for unemployed people. From mid-1996 this is called 'job seeker's allowance'. As the name suggests, in order to qualify, a person has to make a clear undertaking, signing a 'job seeker's agreement', on the steps he or she will take to try to get work. However, contributory benefits for unemployed people have always been limited by strict previous contribution conditions, rules which disqualify a person if there is evidence that the unemployment may be to some extent their own fault, and a time limit to entitlement. With the introduction of the job seeker's allowance, the latter has been reduced to six months. After six months, or if the previous contributions and other tests are not satisfied, job seeker's allowance is means-tested (its rules being broadly those applying to income support; see next section).

At a time of high unemployment, a contributory scheme for those out of work, which has initial qualifying rules and the exhaustion of entitlement after six months, leaves many in need of means-tested benefits. In particular, young new entrants to the labour force are unprotected by the contributory benefit scheme.

Widows have a contributory benefit entitlement, based upon their deceased husband's contributions to widowed mother's allowances if they have children to support and to widow's pensions if they are over 45. For widow's benefits and for retirement pensions during the first five years after reaching pensionable age (60 for women, 65 for men), there are 'earnings rules' which may reduce the income received, on the basis of sliding scales which allow some, but not large amounts of, earnings. These rules apply only to earned income; in this sense they differ from the fuller forms of means tests. Widows lose their benefits on remarriage; there is also a 'cohabitation rule' which may be invoked to treat widows living 'as wives' in the same way as 'married wives'.

NON-CONTRIBUTORY, NON-MEANS-TESTED, CONTINGENT BENEFITS

Child benefit is paid to the parents or guardians of all children under 16 and children between 16 and 18 who are still at school. The only qualifying condition is a residence one. 'One-parent benefits' can be claimed as a modest addition to child benefits for single parents.

There are some non-contributory benefits available to the long-term disabled, which must not be confused with the industrial injury disablement provision or with incapacity benefit. These are the disability living allowance (a combination of the former attendance allowance and mobility allowance), set at various rates depending upon the need for care by another person, and the disability working allowance for disabled people able to work. These are benefits which were started in 1992 to replace attendance allowance and mobility allowance for people under 65. People over 65 may still get attendance allowance if they need long periods of care. There is a range of detailed rules concerning these benefits which cannot be discussed in the space available here.

There is also a benefit available for carers who are not gainfully employed and have to devote a substantial amount of time to the care of someone disabled. This is invalid care allowance, and its rate of pay is low.

MEANS-TESTED BENEFITS

The 1986 Social Security Act, which was implemented in April 1988, radically altered the structure of means-tested benefits. It will be evident from statements above about contributory benefits that means tests are central to the British social security system. In addition, the levels of some of the contributory benefits (flat-rate pensions, short-term incapacity benefit and job seeker's allowance) are such that claimants will often qualify for further means-tested support as well, at least in respect of housing costs.

In addition, many people in work earn insufficient for their needs, and have to apply for means-tested family and housing benefits to supplement their incomes.

The figures in table 5.1 give some idea of the distribution of expenditure on benefits of all kinds. The way these are grouped by recipient category mixes together different kinds of benefits. The 'family' group includes child benefit and family credit. Table 5.2 then sets out the numbers of people receiving various benefits (there will of course be considerable overlaps, as many receive more than one benefit).

Table 5.1 Expenditure on social security benefits in Great Britain, 1994–5

	£ (million)
Expenditure on contributory benefits	40,141
Expenditure on non-contributory benefits	45,080
Total expenditure	85,221
Beneficiary groups	
Elderly	37,926
Sick and disabled	20,424
Family benefits	15,919
Unemployed	9,104
Widows, etc.	1,847

Source: Department of Social Security, 1995, p. 3

Table 5.2 Numbers receiving various social security benefits in Great Britain on a specific date within 1994

Type of benefit	Number of recipients (thousands)
Contributory benefits	
Retirement pension	10,167
Invalidity benefit[a]	1,685
Unemployment benefit[b]	458
Widow's benefit	324
Non-contributory, non-means-tested benefits	
Child benefit	6,995
Attendance allowance	996
Invalid care allowance	274
Disability living allowance	1,308
Means-tested benefits	
Income support	5,675
Housing benefit	4,711
Family credit	536

[a] Now replaced by incapacity benefit.
[b] Now replaced by job seeker's allowance.
Source: Department of Social Security, 1995, p. 4

The main means-tested benefit is called 'income support'. Its means test is based upon a simple personal allowance structure, enhanced in some cases by 'premiums'. The specific personal allowance rates are for a couple, a single person over 25, a person between 18 and 24, and there are three age-related rates for children. Then there are different premiums for families, lone parents, pensioners under 80, pensioners over 80, disabled people, and seriously disabled people. The idea throughout is that the determination of the appropriate overall entitlement for a household should be a simple, predictable process. Additions for special needs have been abolished. Rules determine how any income should be taken into account. People in full-time work (defined as doing 16 or more hours in employment per week) are disqualified from receiving income support, but part-time workers may obtain it. To deal with this, an earnings rule is used, based on net income, which involves disregarding a small amount and then deducting the rest from any entitlement. Similar 'disregards' are used for some other kinds of income, but state benefits are taken into account in full. There are special rules dealing with savings, disregarding small amounts, then applying a sliding scale, reducing benefits up to an upper limit at which they disqualify a person from benefit entirely.

Alongside the income support scheme is a means-tested benefit available to low-paid workers doing over 16 hours a week who have child dependants. This is called 'family credit'. The calculation rules for this benefit are based upon those for income support. The maximum credit is payable where net earned income is equal to, or below, the personal allowance available to a family on income support. Hence the government aim to ensure that most families where there is a full-time bread-winner are better off than comparable families on income support. Above income support level the credit is withdrawn at the rate of 70 per cent; that is, for each £1 of income above that level, 70 pence of credit is lost. There is, however, some relief applied to expenditure on child care costs.

The housing benefit scheme has been designed to be compatible with these two other means-tested benefits. The income support rules are used in the calculation of benefit so that anyone with a rent to pay who is at or below income support income level may get the full housing benefit entitlement. Housing benefit provides support for rent; it does not provide support for house buying. However, owner-occupiers on income support may get some help towards mortgage interest payments (see further discussion in chapter 10).

The housing benefit scheme is, in effect, extended to local taxation. Low-income council tax payers may apply for a reduction in their payments (calculated in a similar way to housing benefit).

The housing benefit maximum is generally the full rent (though this may not apply if the rent is deemed to be unreasonably high or if there are other adults besides the claimant's spouse in the household – there are some complicated rules dealing with these situations) payable to those whose incomes are at or below the income support qualifying level. Similarly, for those with incomes at or below income support level and no adult non-dependants the council tax benefit will provide for the remission of the whole tax liability. Where incomes are above income support level, benefit tapers off proportionately, at the rate of 65 per cent for housing benefit and 20 per cent for council tax benefit.

Under the supplementary benefit scheme operative until 1988 there were provisions enabling single payments to be made to help people with exceptional expenditures – removal costs, furnishing, house repairs and so forth. An elaborate body of rules dealt with these entitlements. The 1986 Act swept away these single payment entitlements, but in their place set up a social fund, administered by a specially trained group of Benefits Agency officers. Under the fund there are two kinds of grants available as of right to people on income support or family credit: a lump sum maternity needs payment and a funeral needs payment (the amount of which depends upon funeral costs). There is also provision for grants to be made from the social fund to assist with the promotion of community care. These may be available when someone needs help in establishing themselves in the community after a period of institutional care, to assist with some travelling expenses to visit relatives in hospitals and other institutions, and to improve the living conditions of defined 'vulnerable groups' in the community. Elaborate guidance is provided to social fund officers to help them determine needs of this kind. They are expected to liaise closely about such matters with social services and health services staff, and to take into account powers these other departments may have to provide assistance in cash or kind. Apart from the grants, outlined above, all other help from the social fund is by way of loans, normally repayable by weekly deductions from benefits. Again, officers have been given elaborate instructions on the circumstances in which they may provide loans. The social fund, excluding the two items of benefit as of right, is 'cash limited'. Within this budget 30 per cent is available for community care grants and 70 per cent for loans. This means that local offices have annual budgets, and are expected to relate a set of rules about priorities to the total sum available. Claimants for help from the social fund, other than claimants for maternity and funeral payments, have no right of appeal to an independent body against decisions, though there is an elaborate provision for internal 'review'.

This description of the structure for the main means-tested benefits does not exhaust the list of benefits. One quite important means-tested benefit administered by local authorities, entitlement to free school meals, had its availability restricted under the 1986 social security changes. Free school meals are now available only to children whose parents are on income support.

Other means-tested benefits include grants to students in higher education, relief from payment of National Health Service charges, and legal aid. Local authority social services departments also use means tests to determine charges for residential care and domiciliary services (see chapter 6).

The Distinctive Characteristics of the British System of Social Security

The British national insurance scheme today bears little resemblance to commercial insurance. There is no 'funding' and investing of contributions. Annual government income from national insurance contributions normally only slightly exceeds expenditure on contributory benefits, and the separate government contribution to the fund promised in the original legislation is no longer made. Incapacity benefit continues for as long as the claimant is deemed to be unfit for work, assuming an initial fulfilment of the contribution conditions. It is impossible to relate flat-rate pensions to contributions. The rate of inflation of recent years has destroyed any correspondence between contributions and payments in terms of the face value of the money involved, and no inflation-proofing assumptions were built into the original scheme. When the state earnings-related pension scheme (SERPS) was set up in 1977, some consideration was given to the future relationship between amounts to be paid out to qualifiers and amounts to be contributed by participants in the scheme whilst in work. Concern about the relationship between these groups in the early years of the next century, when the number of SERPS beneficiaries will increase rapidly but that of SERPS contributors seems likely to be comparatively low, was seen by the Thatcher government as a justification for reducing the benefits offered. This change, together with measures to increase the extent of contracting out of SERPS into private schemes, was included in the 1986 Social Security Act.

The job seeker's allowance scheme maintains a limited insurance principle. But the restrictions imposed upon the availability of contributory benefits to the unemployed, under this scheme and its predecessor, has limited the extent to which unemployed people can avoid applying for income support. At the time of writing, data are not yet available on those getting benefits under the new scheme. But in November 1994 only 12 per cent of unemployed males registering for benefits were getting unemployment benefit alone, while 73 per cent were getting income support only. The remainder consisted of 6 per cent getting both benefits and 9 per cent getting nothing (Department of Social Security, 1995, p. 153). The percentage of females getting unemployment benefit was much higher (21 per cent), but this is because the family means test disqualifies many unemployed women from any entitlement to benefit. This has the effect of artificially reducing the number of women counted as unemployed.

The presence in the British system of a safety net group of means-tested benefits to back up the contributory scheme is by no means peculiar to this country. Such assistance schemes are very widespread, and in many countries they remain under local control, and more closely resemble the British scheme's predecessor, the poor-law. What is perhaps peculiar to the British scene is the complex overlap between the two systems. In Britain the contributory scheme has to be supplemented in a large number of ways.

For those who, like myself, have deplored the erosion of national insurance, the case for a reversal of the shift towards means testing is increasingly difficult to argue. The abandonment of the limitations on the availability of contributory benefits for unemployed people and some relatively slight increases in contributory benefit rates would markedly reduce dependence on means-tested benefits. Yet these changes would be costly to the Exchequer. Moreover, the main effect of increasing the availability of unemployment benefit would be to shift the support of a large group of people from a means-tested to a contributory benefit with little change to their income, whilst a relatively small number of people with other sources of income (those with private pensions who retired early) made actual income gains. Similarly, an increase in contributory benefits relative to income support would produce income gains for a group not among the least poor (not on income support), while merely altering the source of help for the very poor (who would then accuse governments of giving with one hand and taking away with the other).

LEVELS OF BENEFITS

Clearly it is important in assessing a system of social security to look not merely at the structure of the system but also at the level of benefits provided by it. There are examples, for instance, within the British system that look most impressive until one scrutinizes the levels of benefit available. It would be pointless, in discussing the main social security benefits, to provide specific figures, which would be dated by the time many read this section. Instead, some of the general issues about the setting of benefit levels will be outlined.

Reference has already been made to the relationship between contributory benefit levels and income support levels. Hence a great deal of debate about poverty in Britain is concerned not about the contributory benefits as such, but about the means-tested benefit levels and about the people and families whose incomes fall below those levels. There are three ways to try to assess the adequacy of these 'poverty levels': in relation to absolute concepts of need, in relation to other incomes, and over time in relation to the movement of prices and other incomes. In the early years of national assistance, studies which attempted to relate poverty to an absolute standard based upon the cost of providing a basic minimum of necessities were still regarded as providing a sound basis for the fixing of benefit levels. More recently this approach has been discredited. It has been pointed out, notably by Townsend (1979), that poverty is a meaningful concept only when individual standards of living are related to those widely taken for granted in a society. The British bare minimum could certainly equate with a good absolute standard of living for poor people in the less developed countries of the world. At the same time, British views about what is necessary for an adequate way of life change over time. These changes are related to developments in living standards within the nation as a whole. When the national assistance scales – which today, much updated for inflation, form the basis for the income support scales – were first set, in 1948, television was not even available, and few households had refrigerators, washing machines or central heating systems. If a definition of the poverty level is to take into account these considerations, the key questions are, for example: to what extent should those on the official poverty line have incomes that make it difficult for them to share the way of life of the majority of the people? Or how large should the gap be between the incomes of those on the poverty line and average incomes? Or even, what should the relationship be between the lowest incomes in our society, most of which are provided by the social security system, and the highest incomes? In other words, the crucial questions are about relationships between the official minimum level and other incomes.

These issues have been effectively examined by Peter Townsend in his large study of poverty. He persuasively makes a case for regarding large numbers of British people, including both people dependent upon social security and many on low wages, as living in poverty (ibid.). A more recent study by Mack and Lansley (1985, but with an update whose publication is expected at the time this book is going to press) lends support to Townsend's argument. It demonstrates the extent to which low-income people lack things which, according to a public opinion survey, are regarded as necessities.

A variant on this theme of considerable importance in contemporary political debate concerns the relationship between social security incomes and average earned incomes over time. After all, the real political questions are not so much about the setting of levels in the abstract as about the need for, or the amount of, benefit increases. Pressure groups regularly draw politicians' attention to the ways in which, over a period of time, those whom they represent are losing ground. Two important alternative kinds of yardsticks are used for these judgements: indices of earnings and indices of prices. The plural form is used in both instances since there have been extensive arguments about the best ways of calculating these. In particular, it has been argued that a price index for the poor should be rather different from a more general one, since the poor spend their incomes in rather different ways. However, the general problem of choice between earnings and prices as bases for judgements on benefit levels over time is that, while attention to earnings presumes relative positions, it may be important to protect the living standards of the poor at a time when prices are rising faster than earnings.

Before 1973 there was no statutory requirement for government to take specific notice of wages or price movements in determining benefit levels. *Ad hoc* political judgements governed up-rating decisions. However, there was a tendency, over time, for the relationship between short-term benefit rates and wage rates to remain roughly the same (Barr, 1981).

In the Social Security Act of 1973 the Conservatives provided a statutory link between benefits and prices. In 1975 an amendment to the Social Security Act committed the Labour Government to up-rating long-term benefits in line with prices or earnings, whichever was greater, and most short-term benefits in line with prices. Heavy price inflation in the late 1970s did produce some relative gains to social security recipients. In 1979 the Conservatives amended the statutory requirement so that long-term benefits were to be linked only to prices. Also, short-term benefits might be increased by up to 5 per cent less than the inflation rate. These rules relate only to the contributory benefits, but, in most cases, means-tested benefit rates have been up-rated on a similar basis. The changes after 1979 have led to a serious fall in the value of all benefits relative to average wages.

The relationship between social security incomes and low wages is clearly important. Several studies of poverty have related incomes to the level provided by the main means-tested scheme. Apart from drawing attention to numbers falling below it because of a failure to claim benefits, they have shown that there is a significant group who fall below that standard because of low wages. Developments in the family benefits and in housing benefit have been designed to tackle this problem. However, there is an alternative way of responding to it. This is to argue not that something must be done to augment the earnings of the low-wage earner, but that means-tested benefit levels should be kept below the lowest wage levels. This view is linked with a concern to lower wage costs, expressed by those who see the only way forward for the British economy to be to have wage costs comparable to those of very much poorer countries.

It has been argued that few of the unemployed are in fact deterred from obtaining work by benefit payments being above the levels they can obtain as earners. However, there is undoubtedly a relatively small gap between the benefits paid to some families, particularly large families, and the wages paid for low-skilled work. The deterrent effect of this will depend first upon the actual costs of going to work, second upon individual views of the psychological costs and benefits of work, and third upon the benefits still obtainable when in work.

It is difficult to estimate the actual extent of deterrence at a time when jobs are scarce. However, there is a widespread public belief that this deterrent effect actually contributes to our high unemployment rates. Politicians share, or are sensitive to, this belief. It accordingly influences their attitudes to increases in the short-term benefits. However, the government sees the family credit scheme, which provides in-work benefits to parents with dependent children whose net incomes are at or below the income support level, as dealing with this 'unemployment trap' problem. In practice, administrative problems associated with the shift from out-of-work benefits to in-work benefits complicate the situation for those actually trying to make the transition. That has an impact upon take-up, an issue to which we will return.

As well as a concern about the relationship between benefits and other incomes, there is also a concern about relativities within the benefit system. The income support scheme rules make assumptions about the extent to which a couple may live more cheaply than a single person, about the extra needs of elderly and disabled people, about the different costs of children at various ages, and about the lower needs of single adults under 25. Some of these judgements are clearly controversial. In particular, the low income support rate for single under 25s, and the particularly harsh treatment of 16–18-year-olds who have left school, seem to be related to an assumption that such people can live with their parents, and not form separate households. The assumptions about the costs of children made by the rules have also been challenged as unrealistic regarding the costs of teenage children. It seems fair to suggest that considerations of the evidence on actual costs have been mixed, in the determination of some of these rules, with views about who are the most deserving amongst the poor.

SOCIAL SECURITY ASSUMPTIONS ABOUT FAMILY LIFE AND WOMEN'S ROLES

The assumptions about family life incorporated in the poor-law involved a household means test whereby all a household's needs were taken into account and also its resources, so that adult children of a needy couple were expected to contribute to their maintenance. The contributory benefits developed in 1911 treated the insured claimant as the sole beneficiary, providing flat-rate payments at the same level, regardless of his or her family commitments. However, in the 1920s the principle of additions to benefits, taking into account the needs of wives and children, was introduced. The improved contributory scheme developed in the 1940s carried forward this principle, while means-tested assistance shifted from a household means test to a family one. Broadly, then, British social security policies have been developed on the assumption that the typical claimant is a married man with a non-working wife and dependent children. That is not, of course, to say that the system cannot cope with claims from single people, but that it has had difficulty in coming to terms with both female employment and multi-person families constituted other than on the basis of legal marriage.

Until the 1970s, married women were required to pay lower contributions and to receive lower benefits than men. There was additionally an arrangement, now largely phased out, under which they could contract out of all of the contributory scheme except the industrial injuries part. While this anomaly is being eliminated, others remain. Married women cannot claim contributory benefit increases in respect of dependent husbands and children. The continuation of provisions for non-employed wives to be treated as 'dependants' for whom husbands can claim additions to benefits implies that the return which an employed woman receives on her contributions may in some cases be worth only the difference between the full pension or benefit and the addition for a non-working wife. In other words, there are difficulties in securing a fair balance in a scheme that tries, on the one hand, to make provision for dependent wives and children and, on the other, to enable the married woman to be a contributor and claimant in her own right.

The position with regard to means-tested benefits is even more complicated when men and women live together, and perhaps have children, but are not married. A family means test requires judgements to be made about whether a family situation exists. Generally this is straightforward; claimants agree with official interpretations of their situations. Indeed, it is to the advantage of a male claimant living with a non-employed 'wife' and children (even if they are not his) to claim them as his family. However, difficulties arise when claimants, usually female, wish to be treated as independent, but find that the Benefits Agency regards them as the 'wives' of male friends. The Department of Social Security has tried to develop a definition of 'living together as man and wife' which distinguishes stable relationships from more casual ones, but difficulties and disagreements still occur. It is only heterosexual relationships that are treated in this way; in all other cases claimants' needs are assessed separately. The issue here, which, as was pointed out above, also applies to widow's benefits, arises from the family-based approach to benefits. While it would be possible to treat unmarried 'couples' differently from married ones, the only fair way to avoid problems of this kind is to cease to make assumptions about family patterns of support, and instead have a structure of *individual* entitlements (see Dale and Foster, 1986, ch. 6).

A related issue concerns the treatment of single-parent families, most of which are, of course, headed by women. The British treatment of this group has been relatively generous, by comparison with other countries. Income support has been available. Mothers have not been required to become labour market participants until their children reach 16. Absent fathers have been expected to make contributions, though the system has found it difficult to secure these because of the extent to which the fathers are low-income men with commitments to new families.

Charles Murray's tirade against the single-headed household in the United States (1984) was taken up in Britain. Politicians began to attribute the growth in single parenthood to the availability of benefits and housing. This has stimulated a debate, reaching beyond the ranks of the extreme Right, about (a) work opportunities for single parents and (b) contributions from absent parents. Attention to the first issue is difficult at a time of high unemployment, but some efforts have been made to increase work incentives for those on family credit. The poverty trap (see next section) poses a problem for this strategy. The best way forward may be an extension of family benefits which are not means-tested.

The government decided to tackle the issue of contributions from absent parents by means of a comprehensive, formula-driven scheme to replace both the assessments made as part of the administration of the existing means-tested benefits and the assessments made by the courts in determining maintenance on the breakdown of a relationship. It enacted the Child Support Act in 1991, setting up an agency to administer it. Reference was made in chapter 4 to the difficulties this Agency encountered, but that discussion merely spoke of widespread resistance. The main objections to the new legislation were:

(a) that it is retrospective in effect – agreements, including court settlements, made in the past are overturned (a particular problem here is the overturning of agreements in which the absent parent has relinquished an interest in a house in return for a lower maintenance expectation);
(b) that where the absent parent has obligations to a second family, these are given relatively low weight in the calculations;
(c) that the parent with care of the child has nothing to gain from collaborating with the agency if she (it is nearly always *she* in this situation) is on income support, since everything collected goes to reimburse the state; a special problem here is the expectation of co-operation in the supply of information unless there are very strong reasons to protect a woman from further indirect dealings with the father of her child;

(d) that the operation of a rigid formula is unfair when there are regular contacts with the absent parent and a variety of connected expenses.

The enforcement of the Act has not been helped by the income targets imposed on the agency and a programme of work which meant that it started with families on 'income support' and had incentives to tackle the easier cases (that is, the more compliant absent parents).

In 1995 the government brought in amending legislation. It bowed to a vociferous male lobby. It did not change the basic principles of the Act, but it did give the agency some limited leeway to modify its application in relation to the points made in (a), (b) and (d) above.

PROBLEMS OF MEANS TESTING

There is an extensive literature on the problems of means testing. Much that has been written on this subject comes from those who advocate, as an alternative, strengthening the contributory benefits system so that it becomes more universal in its coverage and provides better benefits. We have seen already some of the political objections to this approach. Alternative approaches to this issue are also found. One of these suggests that we could have a structure of 'basic income' whereby all would be guaranteed a minimum income, and some would secure earned incomes (necessarily more heavily taxed) to supplement this state minimum (Walter, 1988; Parker, 1989). This would be a radical departure from our current system. It finds little support close to the corridors of power. Another alternative which has awakened a wider interest is 'negative income tax' (Minford, 1984; Dilnot, et al., 1984). The British 'pay-as-you-earn' system for the deduction of tax would seem to be the ideal vehicle for the development of a system whereby additions, rather than deductions, could be provided in some cases. However, the basis for the assessment of tax would have to be shifted from an annual to a weekly one; arrangements would have to be made for the system to operate when people were both in and out of work; and some more precise information on need would have to be available to the tax authorities.

When the Conservative government announced its radical review of social security in 1983, it seemed possible that the negative income tax idea would be adopted. In practice, the 1986 changes were influenced by this approach, in the adoption of a common set of rules to determine benefit rates and in the use of net rather than gross income (that is, income after tax). But the income tax system itself remains 'untainted' by social security considerations. Hence the standard problems with means testing remain, albeit in a form much affected by the 1986 Act. The general case against means tests is that they confuse, deter and stigmatize those who need help. People prefer benefits to which they have clear-cut rights, and about which they can obtain unambiguous information. Those who have to claim help are often already in trouble, about which they are ashamed or for which their neighbours criticize them; to have to reveal intimate details to an official in order to obtain benefits deepens the sense of 'stigma'. The low take-up of some benefits is attributed both to this stigma and to the complexities surrounding the administration of means tests.

It is undoubtedly the case that take-up levels for means-tested benefits are lower than for many other benefits. But there are also marked variations between the various means-tested ones. Income support take-up rates are relatively high, particularly if the entitlement is likely to be large. Family credit and housing benefit take-up figures are lower. The Department of Social Security estimates that the take-up rate for family credit is about 66 per cent (Department of Social Security, 1995, p. 239). In 1994 the overall housing benefit take-up rate was estimated by the Department of Social Security to be around 90 per cent (ibid.).

Take-up of housing benefit is influenced by two things: whether the household is also on income support and whether they are local authority tenants. In a study done by the Department of Social Security before the introduction of the 1986 Act changes, private tenants not on supplementary benefit were shown to have only a 64 per cent take-up rate, by comparison with a near 100 per cent rate for local authority tenants on supplementary benefit. The disparity between take-up of housing benefit by public tenants and that by private tenants occurred because local authorities, as the administrators of those means tests, can much more easily publicize the former among their own tenants.

Another factor that facilitates take-up of benefits is that income support is regarded as an automatic 'passport' to other benefits. This is most evidently the case with relief from NHS charges. However, this implies a cause for concern about the needs of those just above income support levels, together with those who, in not claiming small amounts of income support, may also be shutting themselves out from ready access to other benefits.

One particular problem with the multiplicity of means tests is that, operating together, they may create a poverty trap. This is a kind of 'tax effect' whereby an individual whose earned income rises may find that tax and insurance contributions increase while benefit income decreases, together diminishing any gain to a very low level. The government stated that one of the main benefits of the 1986 Act was to be that, by taking into account earned income after tax and national insurance deductions and having the main means tests operate with a common framework, they would eliminate the poverty trap problem for most people. However, an individual gaining £1 in income may lose 23 pence from it in tax and insurance contributions (the prevailing lowest rates of each of these have been taken into account, but they increase only a little way up the income range to reach 32 per cent quite quickly). Then the remaining 77 pence will affect family credit entitlement, where a 70 per cent taper is applied. This will reduce the gain to 23 pence. But the housing benefit taper is 65 per cent, and the council tax benefit taper is 20 per cent, so that the eventual gain may be no more than 3 pence. An individual entitled to all these benefits will thus be subject to the equivalent of a 97 per cent tax rate on gaining a pound of earned income. Even an individual without a tax and insurance charge and with housing benefit but no family credit will experience an 85 per cent taper, reducing the gain to 15 pence. These losses are more than twice as large as the marginal rate of income tax on people with the highest incomes!

It is important to bear in mind that the poverty trap effect applies with part-time work, when either of a couple on benefits together gets work, and to temporary work. In other words, there are some complex issues about disincentives to labour market participation which flow directly from the poverty trap effect.

The poverty trap problem must afflict any unified means-testing system, including negative income tax. If the tapering-off effect is to be reduced, benefit receipt will logically spread further up the income distribution, adding to the cost of the scheme. In the last resort this can only be compensated by increasing tax rates, either across the board or through alterations to the higher-rate bands.

CONCLUSIONS

The British system of social security has been built up by the development of a contributory system together with a limited system of family benefits, which were conceived to minimize dependence upon means-tested benefits. However, the latter have not been reduced to the safety net role envisaged for them by Beveridge and others. Indeed, in recent years an alternative strategy has been suggested: to confine expenditure on social security by putting the emphasis upon means-tested benefits. While the main issue for debate about the system seems to be the conflict between the case for a comprehensive system of non-means-tested benefits, probably founded upon contributory principles, and the alternative means-testing approach, this conveys an oversimplified notion of its character. In fact, the two approaches are mixed together in the system, and the overall picture is further confused by a range of *ad hoc* responses to special issues and problems: the needs of disabled people, the compensation of industrial injury victims, the requirements of support for students and schoolchildren, and so on.

The 1986 Social Security Act has simplified the means-tested part of the system. This eases administration. It has limited the opportunities for errors, differential rule interpretation and outright discretion within the main means tests. However, the staff reductions which have occurred, the increases in the numbers of claimants and the high performance targets imposed on staff have meant that error rates in the calculation of benefits have remained high.

The 1986 Act offered an approach to reform around which a broad consensus might have formed were it not for the fact that the government was determined that the new scheme should be no more costly than its predecessors, and that it should make it easier for them to contain the future growth of social security costs. Such simplification inevitably implied rough justice, gainers being counterbalanced by losers. In addition, the very controversial social fund was introduced, with loans as its main form of aid and cash limits, to take up the strain on the system previously imposed by the complex single payments rules.

The growth of means-tested benefits relative to contributory benefits between 1964 and 1986, caused by political reluctance to increase the expensive contributory benefits, and the use of *ad hoc* measures to cope with problems of low wages and high housing costs produced a great deal of turbulence in social security policy. Yet the 1986 Act did not bring in a period of stability. It led to further attacks on the contributory system in the pursuit of more savings. The situation now is one in which any future government which considers attempting to turn back the tide and revert to a modernized version of the Beveridge approach would have to come to terms with the high cost implications of such action.

SUGGESTIONS FOR FURTHER READING

I have published an account of the British social security system (Hill, 1990). The Child Poverty Action Group (CPAG) annual handbooks on means-tested and contributory benefits are the key sources for details, including benefit rates, which change at least annually (and have not therefore been quoted here). Other good, general, up-to-date sources are CPAG's journal *Poverty* and a journal published by the University of Nottingham called *Benefits.*

CPAG pamphlets are useful critical sources of information on the system. Deacon and Bradshaw's *Reserved for the Poor* (1983) is an excellent review of the issues regarding means testing and the various alternatives to it, but is now very dated. Parker (1989) provides a good critique of policy, coupled with advocacy of 'basic income'. The report of the Commission on Social Justice (1994) has much to say about social security policy, particularly in relation to benefits and work.

The best discussions of poverty and social security are Townsend's important poverty survey (1979), Mack and Lansley's book (1985), and Alcock's *Understanding Poverty* (1993).

THE HEALTH SERVICE

THE ORGANIZATION OF THE SERVICE

The first part of this chapter is less concerned than the previous one with what the service does – people are relatively more clear about this – but more concerned with how it does it, and particularly how it is organized. Clearly, the ingredients of the health service are hospitals, the family or primary care practitioners (doctors, dentists, pharmacists and opticians operating outside the hospitals), and other community-based services (community nursing and health visiting, and preventive medicine). One of the most confusing aspects of the health service is the structure that has been designed to contain, and hopefully integrate, these various activities.

Figure 6.1 Basic Structure of the Health Service in England.

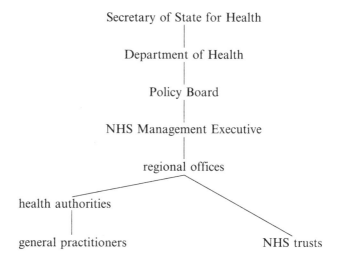

Secretary of State for Health

Department of Health

Policy Board

NHS Management Executive

regional offices

health authorities

general practitioners   NHS trusts

The basic structure of the system in England can be represented diagrammatically, as in figure 6.1. At the top the health service is the responsibility of the Secretary of State for Health. He or she is assisted by a policy board, which he or she chairs. Then, to deal with operational matters, there is a management executive chaired by a chief executive. While this seems to involve a departure from the normal top civil service control structure towards a system which mimics that of a private company, the NHS executive is not a separate agency like the Benefits Agency.

There used to be quasi-independent regional health authorities; now there are simply eight regional offices of the NHS executive in England. Then, at the local level, health authorities, since 1996, integrate the functions of the former district health authorities and family health services authorities. These are purchasers of services for the people in their areas.

In Scotland and Wales responsibility for the service is that of separate ministers (the secretaries of state for Scotland and Wales) and separate departments. This devolved structure allows the omission of the regional management tier in the system. In Scotland the next-tier authorities are called health boards. In Northern Ireland there are four health and social services boards with 'area' responsibilities, each responsible for a number of units. Overall, in the other countries of the United Kingdom, the service and management arrangements are broadly the same as those for England.

The service is organized in a way which splits purchasing of services from provision thereof. The health authorities are purchasers, but only exceptionally direct providers. What this means is that the health authorities are required to enter into specific contracts to secure the services needed for the patients in their area. The providers engaged in this way need not necessarily be in the health authority's geographical patch. The providers are the trusts for hospital and community services and general practitioners for primary care services.

The general medical practitioners operate under contracts granted by the health authorities. Broadly speaking, they are free to decide how they will organize their practices, and are free to accept or reject patients. They are paid primarily on a 'capitation' basis, so much for each patient on their list, plus an allowance for practice expenses and special payments for various exceptional tasks undertaken. The system of payments has been the subject of extensive negotiations and conflict between the doctors and the secretary of state, in the course of which the scheme has been elaborated in a variety of ways to include such things as additional fees for elderly people on doctors' lists and payments for night and weekend work. While the doctors have clearly been eager to secure maximum rewards but to remain within a system that preserves their freedom, the government's objectives in these negotiations have included the encouragement of forms of group practice, the development of health centres and an increase in the number of doctors practising in some areas. In the last few years the general practitioner service has grown much more sophisticated. Isolated independent practice has declined, and group practices, providing a wide range of medical services, have multiplied.

A further complication is that many general medical practitioners (around 40 per cent at the time of writing) are GP fund-holders, with resources which enable them to purchase directly most of the hospital services needed by the patients on their lists without reference to the health authority responsible for their area.

Dentists, opticians and pharmacists are paid on a fee-for-service basis. However, there are problems, particularly as far as dentists are concerned, about the setting of a system of remuneration that rewards most adequately the best practice, is administratively straightforward and can be supervised without detailed surveillance of day-to-day activities.

The dental, optical and pharmaceutical services are, like general medical practice, administered by the health authorities. The latter have responsibilities to see that the various services are available in their district, to help patients obtain practitioners and to deal with complaints.

Prior to reorganization in 1974, the local authorities provided some of the community health services, under the direction of the medical officers of health. They were responsible for community nursing services, the running of maternity clinics, measures to prevent the spread of infectious diseases, and a range of public health matters (controls against impure foods, insanitary living conditions, etc.). There was also a separate school health service, although usually the medical officer of health was also in charge of this. Reorganization left the district councils with the public health responsibilities, but shifted all other services to the health authorities.

The management changes in the 1980s and 1990s have tended to disperse the 'community health' group of activities. In 1974 one possibility was that community medicine would assume a key role in the planning of the service, extending concerns about preventative medicine. Now such specialists are found in health authorities, able to influence contracting decisions but distanced from the management of service delivery. Community nursing services are now generally within trusts, some specifically designed to deliver community services of all kinds, others linked with hospital services. These services may be linked with general medical practice, particularly where GPs are fund-holders.

At local levels there has been some scope for the development of 'primary care teams', groups of health service workers based upon a health centre and sharing a common clientele. But at that level community teamwork is made more difficult by the independence of the general medical practitioners. However, the latter may employ nurses in their surgeries, and increasingly the government has provided them with incentives to provide preventative services (in particular, health checks for their patients). Some issues regarding relationships between the health service and social care services run by the local authorities are picked up in the next chapter.

THE MANAGEMENT OF THE SERVICE

Until the 1980s the managerial arrangements for the NHS could have been described as broadly 'collegial': that is, the various professionals within the service were represented in the management structure. Then, after 1983, each region, district and unit was required to appoint a general manager, on a fixed-term contract. Many of these general managers were already health service administrators, but there were appointments from outside, and in a few cases senior professionals, particularly doctors, but occasionally nurses, have received these posts. These managers were accountable to the relevant appointed authorities. Then, under the changes enacted in 1990, the health authorities were restructured to comprise up to five 'executive members', to include the chief executive and the finance director, and five non-executive members (including a non-executive chairman). Non-executive members are appointed by the secretary of state. Trusts have similar management structures.

Hospital doctors have traditionally exercised a considerable degree of autonomy. Crucial for this is the concept of clinical freedom, which can be effectively extended from a right to determine the treatment of individual patients to a right to plan the pattern of care as a whole. The new managerial arrangements, and the significance of the contracting system for patterns of work, have been seen by some to threaten that freedom (Harrison et al., 1990). It is hard to say how significant that threat is, since a great deal depends upon the internal management arrangements made within the trusts. There is a requirement to make a senior medical appointment, which may place one doctor in a strong position, probably working closely with the chief executive. Alternatively, he or she may be seen merely as a figurehead to represent the consultant group as a whole, without disturbing individual autonomy.

Consultants may be part-time appointees, who combine private practice with NHS work. Junior hospital doctors, below consultant status, are organized in consultant-led teams. Most of them are in short-term appointments, which are seen as building blocks of trainee experience leading to consultant status. There are problems of relatively low pay, heavy duties and insecurity for junior doctors, enhanced by difficulties in advancing to consultancies.

Access of patients to the hospital system is normally by way of general practitioner referral, though direct self-referral is accepted in the event of accidents and emergencies. Once under hospital care, individuals may be treated as in-patients or out-patients. The general notion here is of a hospital-based service for problems that are beyond either the expertise or resources of general practitioners and the 'primary care' teams. However, the lines are sometimes blurred. Modern health centres can often provide services that are elsewhere provided by hospitals. The arrangements for general practice fund-holders may further encourage this development. Community hospitals provide, in some areas, limited service of a kind once provided by 'cottage hospitals', and they may involve general practitioners in their work.

The organizational changes enacted in 1990 created what is often described as an 'internal market' or 'quasi-market' system of health authorities and GP fund-holders as purchasers of services and trusts, together with 'units' within Authorities, as providers. This new arrangement generated considerable controversy; there are difficulties in separating rhetoric from reality to provide a brief evaluation.

The case for the internal market is that the separation of purchasers and providers helps to undermine the tendency for those who provide services to exaggerate their value and hide their inefficient aspects. Bureaucratic allocation procedures have been replaced by a system of contracts, giving purchasers the capacity to make choices between providers and to change them if they do not deliver what is required. A contract involving an expectation of a specific volume of activity at a specific cost forces the provider to pay attention to efficiency.

Those who attacked this system initially argued that to promote efficiency in this way in a caring service is likely to involve disregard of quality and efforts to avoid treatments or kinds of patients whenever there are uncertainties about costs. The simple, readily quantifiable activities of the health service would be emphasized at the cost of care and innovation. This criticism was met by the government by an insistence that purchasers would have to give attention to quality concerns and special needs.

Another criticism was that, far from promoting efficiency, the use of contracts would produce inefficiencies: spare capacity because contracts were fulfilled early, under-use of expensive facilities in hospitals which lost out in contracting processes, and high costs on all sides associated with the renegotiation of contracts (transaction costs). The answers offered to this were of two kinds: first, that there were inefficiencies in the system in any case, some of which would in the long run be ironed out by the new process. There was spare capacity in the service (something linked with changes in the use of hospitals – reductions in the amount and length of in-patient treatment), which the new system would help to get rid of. Some inefficient, or inappropriately located, hospitals would be forced to close. Second, it was argued that some of these problems would arise during the adjustment period of the new system, but subsequently, as contracting skills increased, would be brought under control.

The system that has emerged does not measure up to the aspirations of the market advocates. Political and managerial interventions have sought to allay some of the anxieties expressed by the opponents of the internal market. It has proved to be very much a managed market, with its potential effects upon some hospitals and some services damped down. It has proved nearly as difficult to close hospitals in an internal market system as it was in a bureaucratic system, such is the public concern that this activity raises. Progress is being made towards reducing the number of hospitals in central London, though how much the internal market system has helped the government to grasp that particular political nettle is hard to say. Elsewhere there is no doubt that interventions have occurred to 'steer' the contracting process to ensure continued use of various hospitals or departments within them.

However, it also needs to be noted that the change to a contracting process has necessarily been an incremental one. Purchasers seldom have the capacity to realize the ideal which saw them as fully informed about the needs of their population and about the quality of the services on offer from the providers. Much contracting involves continuing an existing service (looking at what was done in the previous year) with only marginal adjustments. This has led some to argue that a key problem of the new system is the extent to which it is a 'provider-led market' – the providers have a clearer idea of what they want than the purchasers, and are in many respects the main sources of information for the latter. In this respect the general practitioner fund-holders are a maverick element – perhaps able to exert purchaser pressure better than the health authorities, but, because of that, perhaps likely to produce unpredictable distortions in the service (Glennerster et al., 1994).

At the time of writing, research is attempting to evaluate the new system. It looks as if it will survive a change of government. The Labour Party seems to have accepted the basic idea of the purchaser – provider split. It is likely to want to strengthen central control over both parties, and to ensure that contracts are rather more long-term arrangements. It may abolish the arrangements for general practitioner fundholders.

THE FINANCING OF THE SERVICE

The NHS is financed out of national taxation. In 1994 in the United Kingdom £38,657 million was spent on it (this figure does not include any income offsets) (Central Statistical Office, 1995b, p. 15, table 2.2). About three-quarters of this sum was spent on hospital and community services, most of the rest on family practitioner services (*idem*, 1996, p. 146).

Throughout its history, the growth of the cost of the health service to the Exchequer has been a matter of political concern. Demographic changes affecting need, technological changes affecting the quality of treatment, and rising staff costs mean that the cost of the NHS increases without there necessarily being any improvement in the service it provides. Attempts have been made to estimate how much expenditure has to grow each year merely to maintain a consistent level of services to the public. A conservative estimate puts it at 2 per cent, but many suggest that it is nearer 4 or 5 per cent (Robinson and Judge, 1987; see also the discussion of this difficult, controversial subject in Hills (ed.), 1990, ch. 4). This is important in explaining why, in recent years, both the public and NHS practitioners regularly complain about falling standards, supported by concrete evidence from increasing waiting lists for operations, whilst governments claim they are spending more, in real terms, than ever before on the health service. This is a theme to which we will return when we look at trends in public expenditure in the final chapter.

Charges to recipients of services bring some money back to the health service, about 3 per cent of the NHS's total income. Charges cover most of the cost of spectacles and dental treatment and part of the cost of the supply of drugs and medical appliances. They are not applied to hospital in-patients or to children and the elderly. There are means tests that enable low-income people to secure remission of charges.

NEED AND THE RATIONING OF THE HEALTH SERVICE

The British health service is thus, broadly speaking, free and universally available. The general issues raised by the absence of a price mechanism to convert needs into effective demands will be discussed in the next chapter. One of the political preoccupations ever since the founding of the National Health Service has been the apparently limitless character of need.

There seem to be two crucial problems that were given insufficient attention by those who forecasted a decline in need for health services. One is that everyone whose life is saved lives on to become ill again. More precisely, increases in life expectancy bring with them the likelihood of increased work for the service in dealing with the chronic illnesses that particularly affect elderly people. The size of this group has grown rapidly over recent years. Over-65s now constitute 18 per cent of the population, and over-80s 4 per cent (Central Statistical Office, 1996, p. 39, table 1.5). The growth in the proportion of elderly people has temporarily stopped, but will start again just after 2010, as the post-Second World War baby boom population begins to reach 65.

The other problem in predicting need for health services arises from difficulties in defining need. There is a growing understanding that the relationship between having a medical need and seeking medical attention is complex and obscure. Individuals may experience considerable suffering from a condition that manifests no pathological abnormality. Conversely, they may have serious medical problems, yet experience little suffering. Perhaps more significantly in quantitative terms, minor deviations from 'good health' are tolerated by many people for long periods of time without medical attention being sought. This applies, for example, to problems like indigestion, recurrent headaches and skin complaints. It is important to recognize that 'Illness is the subjective state which is experienced by an individual, a feeling of ill-being. Disease is a pathological condition recognized by indications agreed among biomedical practitioners' (Stacey, 1988, p. 171).

The definitions of 'biomedical practitioners' are no more valid than people's subjective judgements. They are subject to variation over time and between 'experts', and are conditional upon the dominant paradigms in medical knowledge. They are, however, crucial in influencing demand for health services. This is the sense in which there may be a problem for health services about 'producer'-determined demand, deriving from 'biomedical practitioners' claims to competence and, in some circumstances, their tendency – encouraged by public faith in medicine – to 'medicalize' social problems.

There is a choice between the policy conclusions to be drawn from these findings. One is that a great deal more should be spent on the health service, and, in particular, many more efforts should be made to screen for unidentified illness in the population at large. The quite opposite view is that the fact that many people manage without medical treatment for many complaints suggests that those who do 'bother' doctors with similar problems should be encouraged to become more self-reliant and to make more use of self-medication. A less extreme version of this view suggests that, since medical resources are clearly limited, it is important to control access to the services in such a way that the more serious complaints are treated, while doctors are not overburdened with the trivial. Another issue on the agenda is the exclusion of some kinds of treatments from the NHS, a much-debated example being treatment of infertility.

At the moment the system depends primarily on general practitioners' judgements for controlling demand upon the system. Are there ways of pushing the responsibility for demand back on to the patients? This provides one argument for the exploration of the case for a 'cost sharing' charging system to control demands upon the service. One possibility is the introduction of 'hotel charges' for hospital stays. The problem with this is that stays are becoming shorter. The administrative costs of billing and collecting charges for the very many very short stays would be considerable. Further complications would be introduced if, as with prescriptions, some patients were not required to pay. A case for health service charges is also argued in terms of the desirability of choice and competition. This case has been made most cogently in the United States by Eliot Friedson (1970), who sees the power of the consumer as enhanced by a relationship with the doctor in which he or she has the capacity to 'hire or fire'. In Friedson's view, the British model of health service organization places individuals in a very weak position in dealing with doctors, and provides the community at large with an absence of weapons for bargaining with a medical profession that would not be so united were doctors in competition with each other. The new purchaser–provider system is designed to try to come part way to solving this problem, but of course it does not give the hire-or-fire power directly to the consumer.

The fundamental point in favour of a free service is that charges may deter people from seeking necessary help (Abel-Smith, 1976). This is particularly likely to be the case with people on low incomes. Moreover, one of the effects of ill health is naturally to reduce income and to increase other costs. The issue at stake, therefore, is not simply one of inequality in general, but specifically of inequality between the sick and the well (regardless of other determinants of income and expenditure). Clearly also, while in other areas of life people may be expected to make choices between different ways of spending money, serious illness leaves little choice. Individuals will bankrupt themselves to save their lives and those of their loved ones.

Where much of the health service is still 'in the market place', as, for example, in the United States, the issues are rarely actually as stark as these. There are two reasons why not. One is that many people insure themselves against sickness. The other is that a 'safety net' means-tested medical system exists for the poor. Arguments in favour of a free service must therefore deal with the weaknesses of these two alternative forms of provision.

The key problems with insurance schemes are that they will not insure the 'bad risks'; they often exclude some conditions (especially preventable ones – for example, pregnancy); and they may collapse. These schemes may reduce the powers of doctors, making them dependent upon the patronage of the insurance agencies; but the latter often encounter the same problems of provider-determined need as the British system has been alleged to suffer from. Moreover, they do not necessarily curb trivial demands, since subscribers may be determined to obtain their money's worth. It is the exclusion of certain groups from insurance cover, however, that is the main problem. In the 1980s the case for an insurance-based approach to health care re-emerged on the British political agenda. Private insurance schemes had grown rapidly, facilitating the growth of private hospitals (Higgins, 1988). Debate developed, therefore, about the extension of such schemes nationwide. Those advocating such an approach argue that individuals should be required to insure themselves privately, and that the state should underwrite such schemes and make special means-tested provision for those for whom they cannot cater. This approach was given very serious attention by the Conservatives in their review of policy before their 1990 changes to the system. The creation of a tier of potentially autonomous providers (the trusts) opens the way to such a development, and certainly encourages mixed arrangements, some of which are outlined in the next section.

The problems with a means-tested health service are the requirement of a test of means before treatment, the likelihood of situations in which individuals will have to abandon resources – or wait to 'hit the bottom' – before they can get treatment, and the probability that (as was the case in Britain when such a system operated) two classes of health service will result. In the last resort, as implied above, the case for a free service is not that it helps to distribute resources from the rich to the poor, but that it enables the healthy to support the sick. If it is believed, on the other hand, that it is in the interests of the evolution of society that the 'weak should go to the wall', it will of course be comparatively easy to take an alternative view.

EQUALITY OF TREATMENT

The impact of the private sector

In the atmosphere of concern about rising health service costs and advocacy of privatization by the New Right, there is considerable concern in Britain on two related issues: the most appropriate relationship between the health service and the residual private medical sector, and the extent to which the health service provides equality of treatment to all the population.

These two issues are related, since the diversion of medical resources into a private sector, largely accessible only to the better off, reduces the resources available to other sectors of the population. However, the defenders of private medicine argue that the resources involved are, in a sense, extra ones, which would not necessarily be diverted into public medicine in an entirely nationalized sector. Particular bones of contention, however, have been not so much the right of the private sector to exist, as the support that sector receives from a variety of special links with the health service.

Both general practitioners and consultants are able to take on private patients as well as health service ones, and now NHS trusts may venture even more boldly into private services for patients from home or abroad. This enables health service resources to be used in various ways in support of private medicine. It facilitates the undertaking of public and private work side-by-side, the use of public resources (such as expensive equipment) for private patients, and 'queue-jumping' when public beds are scarce. The way in which doctors with both public and private work distribute their time between the two may also result in subsidy to the latter, in that they may neglect NHS duties to enhance fee earning. Also, situations arise in which it is possible for doctors to say to people that, whereas health service treatment will be inadequate or long delayed, they may secure a better deal by becoming private patients.

The growth of private insurance raises the question of the overall impact on the state service of alternative ones. Is there scope here for desirable competition? Is it a valuable addition to consumer choice, enabling people who are so inclined to pay a little extra for a superior service? Or does it threaten the basic service, and reduce its capacity to meet the needs of all?

It should be added that the new system also allows situations to arise in which private hospitals and other health services can become providers for the NHS. While it may be argued that this is just enabling the NHS to get public services – at lower cost or where public providers are unavailable – such arrangements may implicitly subsidize the private sector, and may be (as implied in the last section) the thin end of a wedge leading to the transformation of the free health service.

Inequalities in health and medical treatment

The health service's capacity to meet need has been subjected to extensive scrutiny. Epidemiological studies of the differential impact of mortality and morbidity have been of importance here. These show considerable differences in the experience of ill health between different regions of the country, between different social classes (Townsend et al. (eds), 1988), and between different ethnic groups. The statistics on infant deaths have been given particular attention. Twice as many children of unskilled workers die in the first month of life as children of professional workers. The infant mortality rate (deaths in the first year of life by 1,000 live births) varies widely from region to region. In 1994 the highest rate in England was 7.2 in three regions (West Midlands, Yorkshire and Trent). The lowest rate was 4.5 in South West Thames (Central Statistical Office, 1995a). This range is very much less than that quoted in earlier editions of this book; and progress is clearly being made in reducing regional differences. However, there may be great variations within regions. Certainly studies of death rates and experience of illness in other age-groups have shown these. Recent work concentrating attention on quite small areas (local government wards) has shown (a) differences which it is possible to correlate with other indices of deprivation and (b) a tendency for these differences to widen in the last few years (Phillimore et al., 1994).

The policy questions this evidence raises obviously concern:

1 the extent to which these differentials are attributable to differences in the availability of health services;
2 inasmuch as they are attributable to other factors (low income, poor housing and so on), to what extent better health services can and should offset these disadvantages.

On a narrow interpretation of the first of these questions, there is evidence of differences between different parts of the country in terms of the availability of health care. There are variations both between and within regions. Similar disparities may be noted in numbers of doctors and other health service practitioners per head. It should be stressed, however, that these figures do not clearly correlate with the data on mortality. Expenditure on health care and numbers of doctors need to be related to the differential incidence of needs, taking into account such factors as the age structure of the population.

The government, after the reorganization of the health service in 1974, set up a Resource Allocation Working Party (RAWP) to develop a formula to facilitate comparisons between the resource needs of different regions. This used population estimates weighted to take into account differential mortality and different utilization rates based upon differences in the age and the structure of the population (Department of Health and Social Security, 1976). Allocation of new money to the regions was based upon the RAWP formula, and allocations by regions to districts were based upon similar principles.

This proved a difficult, controversial exercise in light of the inadequacy of the statistics available, the difficulties in relating such data to needs, and the uncertainty about the relationship between costs and effectiveness. The 1990 changes brought the RAWP procedure to an end; some of the problems that it had had to deal with in relation to 'flows' of patients across boundaries were solved by the contracting procedure. The allocation of money to health authorities is now based upon population numbers, but is still weighted to take into account some of the considerations about differential needs.

While efforts to tackle some of the problems of 'territorial injustice' that have beset the National Health Service since its foundation have been widely welcomed, there are some other issues about the availability of services that require attention. Social class differentials in the use of health services suggest that efforts need to be made not only to ensure that adequate resources are available in underprivileged areas, but also to facilitate access to the use of those resources by all in need. This raises policy questions about the siting of surgeries and hospitals, the arrangements made by doctors to enable patients to secure appointments, the extent of the use of health service personnel – such as health visitors – who actively seek out those in need of health care, the extent of health education, and the significance of screening services.

Finally, these questions lead on to the other question raised: the extent to which there might be an expectation that health services should be better in some areas, or for some people, to help to compensate for other social disadvantages. Alternatively, to what extent should the concept of a state health service embrace a responsibility to point out how other social factors contribute to ill health?

These last questions have led some critics of the National Health Service to say that it is really a 'national illness service' (HMSO, 1979, p. 15). Academic studies of the health progress of the nation have suggested that changes in the environment and in behaviour have been more important than medical advances (McKeown, 1980).

There are a number of interrelated approaches to the prevention of ill health. Healthy life-styles may be regarded as a matter of personal choice. It is evident that many people have become aware of the need for exercise and the need for a healthy diet. Yet life-style options are influenced by income and environment, constraining choices. They may also be influenced by the practices of the food and drink industry, the additives they use and the things their advertisements promote. Other aspects of our living and working environments may be quite outside our control. It may be argued that governments have important regulatory responsibilities to help protect our health. The limited list of points above about this vast subject indicates that the health of the nation depends upon much more than the efforts of the NHS. Some slight efforts are being made to address these issues: the work of the Health Education Authority at the national level, the 'healthy cities movement' at the local level, and the encouragement of health promotion work by GPs (see Ranade, 1994, ch. 8).

THE REPRESENTATION AND PROTECTION OF THE PUBLIC

When the formation of the National Health Service was debated in the years before 1948, many doctors made clear their opposition to local government control. While some community services were kept within local government between 1948 and 1974, the main forms chosen for the local control of the health service were hybrid organizations in which ministerial appointees served alongside local authority nominees. Since 1991 the arrangements for direct local government representation on health service governing bodies have disappeared. Public representation is therefore only at the national government level.

An interesting innovation in 1974 was the setting-up of locally based community health councils (CHCs) to enable the public viewpoint to be expressed. But the status of these bodies is that of officially recognized and subsidized pressure groups, with rights to make representations and to seek information. Such power as they have primarily rests upon their capacity to embarrass health authorities. Even in relation to this weapon, they have an awkward choice to make, between seeking a close day-to-day working relationship, which may inhibit its use, and remaining more aloof, but thereby losing opportunities to secure information and to make informal representations. They also have difficult choices to make between concentration on individual grievances, the passing-on of views of all kinds from the local groups which form their 'constituency', and the development of a carefully documented, informed critique of the service. Their low resources exacerbate these choice problems.

One point not to be forgotten about CHCs is that they are not themselves representative bodies in any of the senses in which that term is used in democratic theory. Half their members are appointed by local authorities, one-sixth by the Department of Health; the remainder are elected by relevant voluntary organizations (by means of rather haphazard election processes which do nothing to ensure that they are representative of the patients in their areas).

The Labour Party has attacked the political influences upon the selection of non-executive directors for authorities and trusts. There are promises of a more open approach in future – but a system of appointment by the minister is bound to be open to political manipulation. If a new government simply replaces 'their' people by 'our' people, no real progress will be made towards opening up the system.

The separation of purchasing and providing could facilitate the development of a new approach to the issue of democratic control. Since a purchaser is not a direct employer of clinicians, the medical objection to direct control by local politicians has little validity now. Local authorities could become purchasers. Alternatively, since the credit of local government is (rightly or wrongly) at a low level, a system of direct election to health authorities could be developed. A likely scenario under an alternative government is a return to some sort of hybrid arrangement, with local authority (again) or CHC representatives on health authorities (see Wall, 1996, for a further discussion of some of the options for increasing accountability).

However, for many members of the public, what matters more than representation is protection from abuse and malpractice and the chance to be heard when dissatisfied with the service provided. Apart from the general opportunities to make representations, which apply to all the public services, there are, for the health service, a number of special procedures available. Practitioners and hospitals may be sued for tort damages, and professional malpractice may result in debarment from practice by the relevant professional organization. Patients may complain to the health authorities that primary care practitioners have acted in breach of their terms of service, and penalties may be imposed, including, at worst, 'sacking' from health service employment. Complaints against hospitals have to be formally investigated. Finally, a patient may complain to the Health Service Commissioner, though the powers of this official broadly preclude investigations in areas where other forms of investigation or litigation are available.

There is thus no absence of avenues for further action by individuals with grievances. However, the multiplicity of procedures is confusing to patients; and all involve formal approaches which deter action. This formality is regarded as important for the protection of vulnerable professionals from frivolous complaints. But the general problem here is that evidence that things are going wrong in particular parts of the service, particularly the family practitioner parts, does not come to light easily, and thus attract corrective action, when complaints involved are insufficiently serious to activate the formal machinery. At the time of writing, the government has enacted reforms which should systematize and open up a little the way the health service deals with complaints of all kinds.

There are other, more 'internalized' systems for reviewing practice within various parts of the health service. There is a requirement that systems of 'medical audit' be used in hospitals to monitor the activities of doctors. These are controlled by the profession, however, and 'findings' are kept within its ranks. There is also a health advisory service, accountable to the secretary of state and staffed by seconded professionals. It is required to conduct a limited audit of the operation of particular services. This body is concerned with the overall performance in specific areas, particularly where long-term institutional care is involved, and not with the scrutiny of individual professional decision-making. The Audit Commission is also able to conduct investigations within the health service. All these approaches could be developed into a more all-embracing, and more public, health service audit system.

CONCLUSIONS

Long ago, an American student of the British National Health Service described it as 'something magnificent in scope and breathtaking in its implications'. He went on to say:

> In the light of past accomplishments and future goals, the Health Service cannot very well be excluded from any list of notable achievements of the twentieth century. So much has it become a part of the British way of life, it is difficult for the average Englishman to imagine what it would be like without those services that have contributed so much to his physical and mental well-being. (Lindsey, 1962, p. 474)

That expresses rather well the peculiar mixture of utopian expectations and of taking the service for granted that gives a slightly exaggerated quality to British discussions of policy issues in the health service.

We have expectations of the service that often go quite beyond any capacity to deliver results. We oscillate wildly, therefore, between pride in our system and disquiet about its waiting lists and overcrowded wards. We put doctors on a pedestal as the magnificent experts who dominate the system, and we get angry about their arrogant presumptions. We demand more and more from the service, and we get worried that we are perhaps becoming a nation of hypochondriacs who can too easily make demands upon it. These mixed emotions colour the reactions of both politicians and the public to the main policy dilemmas that inevitably confront the service.

Undoubtedly a public approach to medicine involving disproportionate expectations about its capacity to solve the problems of suffering and death lies at the root of some of our difficulties in putting health policies in context and coming to terms with the strengths and weaknesses of our health service. There are signs, however, that a 'demystification of medicine' is beginning to occur. This is helping us to assess much more realistically decisions about the allocation of resources between the hospital service and the community services, and between the health service and other public policies. Some of these issues have been considered in this chapter. Others are given attention in the next chapter.

We are beginning to ask whether we have not so far been too ready to delegate decisions involving moral questions as well as medical questions to professional practitioners. We are beginning to achieve a better understanding of the extent to which many of the determinants of the health of the nation have little to do with the quality and nature of its clinical medical services. But the debate about these issues is inevitably conducted in the shadow of concerns about the continuing rise of health care costs. Questions about what the NHS *should not do* have to be considered in a context dominated by questions about what the NHS *can afford to do.*

SUGGESTIONS FOR FURTHER READING

Wendy Ranade's *A Future for the NHS* (1994) offers a good up-to-date review of all aspects of health policy. Two long-lasting textbooks which are regularly updated are Christopher Ham's *Health Policy in Britain* (latest edition, 1992) and Rudolph Klein's *The Politics of the NHS* (latest edition, 1995). A further recent contribution on this subject is Harrison et al.'s *The Dynamics of British Health Policy* (1990).

A thorough discussion of the implications of the arrival of the trusts is still awaited, but Glennerster et al. (1994) offers a thoughtful review of the early years of the GP fund-holder system.

The Black Report on *Inequalities and Health* and Whitehead's *The Health Divide* are vital sources on the activities and performance of the health service. They are published together in a book listed in the bibliography as Townsend et al. (eds), 1988. Issues about finance and performance are well examined in the relevant chapter of Hills (ed.) (1990) and in Glennerster's *Paying for Welfare* (1992). Stacey (1988) explores the wider sociological issues which need to be taken into account in any evaluation of health policy.

The Personal Social Services

INTRODUCTION

This chapter deals with those services which are the responsibility of the local authority social services departments in England and Wales. The decision to treat the personal social services sector as equivalent to that of the local social services departments is an arbitrary one, justifiable only in terms of existing departmental boundaries in England and Wales. In Scotland, for example, the relevant departments are the 'social work departments', and their responsibilities include duties carried out by the probation service in England and Wales. The justification for refraining from giving attention to the probation service is that a proper consideration of its role raises issues about its relationship to the courts and to other aspects of penal policy, which it is not intended to cover in this book. In England and Wales, before the creation of social services departments in 1971, a chapter like this would have had to deal with activities carried out within several public departments. There are still some variations among authorities in the services that are the concern of the social services departments – a few departments have taken over the education welfare service, and child guidance remains an interdepartmental 'hybrid' service – but broadly the activities of these departments can be made the focus of attention.

In Northern Ireland there are integrated Health and Social Services Boards in which the activities described here are managed side by side with the health service.

One way of classifying the personal social services is in terms of their contributions to the needs of specific groups in the population: elderly people, physically handicapped people, mentally ill people, people with learning difficulties (a group which used to be called 'mentally handicapped'), and children. An alternative classification is in terms of kinds of services: residential care, day care, domiciliary services and field-work. These two modes of classification can, of course, be related to each other. A two-dimensional table could be drawn up, relating kinds of clients to kinds of services. This is difficult only where client groups fall into two or more categories – where elderly people are also physically handicapped, for example – unless the service is seen as being provided for families rather than for specific individual clients.

The data on personal social services expenditure is set out in this way in table 7.1, which gives figures for England in 1994.

Table 7.1 Personal social services expenditure in England, 1994, by client group

Client group	Percentage spent on residential care	Percentage spent overall
Children	27.0	31.3
Elderly people	50.0	42.7
The young physically handicapped	5.7	6.2
People with learning difficulties	15.5	13.9
Mentally ill people	1.9	4.7
Others	0.0	1.1
Total expenditure	£1,846 million	£5,656 million

Source: Department of Health, 1995, p. 116.

Alternatively, services may be seen in two distinct groups: those for children (broadly governed by the Children Act of 1989) and those for adults (broadly governed by the National Health Service and Community Care Act). This legislation, particularly the latter, has largely undermined the aspirations towards an integrated service with general commitments to families embodied in the legislation which set up the social services departments in England and Wales and the social work departments in Scotland. In recognition of the fundamental importance of this new divide in the services, the first part of this chapter will (unlike its form in earlier editions of this book) look separately at these two groups of services. It should be noted that the group of services for adults is often called 'community care', and that this title is used regardless of whether or not the care is residential or domiciliary.

CHILDREN'S SERVICES

The Children Act of 1989 (and a Scottish Act enacted in 1995) consolidated previous legislation on the protection of children. The complex legal framework in this Act tries to ensure that children are protected whilst at the same time recognizing that public interventions into family life should be kept as low as possible. It carries forward a long-standing concern to minimize the likelihood of the removal of children from their family of origin. The Act identifies a wide range of ways in which authorities may spend money to try to avoid taking children into direct care.

Social workers in the social services departments have a crucial role to play in situations in which evidence comes to light that children may be at risk of ill-treatment, abuse or neglect. Their most draconian powers are those which enable them to activate procedures under which children may be taken into the 'legal' care of a local authority because parents are unable to care for them or are deemed to be unfit to care for them. Care decisions are the responsibility of the courts, but most action to take children into care will have been initiated by social workers in the social services departments. Once a child has been taken into care, the local authority will seek to ensure a settled future for him or her. In some cases this will mean return to parental care under supervision. Where this is not possible, foster care is widely used. Hence, institutional care is likely to be regarded as a temporary expedient in many cases, while the situation is assessed and longer-term plans are made.

A large proportion of the children who are in legal terms 'in the care of the local authorities' are not in fact in any kind of institution; indeed, a significant proportion of them are living in their parents' homes. There were about 50,000 children 'in care' in England in 1988. Of these, 64 per cent were boarded out with foster parents. About 17 per cent were under the 'charge and control' of a parent, friend or relative. The remainder, only about 19 per cent, were in some sort of institutionalized care (Department of Health, 1995, p. 72, table 5.45).

Amongst the children who may be deemed in need of statutory care is a group of generally older children who are considered to be out of parental control. Under the 1969 Children and Young Persons Act local authorities acquired increased responsibilities for the care of children brought before the courts for delinquent acts. The object of this legislation was to move away from labelling young offenders as criminals, and to make the issue for decision by the juvenile courts one about responsibility for care rather than punishment for crime. Social services departments may now have to undertake the 'supervision' of such children, or they may be given legal custody of them under a 'care order'. They may fulfil the parental responsibilities entailed in a care order in a variety of ways, including the supervision of a child within a residential institution. The former remand homes and approved schools became specially staffed 'community homes' under this legislation. Since many local authorities do not possess the residential resources to fulfil responsibilities of this kind on their own and, in particular, lack the necessary range of resources, which must include (exceptionally) a 'secure' institution, regional planning committees have been set up to facilitate the use of homes by authorities other than those responsible for their management.

Where the care responsibilities of local authorities are discharged through the use of foster parents, payment will be made, and the arrangements will be supervised by social workers. Some children in the various forms of care may eventually be legally adopted into another family. Social workers have responsibilities to organize and supervise adoption procedures.

In very many cases prevention of child abuse or neglect requires activities other than the formal institution of legal procedures to transfer formal responsibility for the care of children. Social workers have a number of ways in which they may try to do this. They may themselves try to offer support to families – visiting regularly, making suggestions about how to deal with stresses in the household, listening and counselling, and generally responding to cries for help from families under pressure. In doing this, they may be able to mobilize resources: domestic help, day care for children, grants or loans (see further discussion below), help in kind. They may also try to secure help for the family from other statutory organizations: for example, better housing or attention to educational or health problems. There may also be voluntary organizations which they can mobilize to help: support groups, charitable help in cash or kind.

Day care is a service for children which could be within the general remit of the statutory sector. Local authority day nurseries were largely developed during the Second World War, but this service has not grown since then to a really effective level. Places are few, and are generally given only to children from very deprived backgrounds. This is essentially a resource for efforts to prevent child abuse and neglect. In recent years there has been a considerable growth of private provision for day care for young children – daily minding, day nurseries and play groups – for which the social services departments have supervisory responsibilities. In 1990 there were 830,000 maintained or registered day care places for children under 5 (not to be confused with nursery school places) in England. Only about 22,000 (4 per cent) of these were in local authority-maintained day nurseries or play-groups. Of the remainder, 531,000 (67 per cent) were in registered day nurseries and play-groups, and 357,000 (29 per cent) were with registered child-minders (Department of Health, 1995, p. 76 table 5.51).

There are also undoubtedly large numbers of unregistered child-minders!

ADULT SERVICES: 'COMMUNITY CARE'

Social services departments (and social work departments in Scotland) have a wide range of responsibilities for social care of adults. Their predecessor departments (local authority welfare or health and welfare departments) inherited residential care responsibilities from the poor-law in 1948. To these were added a range of domiciliary services, as it became recognized that care concerns might be better met in this way rather than by admission to an institution. The restructuring of both social services and health services in the early 1970s brought further developments: the evolution of services outside health service institutions for mentally ill people and adults with learning difficulties and the aspiration to use skilled social work services effectively in the care of adults.

In the early 1980s, whilst the public residential care sector was continuing to contract and hospitals were increasingly reluctant to become involved in long-term care, the number of private, voluntary residential care facilities began to increase rapidly. This growth in independent (that is, private and voluntary – these expressions will be used interchangeably in the following discussion) care was stimulated by the availability of social security benefits to enable people (in particular, elderly people) to pay independent home charges. It was an uneven growth. In some areas it dramatically reduced the demand for local authority care. In others its impact was quite slight. An Audit Commission report on this issue in 1986 described this growth as a 'perverse effect of social security policies', distorting efforts to get the balance right between residential and community care. People might get social security subsidies for residential care in circumstances in which social services departments would not regard them as in need of such care. The social security authorities were not concerned with this issue; they merely carried out a test of means. This development increased regional inequalities. The greatest growth of independent care was in the south and west of England, particularly in sea-side areas. The Audit Commission pointed out, for example, that 'there are now nearly ten times as many places per 1,000 people aged 75 and over in private and voluntary residential homes for elderly people in Devon and East Sussex than there are in Cleveland' (Audit Commission, 1986, p. 3).

An odd situation had thus developed by the end of the 1980s, to which it was necessary for the government to give attention. Local authorities had been seeking to extend forms of care within the community. The local authority burden had been reduced, relatively, in the 1980s, but not particularly through the evolution of community care. Rather, an independent sector had grown up, unconstrained by public authorities' concerns regarding the importance of maintaining people in their own homes and confining the use of residential places to the most needy. The government's response to this was contained in its White Paper, entitled *Caring for People* (HMSO, 1989), and legislation was enacted in 1990 to try to deal with the situation. What was decided was that local authorities should be responsible for assessing need for care (for all who needed publicly supported care), and should then purchase that care. Hence they would be responsible for determining whether residential care was necessary or, alternatively, whether some lesser form of domiciliary care should be provided (or, of course, nothing), and also for determining who should be the provider. The subsidy of independent residential care through the income support scheme was to cease, but housing benefit should be available for the 'rent' element in this care.

This transferring of responsibility was a complicated process. It involved mechanisms to shift resources from the social security budget to local authority social services budgets over a period of time, leaving arrangements for people already in independent care undisturbed. The new system came into full force in April 1993.

This account of events has laid a strong emphasis upon the anomaly that developed because of the social security subsidy of the independent care system. I believe that the government's concern to reform the system of care stemmed particularly from the problem it had in controlling the growth of social security expenditure on independent care for elderly people. However, the case for reform was expressed in wider terms, which suggested that there was a need for the rationalization of social care as a whole. It was proposed that there were problems about the boundaries between health and social care to be resolved (see further discussion below). It was argued that there was a need for better planning, to maximize care *in* the community and participant involvement in decision-making. It was even suggested, though there is little evidence that what was enacted achieves this, that there was a need for the system to be more responsive to the wishes of the consumer. Hence it was possible for practitioners to try to seize upon the 'community care reforms' as an opportunity to give those in need of care and their carers a better deal.

All this occurred against a background of a growth in the numbers of those in need of social care (particularly amongst the elderly), a search for economies in the health service which contributed to reducing that system's contribution to care, and a central attack upon local government expenditure. The specific proposals for change were laced with new pro-market language. Social services departments were to become 'purchasers', making contracts for the supply of services with 'providers' ideally (from the government's point of view) from the private and voluntary sectors, but if not, then from separate units in their own departments. The government's aim was to shift the system to a 75–25 split of provision in favour of the independent sector. Not surprisingly, therefore, the process of change has been a complex one, about which claims are made as to greater efficiency and greater responsiveness to the needs of the consumer, whilst critics see only a deterioration of services and a pushing of social care problems back on individuals and their families.

In the next few paragraphs I will try, with some difficulty because of the state of change, to outline the kinds of services available in terms of the categories of residential and domiciliary care.

In 1994 there were about 273,000 people in residential places for elderly or handicapped people (Central Statistical Office, 1996, p. 153). Most of these were partly supported by public funds. The word 'partly' is important here, because all these places are means-tested. Residents are required to contribute to their care costs from their income and capital. About 56 per cent of these places were in private or voluntary homes (and the percentage is growing). These institutions have contracts with local authorities to take people who are judged by a social services department to be in need of care. The social services departments are also responsible for the registration and regular inspection of all private and voluntary care homes. They have powers to cancel a registration. Home-owners have a right to an appeal to a tribunal against refusal of registration or de-registration.

A distinction can be made between 'care' homes and 'nursing' homes, but there may be institutions which are both. In the old public sector, before the community care legislation, there had been a problem about maintaining a distinction between the population of local authority homes and the patients of the overburdened geriatric wards of hospitals. Under the new legislation, whilst supervision of 'nursing' homes comes under the health authorities, people in those institutions have to have their needs and means assessed by the local authorities. Long-stay hospitals are rapidly disappearing, being replaced by independent sector nursing homes as far as the elderly are concerned and by a variety of forms of community care as far as those who are mentally ill, physically handicapped or with serious learning difficulties are concerned (we will return to this theme below).

Social services departments organize or purchase from independent providers a variety of day care services. For the elderly there may be day centres where people can go for company, social activities, occupational therapy, perhaps cheap midday meals, and perhaps some aid or advice. Similar facilities are often provided for handicapped people. For the younger handicapped, and particularly for people with learning difficulties, there are centres where company and therapy may be accompanied by productive activities. In many cases these are more or less sheltered workshops, doing commercially sponsored work and paying pocket money to handicapped people. There are some difficult distinctions to be drawn here between sheltered work, therapy and provision for some daytime life outside the home. Under the new community care legislation the government's expectation is that local authorities will become more flexible about the range of help they provide *in the community,* and of course that they will make use of an increasingly wide range of non-statutory providers.

The primary form of domiciliary care supported or provided by social services departments is home help services. These have developed remarkably from a service conceived primarily to help in maternity cases to large enterprises serving predominantly the elderly, and thus playing an important part in helping old people manage in their own homes. Local authorities in England provide, directly or through independent agencies, nearly half a million households with home help (Department of Health, 1995, p. 83, table 5.58). The development of the services has, however, been uneven. According to the Audit Commission (1986, p. 24) 'home help provision varies by a factor of six or more among authorities – from under seven full-time home helps for every 1,000 people aged over 75 (equivalent to less than eight minutes of actual help every week for each person aged over 75) to 44 full-time home helps'. Of course, people may purchase their own domestic help unaided by a local authority, and where services are inadequate, the gap is likely to be filled by large amounts of unpaid work by relatives and neighbours. Local authorities may charge for home help services, and may use means tests to determine the level of the charge. In the aftermath of the community care changes, there is a serious need to rationalize charging and means-testing practices.

Local authorities may also support the provision of meals, taken to people in their own homes. These 'meals on wheels' services are often provided through a voluntary organization. Again, the extent of coverage varies widely from area to area, from, at one extreme, a 'token' meal a week to, at the other, the provision of a comprehensive, seven days a week service. Local authorities may set charges for this service, and the extent to which they subsidize it is also variable.

Local authorities provide a range of other 'benefits in kind' to assist with the care of people within the community. The Chronically Sick and Disabled Persons Act of 1970 suggests a wide range of services that local authorities may offer to handicapped people. Despite the emphasis in that Act upon local authority duties, the word 'may' in the last sentence is appropriate. There are wide variations in the adequacy of the help provided. Authorities may provide, and pay the rental costs of, telephones; they may adapt houses to meet the needs of disabled people; and they are able to provide a variety of aids to daily living. They tend, however, to impose budgetary limits that ration quite severely the money available for such benefits. However, a further piece of legislation, the Disabled Persons (Services, Consultation and Representation) Act of 1986, increases the rights of disabled people to be informed about provisions and consulted about their needs. This should have the effect of increasing the flow of services to the disabled, but it has not been brought fully into operation.

The administration of these diverse mixes of services requires social services departments to have a large work-force. The new purchaser–provider split means that the purchaser role in social services departments has to be undertaken by 'care managers', who assess needs and commission services from the available providers. A further discussion of this role is contained in a separate section on 'field-workers' below.

THE RELATIONSHIP BETWEEN PERSONAL SOCIAL SERVICES AND THE HEALTH SERVICE

In many respects the concerns of the health service and those of the social services departments overlap. People are likely to need mixtures of health care and social care. Increasingly the NHS is trying to limit its care to what may be described as 'treatment'. Where possible, in-patient treatment is being replaced by out-patient treatment. Hospital stays are getting shorter, the aim being to send patients 'home' as soon as high inputs of specialized treatment are no longer necessary. The mentally ill are hospitalized as little as possible. It is broadly accepted that there is only very exceptionally a case for hospital care of those with severe learning difficulties. In general there is a concern to maximize care 'within the community' rather than in hospitals. There is some confusion engendered by the fact that care outside hospitals is not necessarily care in the community in the obvious lay sense of the term; it may be care in an institution of some kind. In some cases, moreover, that institution may be a nursing home.

Many people are in receipt of a combination of health treatment from general practitioners and community-based nursing staff, on the one hand, and social care, on the other. Deficiencies on either side may have to be made up by extra services on the other.

The discharge of patients from hospital in itself has substantial implications for personal social services provision. It is important that social support services are readily available at this stage. Hence day-to-day co-ordination between the two services is crucial.

In this context there is a special problem when residential, including nursing home, care may be necessary. Hospital care is still free, whereas residential care deemed necessary by social services departments is not free. Charges are determined by means tests. Those means tests take into account capital assets, including the value of owner-occupied houses in some circumstances. The changes described earlier, in the arrangements made for residential care together with the increasing unwillingness of the heath service to keep people in hospital, is creating situations in which people are discovering that they have to pay substantial amounts for social care in situations in which, in the past, they might have expected free hospital care.

The importance of the overlap between health and social services has led the Department of Health to encourage, and the local agencies to adopt, a variety of means of developing links. At the service planning level, the Department of Health has led the way by emphasizing the need to look at the health service and personal social services together. Within individual localities, they have encouraged the development of formal joint planning activities. A particular stimulus to this has been provided by 'joint financing'. Money from the health service budget is made available to help finance projects within the social services departments that can be considered to meet needs that might otherwise have to be met by the health service. In the long run, social services departments are expected to take over the full cost of these ventures. However, where positive progress can be made in the shift of people from institutional to community care, a more direct transfer of resources from health to personal social services may occur (but only to cover the costs of those transferred).

Finally, it is appropriate to include in this section a very different example of the need for inter-service co-ordination and co-operation. This is supplied by the problem of child abuse. Non-accidental injury to children is frequently discovered by doctors and health visitors; yet it is the social services departments that have the responsibility for preventative and legal action in these circumstances. On the other hand, where social workers suspect child abuse, they may need medical confirmation of their suspicions. Once child abuse is suspected, continued vigilance is necessary. Sometimes it is a health service worker who is best placed to maintain a watching brief; sometimes it is a social worker. In many cases both departments accumulate evidence on the problem; it is important that they share that evidence both formally through case conferences and informally (Hallett and Stevenson, 1979).

NEEDS AND PRIORITIES

The new community care policies require local authorities to engage in planning exercises. At the same time, the increased central control over local authority finance (discussed on pp. 60–1) involves the centre in making clear what it considers social services should be at the local level. There is an inevitable conflict, given that the grant to local authorities is largely non-specific, between this and local government autonomy.

The increased recognition in the 1980s of the limited funds available for public services and the relationship between this and the growing need for social care (as a result, for example, of the growth of the numbers of very elderly people) have sharpened concern to find ways of balancing the respective contributions to the 'mixed economy of welfare'. While this is sometimes presented as a new issue, social care has always involved some combination of care within the family and the community, care which is bought, care which is provided by voluntary and charitable agencies, and care which is provided by public agencies. What is perhaps new is acceptance that the contribution from the last source is inherently limited – hence the development of a lively debate about the roles of the other forms of care.

An important part of that debate concerns the search for ways of defining need, and identifying how public agencies should respond to it. Economists have a distinctive approach to this issue. Instead of attempting to tackle the concept of 'need', they emphasize the concept of demand, which they define as a willingness to buy at a given price. This approach emphasizes the price mechanism as a means of adjusting services to demands. If there is a high demand for a particular thing, then this will be reflected in a willingness to pay higher prices. Higher rewards will attract more suppliers, and may ultimately bring down the price. Always, however, an equilibrium is maintained in which supply and demand are balanced by the price mechanism. To what extent does this offer a solution to the problem of needs in the social services? Clearly it does not if the local authority is the only supplier of a particular service or the controller of access to that service. Equally it does not if that authority is the funder of the service for low-income people without the resources to purchase it themselves. Conditions of monopoly or near monopoly then exist, in which, in theory, the supplier can determine the price, and those unable to pay must go without. The attempt to identify real needs regardless of ability to pay is the hallmark of the public service here. Rationing according to the capacity to pay is quite widely regarded as a bad way to distribute many such services. The price mechanism solution is also inappropriate where it is arguable that people who need particular services are either unlikely to recognize the need or to translate it into an effective, money-backed demand. Social work services designed primarily to protect children from their parents fall into this category. There remain, however, services like the home help service that are provided both by the statutory authorities and by the private market. In some sense, the need for these services can be regarded as fairly limitless – most of us would like our domestic chores to be done by someone else. The price mechanism seems to offer a basis for distinguishing absolute need from effective demand, and of allowing for the existence, side by side, of a public and a private sector.

The use of the price mechanism may be fair enough in theory, but what happens to those with high needs, in some absolute sense, but a low capacity to pay? There are two possible answers to this objection to the use of the price mechanism. One is that social affairs should be arranged in such a way that what are really income maintenance problems do not have to be solved by the provision of subsidized services. This is an attractive argument, but one that matches poorly the real world. The other is that means tests should be devised to enable cheaper services to be given in some cases. The trouble with this latter solution is that it can cope with situations in which only a minority have to be helped outside the market-place, but it quite destroys the market concept when it has to be very widespread. The reality is that for many of the personal social services (including the home help service) some more fundamental way of defining need is required: a minority can buy the services on the open market; but there remains a large group who appear to need them free or at a reduced price, only some of whom actually receive them. The problem remains of determining how much the service should expand to meet the unmet needs (see Judge, 1987; for a strong pro-pricing line see Harris and Seldon, 1976).

This digression into the market approach to need was necessary, first because it has significant advocates, and second because it offers a challenge to the definition of need. The alternative is the ascertainment of some more absolute way of determining need. In some cases this does not seem too problematic; in relation to some diseases, for example, there may be a finite group whom it is generally agreed are in need of treatment. But in other cases the problem is one of making a distinction between 'absolute need' and some more limited concept. While I may contend that I need my house cleaned in order to free me to write books, you may argue that I am still physically capable of doing this work while others are not. They, you will say, are the ones really in need. But would this be a disagreement about needs or about priorities?

For the personal social services, then, the determination of needs is complicated first by the fact that the departments do not have the sole responsibility to meet certain kinds of needs, and second because their views of needs must be determined by their views of priorities. Neither of these problems is one that can be solved by more and better research. Research may be required once the departments have begun to answer the more fundamental questions; but first they have to resolve difficult issues about the limits of the statutory social services' contribution to the solution of the social problems and about the importance of any specific service relative to others.

Theoretically, the purchaser–provider split in community care requires the care managers to take decisions about need, based upon some of the ideal considerations set out above. They must then commission the services they regard as appropriate. At that stage means testing is likely to occur. But to what extent can this split system operate in this way in reality? Local authorities have, in general, gained modest increases in their central grant as a result of the community care legislation. But individual local authorities may in practice have gained little, or even lost resources, because theoretical community care grant gains have to be offset against general grant losses. At the same time the NHS is sharply reducing its contribution to long-term care. In these constrained conditions, those who determine needs will be unlikely to operate in ways unaffected by their knowledge of resource deficiencies.

FIELD-WORK IN SOCIAL SERVICES DEPARTMENTS

The services provided by local authorities that were described above as 'field-work' include visits by social workers, social work assistants, occupational therapists, and volunteers recruited and organized by social services departments. Since the coming of the new community care policies, a significant element of this work involves what is described as 'care management': assessing needs and organizing the commissioning of services.

The social work aspect of local authority field-work is often emphasized; in Scotland the departments are called 'social work departments', while in England and Wales social workers occupy many senior management roles. But it is important to recognize two things: first, that the support of people in their own homes is carried out by a variety of workers, not all of whom are, or should be regarded as, social workers; and second, that the coming of the care management task has led to a challenge to social workers as front-line caseworkers. The practical tasks of identifying what are often straightforward, readily identifiable needs and securing the services needed to meet those needs may be performed by workers without the specific training given to social workers. Local authorities may find it more practical, and cheaper, to use other staff in these roles.

In general, the distinction here between the social work task and other tasks is a difficult one to make. The public often makes no distinction between social work and many other 'caring activities'; yet social workers are increasingly preoccupied by a concern to define their task. This has implications not only for social workers' 'professional' aspirations, but also for the costs of various services, since trained social workers are relatively expensive.

There are some forms of field-work which are seen as needing social work skills. Attention has already been drawn, in the section on children's services, to the special skills needed to determine whether children are at risk and in preventative work in these circumstances. Social workers also have statutory duties under the 1983 Mental Health Act to assess and take appropriate action when mentally ill people appear to require compulsory hospitalization.

In the reorganization of the National Health Service in 1974 the local authority social services departments were given responsibility for hospital social work. This service had evolved from two very different traditions. In connection with the more advanced mental hospitals, a quite sophisticated psychiatric social work profession had developed, often leading the way in the provision of casework both in hospitals and among their out-patients. In the general hospitals, on the other hand, social work had its origins in the activities of almoners, required, before the coming of the National Health Service, to assess patients' capacities to pay fees. Once hospital treatment was free, this group of social workers took on a variety of different jobs. In many cases they were regarded primarily as important for links between hospitals and the community, and in particular, therefore, for arrangements regarding the discharge of patients. Yet others, particularly in the more sophisticated hospitals, developed forms of casework and counselling, to help patients deal with the psychological and social problems that often accompany medical ones. Hospital social work therefore has very mixed traditions, and is very patchily developed today. An important issue for them now is how to integrate with community-based social work while remaining one of the professional groups involved in the hospital service (Department of Health and Social Security, 1974). They share this last problem with social workers employed in the child guidance service, who are social services employees working alongside psychiatrists from the health service and psychologists from the education service within administrative arrangements that are a product of local compromises between the three services involved.

One of the most difficult elements for determination of priorities within social services departments is that part of the service which is provided by social workers and related staff. Many of the needs for social work help are seldom expressed – at least not in any straightforward sense. The pressures that lead to calls for more social work come from the anxieties of the public and politicians about child abuse, the deterioration of old people who live alone, or the disturbance caused by aggressive, mentally ill people, for example. These are issues of social control as much as of service. Pressure also results from the many requests that come to social services departments that are not so much for specific services as for help with a wide range of problems of poverty and deprivation. Social work is seen as having a contribution to make to the problems of underprivileged communities in many different ways; indeed, these expectations often go way beyond the profession's capacities, particularly when political and economic problems are perceived as social or individual ones.

There is a wide but essentially diffuse demand, therefore, for the services of social workers. Forward planning exercises in social services departments find it difficult to categorize the actual contribution made by social workers. Social workers, inasmuch as they seek to protect their day-to-day activities from hierarchical scrutiny and control, contribute to this imprecision. It is also fostered by their own uncertainty about their work, and by controversy within the profession about the essential ingredients of the social work task.

There has been an extensive debate about what social work is, and a related one about whether it can be practised within local authority social services departments. This seems to have various interlocking dimensions. There is a concern about the relationship between social work and a variety of, perhaps more mundane, supporting tasks that may be performed. Thus Butrym distinguishes between:

'provision for the quality of inner life', which she regards as the social work task, above all;

providing 'support and containment', which is partly a social work task, but may also be performed by others, including volunteers;

dealing with 'matters of right and entitlement', where social workers need to know of the services available, but should not be concerned with their day-to-day administration;

dealing with other agencies, where the social worker's task is to transmit relevant needs 'to appropriate institutions and to press for necessary changes to policies'. (Butrym, 1976, pp. 10–11)

A British Association of Social Workers working party has likewise published an elaborate attempt to distinguish some of the more complex tasks which require special skills, including, in particular, skills in dealing with interpersonal relationships, from more mundane activities (1977). A quasi-official investigatory committee which looked at this issue, in response to growing criticism of social work, broadly endorsed, in a report published in 1982, these attempts to distinguish a core of social work expertise from the wider activities surrounding it (Barclay, 1982).

But critics of social work have condemned the quasi-psychiatric emphasis in some of this theorizing, suggesting that above all social workers should give relatively straightforward, practical help to people trying to cope with problems of deprivation (Wootton, 1959; Sinfield, 1969). The significance of this debate is:

1 Its implications for the balance to be achieved by departments between the use of trained social work staff and of less trained personnel (including, perhaps, volunteers).
2 If at the core of the social work task lies intensive work with individuals with special problems, to what extent can such work be done in public authorities; and if it can be done there, what arrangements need to be made to protect this casework from other pressures upon social work time?
3 Alternatively, if a wide range of work with problems of deprivation is to be performed by social workers, how are the boundaries of this work to be determined, and what are the implications for relationships between social services departments and other agencies?

A related debate has concerned the extent to which, in working with an individualistic model of social pathology and an anxiety about deviation from 'normal' behaviour, social work may reinforce the *status quo* and encourage models of behaviour which are class- or race- or sexual orientation-specific (Corrigan and Leonard, 1978; Williams, 1989).

The traditional model of social work, with its concern with individual problem solving, sees as its key method 'casework', requiring intensive relationships with individuals and families. But two other approaches to social work are 'group work' and 'community work'. To these should be added a fourth, an 'integrated' approach embracing all the other three approaches according to the demands of the situations (Specht and Vickery, 1977). Group work clearly has a place within the statutory framework for local authority social work. It has particularly taken the form of 'intermediate treatment', involving help to delinquent children through shared activities with others. The position of community work is more controversial. This involves working with communities to help them solve their own problems. There is, however, a radical school of community work which stresses the importance of mobilizing groups against the power structure in the community. There is scope for argument, first, as to whether this work really is social work and, second, as to whether it has a place within the framework of the local authority social services department. Schools of social work offer community work training or a community work option to their students. But community workers are also trained in other ways. Local authorities employ community workers to some extent, and some authorities tolerate relatively radical activities. They vary in the extent to which they see a need to integrate this work with social work. The case for a more radical approach to social work is particularly pertinent where traditional casework methods come up against cultural differences, as in ethnic communities.

There is one further dimension to the debate about the social work task which must be mentioned here. Before the integration of local authority social services departments, many social workers specialized by client group; indeed, this specialization was determined largely by the department in which they worked. Part of the case for integration of the personal social services was the argument that social work involved skills usable with, or transferable to, varying client groups. The new generic departments matched a generic concept of social work. The initial problem for most departments was to get social workers from different backgrounds to work together. To this end the generic approach was emphasized. Once the achievement of integration was no longer an issue, social workers began to explore the scope for specialization within the generic department. This specialization may be in terms of methods of work or kinds of problems tackled; but it may also be a return to client group specialization.

At the same time, however, an informal, *de facto* kind of specialization has developed within departments. Child care work is particularly seen as deserving of expert attention. This may be attributed to the clear statutory requirements regarding visiting and reporting where the courts are involved with child care problems and the very high anxieties experienced within social work and the public at large by child abuse and neglect. Mental health work is also seen as important, and its underlying significance is emphasized by the emergency powers possessed by social workers and by the recognition, in the 1983 Mental Health Act, of the need for special additional training for this work. Work with people who are handicapped or elderly, on the other hand, is seen as less pressing and more routine. The consequence is that child care work and mental health work are seen as requiring the attention of the most experienced qualified staff, while the other activities are more readily delegated to others. The changes to community care and the emergence of the new care manager role have reinforced this division, and may be in the process of undermining the earlier aspiration to make social work 'generic'.

THE RELATIONSHIP BETWEEN THE PERSONAL SOCIAL SERVICES AND INCOME MAINTENANCE

Some of the functions that today fall within the social services departments have at earlier times been within local authority health, education or even housing departments. However, further back in time, before 1948, there was a strong association between the personal social services and income maintenance within the poor-law. It is worth looking a little more at the separation of these two services that exists today, and at some of the factors that partially undermine that separation, particularly because they have important implications for some of the dilemmas about the social work role.

The political commitment, in the 1940s, to separating income maintenance from the personal social services was influenced by a hatred of the poor-law. It was seen as possible to develop services for all freed from the stigma of the means test and the workhouse when the National Assistance Act of 1948 gave all income maintenance responsibilities to a national body and the duty to provide residential and domiciliary care to the local authorities. The services for children were given a quite distinct identity by the Children Act of 1948, and developed their own special approach to community care within the children's departments of the local authorities. A concept of social work was able to develop that was very different from that within American welfare departments, where income maintenance and social work are closely linked. Social workers, regardless of their political persuasion, have come to see it as very important that they are able to give aid, advice and support to their clients without at the same time having responsibility for their incomes. What this implies is that, whereas personal social services under the poor-law were essentially for the poor, and were very involved in the control of the lives of the poor, today in the British system it is possible to conceive of the benefits of the services as available to all without discrimination.

That, then, is the ideal; the reality is a little different (Jordan, 1974; Hill and Laing, 1979; Becker and Macpherson, 1988). It is clearly the case that a very high proportion of the users of the personal social services are low-income people. It is hard to envisage a situation in which it could be otherwise. The peculiarity of the personal social services is that they are concerned with a range of benefits that is also provided in other very different ways, by both commercial enterprises and voluntary activities. The very existence of a statutory group of services of this kind poses some delicate questions about the nature of the balance between this and individual, family and community provisions. The assumption is that the statutory provisions are necessary when the others fail. Politicians get worried about the possibility that private responsibilities will be abandoned in favour of public ones or that public service 'dependencies' will be engendered. This is possible; it is in the nature of statutory intervention in areas generally the realm of private action that it may alter behaviour. However, the evidence is that, typically, those who seek help from the personal social services do so only when other possibilities no longer exist. An absence of other ways of meeting such needs is particularly associated with poverty.

Several connections between income maintenance and the personal social services therefore exist. Most services are rationed by means of charges. Indeed, as noted above, the new community care legislation, together with financial pressures upon local government, have increased the importance of charges. If charges are not to deter the poor, however, they must be abated through means tests. These need to be related to the other means tests within the social security system.

That is one connection. The other is more complicated, and more clearly explains the social work concern about the separation of their services from income maintenance. There is a correlation between the forms of pathology that come to the attention of social workers – delinquency, child abuse, even publicly threatening mental illness – and poverty (Holman, 1978). It is difficult to summarize here a very complex, and deeply value-laden, debate. Strands within it include arguments about the extent to which the rich can hide their pathology, or seek help from sources other than social services departments; about the extent to which poverty *causes* social pathology, and vice versa; and about the extent to which this 'deviance' simply involves labelling the non-conformity of the poor. The fact is, however, that it is primarily low-income people who become the clients of publicly employed social workers.

It is this fact that leads many who have written about social work to stress the importance of a relationship with the poor that does not include responsibility for their incomes (Jordan, 1974). Yet, at the same time, many social workers recognize a need to help clients with their income maintenance problems. There is a power under the 1989 Children Act (carried forward and enlarged from earlier legislation dating in the first place from 1963) and under a related but rather more all-embracing provision in Scotland enabling money payments to be made to help social services clients where these might assist in keeping children out of care. Here, then, is a statutory recognition of a connection between lack of money and social pathology. Yet this power is used comparatively little, and several writers have drawn attention to the danger that it might be used to reward good behaviour and become a social control device within social work (ibid., also Handler, 1973). In general, an alternative approach is preferred, in which social workers and other social services staff assist clients in claiming benefits from other agencies. Such work is generally described as 'welfare rights work' (Fimister, 1986). To some degree, in many authorities, specialist workers who are often not social workers have been taken on to do this sort of work. There has also been a considerable growth of aid and advice work on welfare benefit problems in voluntary agencies and advice bureaus. However, social workers are bound to have to take on some of this work; some do so with great commitment, while others feel that it distorts their activities and pulls them away from 'real' social work.

The character of welfare rights workers has changed as the social security system has changed. Before 1980 the concern was to get supplementary benefits officers to exercise their extensive discretionary powers. After 1980 the complex structure of apparent 'rights' required that poor people secure help in finding their way through the regulations, identifying things to which they were entitled, and getting the increasingly hard-pressed social security administration to grind into action. The social security changes brought in by the 1986 Act threw social workers and welfare rights specialists into turmoil. Rights to single payments more or less disappeared. The social fund scheme seemed to require social services personnel to replace the conflictual pattern of behaviour required to secure rights by collaboration with social security officers to determine need for community care grants. The loans provisions for other forms of help, administered by officers with high levels of discretion, similarly suggested a need for a very different approach to getting resources for clients. The position is further complicated by the fact that social services departments retain their power to make grants described above. In practice, this power is little used, and most departmental budgets for this item are limited. If this were to change, or if social workers were to be co-opted into helping determine needs for social fund grants and loans, then social workers could be back into money rationing responsibilities in a big way. This development was feared when the social fund was introduced; but in practice, social workers seem to have coped with the conflict, very often by turning a deaf ear to material needs.

The complicated system of benefits for disabled people, which may interact in complicated ways with provisions for institutional care and the provision of caring services, also poses a number of problems for social services clients where welfare rights advice can be invaluable (see Fimister, 1995).

THE ROLE OF THE VOLUNTARY SECTOR

Reference has already been made to the mixed economy of welfare. In this economy, voluntary agencies are, alongside family, community and private enterprise, an element of considerable importance. Voluntary organizations carry out many functions on behalf of social services departments. Under the new community care provisions they may be providers, entering into contracts with social services departments. These entail large grants, and in some cases the truly voluntary component of the work is small. Increasingly, services for elderly people and for specific groups of handicapped people are provided by voluntary organizations, some of which have a nation-wide remit. Similarly, voluntary organizations are substantial providers of residential care.

There is a variety of ways in which individual volunteers are used in the personal social services. They may be deployed under the auspices of voluntary agencies. They may be organized under schemes requiring community service of convicted offenders, or schemes to provide work for the unemployed in return for special allowances (should those in these two categories properly be called volunteers?); or they may be individuals who undertake, by direct arrangements with the departments, to help with particular tasks. A wide range of tasks may be involved: supportive visiting of clients, taking people from residential homes out in cars, helping social services clients with decorating or gardening, helping to run clubs and day centres, and so on.

All this voluntary input into the personal social services may be seen as helping to multiply the amount and range of services available for a given amount of public expenditure. It may also be seen as adding a community dimension to a service that is in danger of becoming too bureaucratized and professionalized. Some of it is a logical extension of the way in which the personal social services are called in to replace or buttress independent caring in the community. In this way it may be seen as helping to put back a community support system that, in the best of all worlds, should have been there all along.

However, there are problems with this balance between statutory effort and voluntary effort. The latter may be seen as a way of achieving personal social services 'on the cheap'. People often support voluntary organizations because they want to add something extra to the statutory service, perhaps something that it cannot or will not do. They may feel that their efforts and their donations are being used simply to meet needs that the state should meet.

While it was suggested above that volunteer services may be better than bureaucratic or professional ones, they may also be worse. Social workers who are reluctant to make use of volunteers suggest that they may be unreliable; they may be indiscreet; they may give gratuitous advice where none is desired; and they may give bad advice and interfere in problems they do not understand (Holme and Maizels, 1978). Voluntary help often comes from people who are very unlike the people who need help, the middle-class and the middle-aged being prominent among the ranks of volunteers.

It may be argued that what is needed in many situations is the development of community-based self-help activities, not the importation of volunteers from outside. On the other hand, it would be rash to suggest that this form of voluntary activity is without its problems. Some of the points about unreliability and indiscretion certainly apply to this form of voluntary activity. Equally, encouraging situations in which communities help themselves may also be seen as providing social services on the cheap. If it is not to be seen like this, then another problem must be confronted: namely, that community self-help may also entail the making of demands for new services from the departments. This form of voluntary activity may therefore entail situations in which departments subsidize their own pressure groups. Some social services departments have been able to accept relationships with the voluntary sector that involve this. However, many others have been unwilling to see volunteers in other than traditional, supplementary service-giving roles.

CONCLUSIONS

The responsibilities of the social services departments in England and Wales and the social work departments in Scotland involve a wide range of activities. These extend from the provision or commissioning of relatively precise benefits and services, through a variety of residential and day care facilities, to a number of very personal, individualized services. They include a high proportion of the social work practised in these countries.

This mixture of activities has grown rapidly. The growth is perceived with quite considerable anxiety by the public, since most of the activities were hitherto undertaken outside the statutory sector, within the family and the community. One interpretation of this growth is that public services can now be provided to help strengthen family and community life. If this view is taken, then residential care replaces the neglect of the isolated old, and social work helps families to cope with crises that would hitherto have destroyed them, and so on. But there is an alternative view, that the growth in these services is itself an index of social pathology, that people are not coping so well with aspects of life that in the past were of little concern to public services. This ambivalence is compounded by widespread uncertainty about what social services departments do (indeed, they are often confused with social security departments), a very vague conception of the social worker's role (shared, it seems, by many social workers), and a deep uncertainty about the circumstances under which help may be sought from the various specific services.

The implementation of the new community care policies complicates the position. In some respects, hidden behind the rhetoric of 'care' is a concern to push responsibility back on to the 'community', the latter meaning, in practice, often hard-pressed relatives.

Social services in Britain are going through an intense period of change, which it is hard to portray accurately. Different departments are changing at different rates. Two new fissures are occurring in the departments which many tried to integrate in the late 1970s and early 1980s: between children's services and adult services and between those given purchaser roles and those given provider roles. In the long run, the departments may split, or provision may become so completely detached that they become merely commissioning agents.

SUGGESTIONS FOR FURTHER READING

Two general books on the personal social services which are recommended are Christine Hallett's *The Personal Social Services in Local Government* (1982) and Adrian Webb and Gerald Wistow's *Social Work, Social Care and Social Planning* (1987). However, both these have become rather dated, without an obvious replacement appearing on the scene. On the community care side there is one book which fills this gap, Means and Smith's *Community Care* (1994).

The Barclay report (1982) on the social work task gives a portrait of the activities of field-work teams, as does Goldberg and Warburton's

Ends and Means in Social Work (1979). A variety of different perspectives on what the social work task should comprise are provided in books by Butrym (1976), Specht and Vickery (1977), Jordan (1974), and Corrigan and Leonard (1978).

The issue of the 'mixed economy of welfare' is explored in an article by Judge (1982). Issues about community care and public expenditure in the social services have been explored in Webb and Wistow's *Planning, Need and Scarcity* (1986) and in Glennerster's *Paying for Welfare* (1992).

Unfortunately, much of the work on social work and social security pre-dates the social fund, though the collection edited by Becker and Macpherson (1988) is a partial exception to this. As far as community care and social security is concerned, however, Fimister (1995) is a valuable up-to-date source.

CHAPTER 8

EDUCATION

EDUCATION POLICIES AND THE ORGANIZATION OF THE SYSTEM

The state's role in education is a dual one; it is the major provider of education, and has also assumed a responsibility to supervise it in the sector for which it is not directly responsible. About 6 per cent of the United Kingdom's schoolchildren are in private schools.

As in the health service chapter, it will be taken for granted that readers are generally aware of the basic services provided by the system. The organizational structure of the state education system has been subject to recent changes, which make it less straightforward than it used to be.

There is a dual system for the provision of state schooling. The majority of schools are, as has long been the case, the responsibility of local government in Britain. They come under the counties, the metropolitan and other single-tier districts, and the London boroughs. In Northern Ireland they come under appointed education and libraries boards.

But since the 1988 Education Act it has been open to schools (with the agreement of a majority of parents) to apply to become grant-maintained. Such schools are funded directly by central government, through funding agencies. Their everyday management is then the responsibility of their own governing bodies. Envisaging a steady movement towards a grant-maintained system, the government provided in the 1993 Education Act statutory arrangements under which, if 10 per cent of schools in a local authority area secured this status, the funding agency then assumes joint responsibility for the planning of educational provision in the area. If 75 per cent achieve that status, the funding agency takes over full responsibility for provision for the area. The number of schools which have secured grant-maintained status is comparatively small (about 1,000 in England by 1994), and there are signs that requests to change status are now coming through very slowly.

There are also a small number of city technology colleges in England and Wales (15 in 1993), which the government set up as new institutions, ostensibly on an experimental basis, also to provide some independently managed, centrally funded secondary education.

Whilst the great majority of schools remain, at the time of writing, in the local authority sector, legislation forces local authorities to fund schools on the basis of a centrally determined formula and to delegate significant management responsibilities to their governing bodies.

Higher education and further education are outside local authority control. In England and Wales two government-appointed funding councils deal with the financing of these two sectors, and thus in various respects control them. There are separate, but broadly similar, funding councils in Scotland and Northern Ireland.

In Scotland, Wales and Northern Ireland, education is the responsibility of the Scottish, Welsh and Northern Ireland offices respectively. In England the relevant central government department is the Department for Education and Employment.

The school system can be identified as involving three sectors: a small pre-primary sector, primary education and secondary education. In most cases these sectors can be identified respectively with the education of children under 5, between 5 and 11, and between 11 and the school-leaving age of 16 (with many pupils continuing at school until 18). However, some authorities have developed systems that deviate from the strict break between primary and secondary education at 11-plus. These have generally introduced an intermediate, middle-school system, for children in two or three of the year bands between 9 and 13. A few have developed separate schools to split the secondary age-group.

One innovation of the latter kind has been the introduction of 'sixth form colleges' for the over-16s. The educational arrangements for those over the minimal school-leaving age is further complicated by the fact that some further education colleges offer both practical and academic courses for people in the 16–18 age bracket.

The arrangement for the starting of compulsory education at the age of 5 differentiates Britain from many other countries, which do not make it compulsory until 6 or 7. However, the concomitant is that public pre-school education is ill-developed. Despite considerable public pressure and considerable emphasis by educational experts on the importance of the preparation for education that may be provided in nursery schools, and may thus particularly assist those children who receive but limited help from parents, the public pre-school system has remained small. There has been a considerable growth of private activity in this field, from simple play groups to effective schools. At the time of writing, the government has just launched a voucher system, which will enable parents of 4-year-old children to buy private provision or use their vouchers for any available public provision. Clearly this will stimulate private activity, but it may merely alter the funding arrangements for public activity without increasing the number of places significantly, since the sums of money being made available do not cover the full costs, and will therefore be insufficient to facilitate new local authority initiatives. Parents with children in state nursery schools, currently able to get free education, will merely have to hand on their vouchers to the local authority.

The main point of note about policies for primary education has been the extent to which, very often on the basis of local initiatives, innovatory approaches to education have been developed. Many primary schools have been transformed over the last twenty to thirty years, from formal institutions in which uniformed children sat in straight rows in classes streamed on the basis of tests of educational ability to very informal places where pupils move about freely to work together in little clusters drawn from mixed-ability classes. The gradual elimination of selection at 11-plus has clearly contributed to this 'liberation' of primary schools. It is an interesting example of a change that developed from the bottom, and has never required any formal recognition in legislation, which may nevertheless be regarded as a major policy development. Its implications are now beginning to receive attention. Politicians are starting to ask whether this largely professionally motivated innovation has gone too far. There is a growing concern about levels of literacy and numeracy, and responsibility for their alleged inadequacy is sometimes attributed to this educational revolution. The increased controls, involving testing and a national curriculum (see below), under the 1988 Act, were a response to this concern, and may now be reversing the trend towards informality.

In chapter 2 it was shown how the idea of the comprehensive secondary school gradually replaced the bipartite or tripartite system envisaged at the time of the passing of the 1944 Education Act. By 1979 the development of comprehensive education was nearing completion. The Labour government had, in the 1976 Education Act, required local authorities to develop plans for comprehensivization. A minority of authorities were holding out on this. But, on coming to power, the Conservatives repealed this law. This had the effect of stemming the tide, but, as the figures below indicate, not reversing it. In 1994–5 about 85 per cent of secondary school children in the public sector in the United Kingdom were in comprehensive schools (Central Statistical Office, 1996, p. 70, table 3.10). At the time of writing, the government is encouraging a partial return to selectivity, mainly by enabling schools to reserve a small proportion of their places for pupils with identified higher abilities in general or in specific subjects such as music.

The growth of the idea of the comprehensive school was identified with that same development in professional educational thinking that created the 'progressive' primary school. But this change in policy required much more positive decision-making by local politicians. The internal organization of a school may be changed gradually and subtly over a period of time by its head teacher and staff. Change in the organization of the local education system requires more centralized and publicly apparent decisions. Comprehensivization received an impetus not only from new ideas on education, but also from an increasing Labour Party opposition to the divisive character of the old system. Popular support was forthcoming largely, it may be suspected, because of discontent about the inaccurate, necessarily arbitrary distinctions that had to be made between children by tests conducted at the age of 11.

One aspect of the resistance to comprehensive education has involved the argument that the abandonment of selective schools leads to a lowering of educational standards and to a neglect of the needs of the most able children. This view seems to have been taken increasingly seriously in recent years. It has also inhibited the extension of the educational changes going on in the primary schools to the secondary schools. In particular, it has contributed to the maintenance of ability-based 'streaming' in many comprehensive schools. This phenomenon, which can have the effect of creating a divided education system within an apparently integrated school, is further reinforced by the imminence, in the teenage years, of public examinations. These involve a 16-plus examination, the General Certificate of Secondary Education, and the Advanced ('A') level examinations normally sat at 18-plus.

Two further current government initiatives under the 1988 Act strengthened the hands of those who stress the need for formal, probably streamed education. These are the development of a national curriculum and the testing of children at 7, 11, 14 and 16. The curriculum consists of three core subjects – English, maths and science (plus Welsh in Welsh-speaking areas) – and seven foundation subjects – history, geography, technology, music, art, physical education and another modern language (for over-11s). There is also a requirement to provide a programme of religious education, which reflects the 'dominance' of Christianity in Britain. Curriculum councils have been set up to keep these developments under review. The testing system involves the setting of attainment targets, and is carried out under the supervision of the School Curriculum and Assessment Council.

The measures described in the last paragraph represent a marked departure from the philosophy of the 1944 Education Act, which left most education under local government control and issues about the determination of the curriculum largely in the hands of teachers, operating with an eye on the entrance requirements of higher education and the expectations of employers.

Results of the statutory tests are published, providing data on the 'achievements' of individual schools in a form which encourages their presentation by the media in a 'league table'. Since much educational attainment is determined by factors outside the control of the schools, these can be very misleading. Some schools may be securing a considerable 'value-added' element in enhancing the achievements of children. Others may be doing very little for children who, by virtue of their socio-economic backgrounds, are likely to score well in tests in any case. Schools in the former group may be unfairly perceived as achieving little, whilst those in the latter group win unwarranted esteem. These comparisons encourage schools to try to recruit pupils with a high academic potential. Middle-class children, Asian children and girls have been regarded in some places as pupils to attract (see Gewirtz et al., 1995).

Sociological studies of education have suggested that as pupils approach school-leaving age, there are many factors, often beyond the control of the schools, that contribute to divisions between school-oriented 'academic' pupils and an anti-school group who increasingly see their education as irrelevant and who drop out of participation in all school activities (Ford, 1969; Willis, 1977). A relevant concern in secondary education, therefore, is not so much the fate of the brighter pupils – the comprehensive schools have been eager to 'prove themselves' by doing justice to the needs of this group – as the difficulties entailed in providing a relevant education for those at the other end of the ability range. There are related problems here, of course, of absenteeism and delinquency. Overall, the issue concerns the relationship of the education system to the needs of underprivileged groups in our society – for example, low-skilled workers and some ethnic minorities. Since, moreover, such groups are located in specific areas, there is a geographical dimension to this problem. One of the arguments advanced in favour of the comprehensive school is that it is able to take all the children of a limited geographical community. But suppose such a 'community' is manifestly not truly 'comprehensive', and, worse still, suppose atypical residents in that community take steps to get their children educated elsewhere, then new distinctions arise between schools. This is a growing problem for comprehensive secondary education in Britain. It is one which has been intensified by government efforts to ensure that parents have maximum opportunities to choose schools for their children, an issue to which we will return.

The education of handicapped children requires the system to develop certain special resources. However, the trend is to try to integrate the education of the handicapped as far as possible into the ordinary system. There is a significant group of children in each authority who are classified as experiencing 'learning difficulties', as a result of the possession of various kinds of physical or intellectual handicaps. They are required to be carefully tested, and a 'statement' has to be prepared setting out their needs. Parents have a right of appeal to an independent tribunal if they are dissatisfied with the statement. On the basis of the statement, children with learning difficulties will either secure some extra teaching or support in an ordinary school or be sent to a school where there are special facilities and staffing arrangements. There are a variety of special schools. In most authorities there are separate ones designed for children with 'moderate' or 'severe' learning difficulties. There are also some very specialized schools, run by private or voluntary bodies, at which local authorities may buy places.

There are a number of non-teaching activities that make contributions to the overall performance of the education system. Schools may provide meals and milk to children. The former may be available free to pupils whose parents are on income support. The extent to which they should be subsidized for others has been something of a political football, and extensive cuts have been made to these services. Means-tested grants may also be available towards the cost of school clothing, and towards support of pupils in the 16–18 age-group who are still at school.

The welfare of schoolchildren is also given attention through the school health service and the education welfare service. Exceptionally, the latter is a social services department responsibility; more typically, it comes under education departments. Historically, the main concern of this service has been truancy. Today its objectives have been widened to embrace a whole range of problems that may affect educational performance. In this it has the support of the child guidance service, which was described earlier, in relation to the personal social services, as an inter-departmental hybrid. The relationship between social workers and educational welfare officers is a delicate one, since the latter are a relatively untrained group who are anxious to upgrade their skills and abandon the 'attendance officer' image (Ralphs, 1973). An established ethos and working style is hard to change, however, and truancy remains a central problem for the service. There is also a growing set of issues about the exclusion of disruptive children from schools.

The concepts of further and higher education embrace a number of different activities: vocational education, further academic education (both of a kind provided generally in schools and at higher levels) and non-vocational adult education. Education for degrees and for post-graduate qualifications is provided in universities and in colleges of higher education. In 1993–4 there were about 1,064,000 full-time students in higher education (Central Statistical Office, 1996, p. 76, table 3.21).

PAYING FOR THE EDUCATION SYSTEM

Public education in Britain is, broadly speaking, free. There is a system of tuition fees for higher education, but nearly all British students, regardless of parental income, are able to obtain support for under-graduate courses that cover at least these. Post-graduate education is subsidized for some through grants from research councils. There is considerable competition for these; consequently, many students (or their parents) are paying for post-graduate education. Some further, non-vocational education has to be paid for by students, but generally the fees are subsidized.

Clearly the provision of education in Britain makes heavy demands on public funds. Most of this money has to be provided by local authorities, but, of course, a high proportion of local expenditure is actually covered by central government grants. In 1994 education in the United Kingdom cost £36,057 million (Central Statistical Office, 1995b, p. 15, table 2.2). About two-thirds of this (a falling proportion) was spent on the local authority sector (ibid., p. 26).

The gradually falling numbers in school-age groups has, since the mid-1970s, encouraged government and local authorities to see educa-tion as a target area for expenditure cuts. Places in teacher education have also been cut dramatically. In 1981, in advance of the fall in the numbers in the 18–22 age-group, the government also identified higher education as an area in which it might make disproportionate expenditure cuts. Subsequently, the continuing high demand for places led it to change its mind on this, but cuts were only partially restored, and, accordingly, staff–student ratios worsened substantially.

The government has made the quest for greater efficiency in the use of diminishing resources the central thrust of its education policy. Right-wing ideologues have also raised questions about the case for free education. The only practical inroad into this principle has been a tendency for schools to be forced to charge for extra benefits not seen as strictly part of the curriculum – musical instrument lessons, educational trips, and the like. It should be pointed out that expenditure restraints have also increased the extent to which parents, individually or collectively, have needed to purchase textbooks and equipment for their children's education.

Another idea for change to the education system which has come from the political 'Right' is that an education voucher system could be developed which would enable parents to place their children within either the private or the public sector, paying supplementary fees to private schools where necessary. The Conservative government encouraged a local experiment to explore the feasibility of vouchers. It has also enabled local authorities to provide 'assisted places' in the private sector for selected children. Expenditure constraints have kept this last development to fairly modest levels. The emergent voucher arrangement for pre-school education has been mentioned above.

The other major area in which there is serious controversy about the use of public funds is in relation to grants to university students. In this case it is not the basic tuition fees that are at issue (though those too are beginning to surface on the political 'agenda'), but the grants provided to pay students' living expenses. The present system involves means-tested grants, which, unless the student has been self-supporting for three years before restarting full-time study, take parental income and other commitments into account (there are also special, rather anomalous arrangements for the means-testing of married students, which cannot be explored properly here).

In 1990 the government started a loans scheme. It decided that grant increases should be frozen, and that in their place loans should be offered. The amount available in the form of a loan would be increased year by year as the grant fell in value. Interest is charged, but at a comparatively low rate. It was argued that students receive public funds whilst delaying starting to make a contribution to national income. Nevertheless, by studying, they enhance their own future earning potential. It is therefore considered reasonable to expect students to repay all or some of the benefit bestowed upon them in this way. Critics of loan schemes point to the benefit the nation gains from its educated people, and warn that loan schemes may deter some people, particularly people from low-income families, from entering higher education.

The government refused to consider any way of taking future income into account in determining loan repayment rates, other than to accept that nothing could be paid before ex-students obtained work and passed a very low earnings threshold. It aimed to claw back loans fairly quickly. The increased difficulties that graduates face in getting work has meant that loan repayment is not occurring as quickly as expected. There is an increasing problem of loan default.

The government ignored proposals regarding more sophisticated ways to run loan schemes, which would avoid heavy demands on resources early on in a career and allow for the possibility that individuals might go into low-paying but socially useful work (Barnes and Barr, 1988). There are various special problems, such as, for example, the appropriate treatment for a woman whose career and earning power are affected by marriage and child-rearing. Administratively sophisticated schemes might become complex and costly, however.

There is an even less satisfactory situation with regard to the financial support of students outside universities, particularly with regard to those between 16 and 18 years of age. It is mandatory that local authorities pay grants to university students; but other higher education grants are discretionary. This clearly has unfair consequences from time to time. Local authorities may pay limited means-tested maintenance awards to the parents of youngsters who are over the school-leaving age. These again are discretionary, and are not very extensive in coverage. Those who have left school cannot even claim social security benefits. Except in exceptional cases, financial help for 16–18-year-olds is conditional upon entering training schemes. Yet, in some cases, places on these schemes are not even available.

CONTROL OVER THE EDUCATION SYSTEM

The control of education in Britain involves what has been described as a 'partnership' between central and local government. Yet, clearly, that partnership has been partly undermined. At a time when central government is trying to curb local government expenditure, the fact that education accounts for around half of this expenditure inevitably puts it in the spotlight. Furthermore, politicians at national level take a great interest in the way education is organized and conducted. The development of comprehensive education was an issue that fundamentally divided the parties. Governments have also felt it important to take stands on such matters as literacy, the core content of the curriculum, the role of nursery education and the future of higher education. Strong commitments in national politics have been met by equally strong ones in local politics. Hence battle-lines have been drawn up, particularly on the comprehensive issue. Local authorities have even had recourse to the courts to resist what they see as central government interference. An example of this from the days when the major shifts towards comprehensives were occurring was the battle in Tameside in 1976 when, after a local election victory, the Conservatives reversed a Labour plan to 'go comprehensive'. The secretary of state sought to intervene, arguing that the change was too far advanced to be reversed. The court upheld the local authority's position. As it happened, a change of government ended this particular battle. In the early 1990s a local authority (Cumbria) tried to stop a grant-maintained school from being allowed to become selective, arguing that it was undermining the rest of the education arrangements in the area. It lost its case in the High Court.

The uneasy relationship between central and local government is not the only delicate balance of power in the British educational system. At the local level the running of the system involves a number of different groups which are contending for influence or protecting their prerogatives. Each local authority appoints an education committee, consisting primarily of councillors, but including some representatives of other groups interested in education, such as teachers, churches and local universities. It is a generally accepted convention that on contentious political matters the non-councillor members should restrain their intervention. The committee is served by a chief education officer, who leads a team of officials who generally have teaching qualifications. There is thus a strong professionally oriented administrative group at the centre of the system.

Schools are required to have governing bodies. These are required to consist of parents, teachers, co-opted members and local education authority nominees. As pointed out above, these bodies are now responsible for delegated budgets partly guaranteed by the secretary of state. They have significant control over appointments. They can also apply for the school to opt out of local authority control. Even if they do not do this, the government has handed them a weapon which they can use against a local authority which adopts policies with which they disagree. It is worth noting, for example, how this weapon has been used by schools threatened with closure in rationalization exercises.

In the schools themselves head teachers expect a considerable measure of freedom in determining how their school is run and the way subjects are taught. They operate, of course, in consultation with their teachers, but vary extensively in the extent to which they allow staff participation in decision-making. In the last resort, however, the class teacher clearly has some autonomy in determining his or her input and relationship to pupils.

An issue which has received considerable attention has been parental choice of schools for their children. Whilst there were high pupil–teacher ratios and pressure upon school numbers in many parts of the country, the scope for parental choice was fairly limited. But as school rolls have fallen, the situation has changed. In urban areas, in particular, variations in the popularity of schools have often become very clear. In the Education Act of 1980 the government tried to provide parents with some measure of choice over schools. It requires local authorities to give information which will help parents choose, and it lays down an appeal procedure for those whose wishes are not granted. Parental choice seems to be operating as a curb on innovation by teachers; it may also be helping to determine where cuts will be made. Inasmuch as it is more likely to be exercised by middle-class parents, it may be enhancing the tendency for there to be a hierarchy of schools, under the influence of geographical location. Patterns of social and ethnic segregation may thereby be enhanced (Gewirtz et al., 1995).

Overall, the government is squeezing local authority powers both by increasing central controls and by extending governors' powers. Glennerster and his colleagues (1991) have seen this as a key example of a number of processes in which, despite the rhetoric of decentralization, extensive centralization is occurring, since, in the last analysis, an individual governing body is in a much weaker position than a local authority to resist the power of the central state.

EDUCATION AND THE DISADVANTAGED

Education plays a significant role in relation to the distribution of occupational opportunities in our society. On the Left there has traditionally been considerable concern about the extent to which education contributes to upward mobility. There are two versions of this preoccupation. One of these involves a commitment to equality of opportunity, and therefore a demand that the able children of 'lower-class' parents should have access to educational openings. The other is a concern about equality in a more absolute sense. A naïve version of this places faith in the possibility of an education system that can help to create a more equal society. A more sophisticated approach recognizes that education cannot be, by itself, an engine of social change, but stresses that it must play a part by ensuring that children are not socially segregated and that schools attempt to compensate for other sources of inequality.

'Equality of opportunity' is a slogan that finds political support beyond the ranks of the Left. A rather mixed commitment to both forms of equality has informed the evaluation of education policy. Differential educational opportunity and achievement have been extensively studied by sociologists and psychologists. The evidence accumulated by research in the 1950s and early 1960s (Douglas, 1964;

Floud et al., 1956; Jackson and Marsden, 1962) was used in making the case for comprehensive education and for the abandonment of streaming. Later, attention shifted to those problems of underachievement in the education system that cannot be directly attributed to the way that system is structured. Two particular themes were emphasized: the significance of home background for educational success and the extent to which the 'culture' of the school system is alien to some children.

It has been shown that poverty and poor housing conditions militate against educational success (Douglas, 1964; Central Advisory Council for Education, 1967). There is little the education system can do about these problems, but it can try to compensate for them with extra efforts to help deprived children. Home backgrounds are relevant in another sense, too. There are wide variations in the extent to which parents help with the education of their children. Such help takes many forms, involving not only the more obvious forms of encouragement and the provision of books and study facilities, but also a great deal of implicit 'teaching' through interaction with children. The latter starts when babies are very tiny, and one of its most significant ingredients is the learning of language. The children who are most deprived in these respects are often those who are also most deprived in a material sense. But parental educational levels and abilities are also relevant. There is a variety of practical ways in which the education system may help to compensate for these less straightforwardly material disadvantages, both before and after children reach compulsory school age (Halsey (ed.), 1972).

The issue with regard to the culture of the schools is a more difficult one. In part, the problem is one of identification of the needs and special interests of children whose backgrounds differ from that of the white educated middle-class males whose needs have dominated the values of the system. There is a variety of ways in which stories, educational situations and examples can be devised that seem relevant to these children. Hence there is ample scope for change here. Considerable progress is being made to overcome female disadvantages embodied in this culture.

However, as far as social class disadvantages are concerned, there are limits to the extent to which this issue can be fully met, if only because of the extent to which it implies a conflict with the objective of facilitating social mobility through education. If a key concern of education is to prepare children to operate in a middle-class world, even perhaps to join that world, then it may not be particularly functional for it to be concerned to relate to working-class culture. There is a great dilemma here, which is very relevant to the alienation of some children from an education system in which they are becoming the 'failures'. You cannot eliminate the concept of failure as long as you have the objective of enabling some to 'succeed' through the education system. It may be desirable to eliminate the more invidious aspects of competition within the system – to recognize, for example, that progress *relative* to ability may be as important as the easy success of the advantaged and talented – but notions of achievement, and consequently non-achievement, are fundamental to the role of education in our kind of society.

There are some special, and slightly different, issues regarding the culture of education and the needs of ethnic minorities. These will be examined in the next section in relation to the whole range of problems, and therefore policy dilemmas, about the education of immigrant children and the children of ethnic minorities.

The idea of attempting to compensate for disadvantage by providing special resources for the schools in some areas was suggested in a report of the Plowden committee (Central Advisory Council for Education, 1967). Many of the measures adopted did no more than attempt to redress the imbalance of educational resources between run-down inner-city areas, where the schools were old and facilities were limited, and newer suburban areas. Additional money was made available for capital projects and current expenditure in areas where there were high levels of deprivation. In addition, the government provided for extra teachers, above the normal quotas, and special additional allowances for teachers in those areas. Areas were designated on the basis of statistics on the socio-economic status of parents, the extent of absence of housing amenities, proportions of children receiving free school meals, and proportion of schoolchildren with serious linguistic difficulties.

Some action research projects were initiated, to monitor special compensatory education ventures in some of these 'educational priority areas'. These gave particular attention to the value of pre-school education, along the lines of the American 'Headstart' programme. In 1968 the government developed a special 'urban programme' of social policies for deprived urban areas. Under this programme, local authorities could receive grants to expand nursery education and to support pre-school play groups. The emphasis upon this stage of education led eventually in 1973 to the easing of limitations upon the development of nursery education.

The issues with which this section has been concerned have received much less attention in the political climate of the 1980s and 1990s. In updating this book, I could easily have left out some of this discussion had I not thought that these issues remain very important. With diminishing work opportunities for school-leavers, there has perhaps been less room for a generous concern about educational under-achievers. However, as suggested above, the public use of indices regarding examination results and tests has tended to obscure the extent to which a school's results are determined by the social backgrounds of its children. The emphasis upon standards and upon parental choice has been to the advantage of the relatively privileged schools. New resources are tending to follow the most successful parts of the education system, rather than – as demanded by an emphasis on com-pensatory education – the least successful. Comprehensive schools are available almost universally, but in a system in which the gaps between the successful (in terms of conventional results) and unsuccessful schools are widening.

THE EDUCATION OF ETHNIC MINORITIES

Britain has a non-white population of around three million. About 45 per cent of these are British-born. The remainder are predominantly immigrants from the West Indies and the Indian subcontinent. There is thus a substantial non-white school population, concentrated in urban areas. Most of these youngsters are the British-born children of immigrants, since immigration has been tightly controlled since the 1960s. About 97 per cent of Afro-Caribbean children under 15 and 92 per cent of children under 15 whose parents originate from the Indian subcontinent were born in Britain (figures calculated from 1991 census data).

In the period when many non-white children were themselves immigrants, the system saw their language problems and cultural differences as the main issue. Some of these are still evident. But many Asian children are encouraged by parents to make the most of educational opportunities, and many have made remarkable progress within the British system. They face problems, however, in coming to terms with strong contrasts between patterns of home life and those of school life.

Some Asian groups have begun either to make demands for new developments in the education system in tune with their cultural needs (appropriate religious education, courses in Asian languages) or to call for separate state-subsidized schools for their children along the lines of Catholic schools. A look across the Irish Sea to Northern Ireland, where a division in education along religious lines has many of the characteristics of a division along cultural lines, and contributes to the division of that community, gives pause for thought regarding this model of education for a culturally diverse society. Such misgivings are reinforced by the extent to which there has also been interest in independence from white parents eager to minimize the Asian influence upon certain schools.

At one time in the late 1960s and early 1970s a number of education authorities bussed children to other areas, to try to prevent certain schools from having high concentrations of Asian children. Since this bussing was a one-way process, applied only to Asians, it was rightly abandoned as discriminatory. Now, the imposition of rules about regard for parental choice means that local authorities cannot even manipulate catchment areas in the interests of any kind of ethnic 'balance'. Parental choices may enhance tendencies towards segregation.

West Indian immigrants come from a society in which European cultural models have a strong influence, and are reinforced through the education process. It is precisely this bias in West Indian society, and in American Negro society, that has been attacked by those concerned about the development of black consciousness. It is argued that this dominance of a white cultural model contributes to the maintenance of a subordinate self-image. Black leaders in Britain have become deeply concerned about the underachievement of children of West Indian origin. They attribute this to a variety of factors, but see the white ethnic and cultural bias in the education system as reinforcing other aspects of disadvantage.

Hence, whilst the education system continues to see the issues regarding non-white children as issues about *their* characteristics, it may alternatively be suggested that the central issue is *its* ethnic and cultural assumptions, the phenomenon described as 'institutional racism'. An official committee, chaired by Lord Swann, reported on its 'Inquiry into the Education of Children from Ethnic Minority Groups' in 1985. In a brief guide to the report, Lord Swann, whilst not using the expression 'institutional racism', made it very clear that the issue of society and the education system's response was of central importance in explaining the problem of underachievement by non-whites. He argued:

> on the evidence so far there is at least a dual problem. On the one hand, society must not, through prejudice and discrimination, increase the social and economic deprivation of ethnic minority families. On the other, schools must respond with greater sensitivity, and without any trace of prejudice, to the needs of ethnic minority children. (Department of Education and Science, 1985, p. 9)

Lord Swann saw the latter as to be achieved through the concept of 'Education for All'. This meant that

[t]he fundamental change needed is a recognition that the problem facing the educational system is not just how to educate the children of ethnic minorities, but how to educate *all* children. Britain has long been an ethnically diverse society, and is now, mainly because of her imperial past, much more obviously one. All pupils must be brought to an understanding of what is entailed if such a society is to become a fair and harmonious entity. (Ibid., p. 10)

Some Afro-Caribbean groups have set up weekend supplementary schools. In these, children receive a mixture of teaching that emphasizes their black cultural heritage, correcting the European biases of history teaching, for example, and helps with the learning of basic skills. The fact that such a development is viewed as necessary poses a different sort of challenge to the education system from that posed by Asian 'separatism'. It suggests a need to tackle the biases in the system through the encouragement of culturally relevant studies, and accepting that there is a problem about the white view of society. It calls for a sophisticated understanding of the issues by all teachers and special efforts to recruit black teachers. Ethnocentric biases in the new national curriculum (for history, for example) threaten to set back this aspiration.

This last problem about the education of black children links up very closely with the issue of the place which disadvantaged white children find themselves occupying within the system, discussed above, and with the quite concrete disadvantages of children from lower-income homes. Inasmuch as black entrants to Britain have generally been forced to accept many of the poorest jobs and worst houses, children find that the 'inferior' stereotype of the black person seems to be reinforced by their, and their parents', experience. Moreover, the fact that many black parents have had relatively little education themselves, and use a dialect form of English very different from that used in the schools, means that, like comparable lower-class white parents, they are ill-equipped to help their children tackle the education system. There is a web of reinforcing disadvantages here, which makes the development of compensatory education particularly important for this group of children.

Many of the points made here are relevant to other policy areas. In particular, the chapter on the personal social services might have discussed some of the issues about the inadequacies of services for minorities, and explored, in terms not unlike those used about educational separation, the issue of trans-racial adoption, for example. Similarly, the chapter on the health service could have dealt more with the extent to which there is an ethnic dimension to inequalities in health, and explored some of the communication difficulties which arise when white health professionals pay insufficient regard to cultural and language problems. Lack of space prevented those discussions; it has been interposed here because of the particular salience of the issue for education. Readers are urged to think about the relevance of the points made here for those other policy areas.

CONCLUSIONS

The state system of education had roots in a mid-nineteenth-century concern with the training of an effective work-force able to operate in an increasingly complex industrial system and society. Its growth has been inextricably bound up with the development of a democratic society. The original view that the newly enfranchised should be literate has been answered by a belief on the part of the electorate that education holds the key to social advancement. This may be in part an illusion. The opportunity structure is determined by the economy and by the political system. Increased education does not in itself increase the supply of 'top jobs'; it merely increases the competition for them. The fact that educational qualifications are widely used as a basis for discrimination between applicants for jobs emphasizes the link between education and social and economic advancement, regardless of whether or not those jobs require education at the level, or of the kind, possessed by those deemed best suited to fill them. Hence the nature of the education system and the opportunities it provides are of central political importance in Britain.

As job opportunities for young people have diminished in Britain in the 1980s and 1990s, a debate about the role of the education system has been stimulated. This is linked to a long-standing controversy about the extent to which British economic underachievement can be attributed to defects in the education system – insufficient emphasis on science and engineering, high esteem for a cultural education that has no immediate practical use, and so on. This is a complex issue, involving propositions which are hard to test empirically. It cannot be explored properly here. What it does involve is a tendency to assign too much importance to the role of the education system, disregarding the extent to which it has to respond to social and political demands upon it. More immediately, this debate seems to encourage a tendency to attribute the shortage of jobs not to deficiencies in the demand for labour but to inadequacies in the supply of labour – to see the education system as failing the youth of this country. This flies in the face of the evidence that competition for jobs is stimulating 'qualification inflation', that the qualifications needed for many jobs are going up because of the stiff competition for them. It is leading, however, to an ever increasing demand for vocationally relevant education (particularly for the vast majority of publicly educated boys and girls unlikely to move easily into elite jobs).

Demands that 'politics should be taken out of education' are based upon a total failure to comprehend what either politics or education is all about. A study of education policy controversies in the past thirty years demonstrates a great deal about politics and administration in British society. Perhaps some of the demands that politics should be taken out of education come from a sense of individual frustration, in parents and pupils, about conflicts in which they feel fairly impotent. Education is perhaps the sector of social policy that people feel they understand best; they try hard to influence it, but find that many of the key problems elude their grasp. The education system's elusive quality should not, however, be explained simply in terms of the reluctance of political and professional elites to accept participation. Its very sensitive relationship to the economy and society makes controlling its interaction with social change very difficult.

SUGGESTIONS FOR FURTHER READING

For a discussion of education policy with a particularly sociological slant readers should look at Finch's *Education and Social Policy* (1984). Ball's *Politics and Policy Making in Education* (1990) deals with some of the current changes to the system, and has now been supplemented by two good critical research studies: Bowe and Ball's *Reforming Education and Changing Schools* (1992) and Gewirtz et al.'s *Markets, Choice and Equity in Education* (1995).

While it is also now very dated, the literature on education and social class – Douglas, 1964; Floud et al., 1956; Jackson and Marsden, 1962, particularly the last – provides excellent insight into underlying issues that are still with us, despite the near demise of the grammar schools. A more up-to-date edited collection on educational inequality is Dawtrey et al., 1995.

Stone (1981) provides a useful examination of the issues surrounding the education of ethnic minorities, as does chapter 6 of Rex and Tomlinson's (1979) study of race relations in Birmingham. To them should be added the Swann Report, discussed in this chapter (Department of Education and Science, 1985).

CHAPTER
9

EMPLOYMENT POLICY

INTRODUCTION

Britain's manpower policies are the responsibility of the Department for Education and Employment. Local responsibility for services for job seekers is managed by the Employment Services Agency. Training is the responsibility of 82 separate training and enterprise councils in England and Wales and 22 local enterprise companies in Scotland. These are independent companies set up by the government, with their own boards of directors, which have contracts to administer government grants. In Northern Ireland there is a training and employment agency responsible to the Department of Economic Development for Northern Ireland. In the financial year 1994–5 about £3,700 million was spent on employment and training services (HMSO, 1995). That is only about 1 per cent of total public expenditure.

However, it is not entirely satisfactory to see the sum total of government employment policies as a set of explicit employment services. Social security benefits play an important role in employment policy, and, even more importantly, employment policy is in many respects a part of wider economic policy.

This is the first of two chapters in which, as was pointed out in the introductory chapter, a considerable amount of attention has to be given to economic issues. In the next chapter, on housing, it is the fact that a great deal of the provision is through a private housing market which requires attention. In this chapter, what forces particular attention to be given to the interaction between social and economic policies is that, while it is true that employment services are provided by both public and private agencies, employment services represent a form of public intervention in the economy, and job opportunities are determined primarily by the working of that economy, rather than by any specific interventions of the employment services. Effective employment services may contribute to the creation of a healthy economy, but they cannot in themselves 'cure' an unhealthy one.

Many discussions of employment services give little attention to their social role. They are seen as concerned with the effective working of the labour market, not as services which provide social benefits. There are two reasons for disagreement with this approach to the study of employment services. The first is simply a dissatisfaction with the conventional distinction between social and economic policies, as suggested in chapter 1. Economic policies have social effects, and clearly the social effects of a service designed to help people secure satisfactory jobs as quickly as possible are most important. The second is that considerations other than concern to make the labour market operate efficiently enter into the employment services. The alleviation of unemployment is as much a social issue as an economic one. Indeed, economic 'realism' may involve unconcern about unemployment, and even a desire to maintain a 'reserve army of labour', to compete for jobs and thereby keep wages low.

Whilst this chapter deals only with measures to combat unemployment, it is recognized that it could also have discussed measures against discrimination in the labour market as social policies. Under European pressure there has been some progress with these. However, diminishing opportunities for work have tended to blunt their impact.

CHARACTERISTICS OF THE BRITISH APPROACH TO MANPOWER POLICY

A government may manage the economy without making any use of employment services, and the case for employment services as necessary for either economic or social ends is less easy to make than the case for, for example, health services or education. The employment services date from the early years of this century, and have played a fairly low-key role until recently. Even today, employment services expenditure is dwarfed by that on the other services discussed in this book.

In his book *Why Some Peoples are More Unemployed than Others* (1986), Goran Therborn analyses the applicability of various theories explaining unemployment to the marked differences in its incidence in 16 advanced capitalist countries. His conclusion is that one can explain the differences only in terms of 'the self-fulfilling tendency of deeply institutionalised policy orientations' (Therborn, 1986, p. 30). The five countries with records of low unemployment at the time he examined his sample – Switzerland, Japan, Sweden, Norway and Austria – differ from each other substantially with regard to their political systems and political ideologies; but, Therborn argues, all developed distinctive labour market policies even if, as in the case of Switzerland, such policies consisted only of limiting the *supply* of labour.

Britain is one of the cases in Therborn's sample of countries with a recent record of high unemployment. Its policy response to this has been slow, limited and very much *ad hoc*.

Rather more recapitulation of history is needed in this chapter than in most others, to help put employment policy in its wider economic context. In the early twentieth century British governments gradually came to reject the view that the economy, and accordingly the labour market, should be left to work 'naturally'. At the end of the nineteenth century adherents of 'classical' economic theory began to acknowledge that it was perhaps necessary for government to play a role in assisting the 'natural' market system to operate more smoothly. In particular, the problems of adjustment to changing economic situations in the short run began to be regarded as sufficiently serious to justify intervention. One such problem concerned the linking of 'sellers' of labour with 'buyers'. To this end, after 1909, systems of labour exchanges were created.

Between the two World Wars continuing evidence that the economy could not readily absorb all who wanted work kept the issue of unemployment on the political agenda. There were strong pressures that forced the erratic development of income maintenance measures for the unemployed (see discussion in chapter 2), but manpower policies evolved very little. A few very limited job-creation and training schemes were developed, but economic orthodoxy was against the heavy public expenditure on the creation of work that, by the middle of the 1930s, began to characterize the policy response in the United States. Only as preparation for war began to alleviate unemployment did official thinking begin to come to terms with its structural character. This change of approach is primarily associated with the Keynesian revolution in economic thinking that linked unemployment with under-consumption and urged governments to spend, and if necessary to unbalance budgets, to get out of a recession. The primary policy response required was in this case a macro-economic one, rather than a form of manpower policy *per se*. However, at the same time, the special problems of certain regions, particularly those where employment had depended upon declining heavy industries, also began to be recognized.

The unexpected success of economic policies in preventing high unemployment from 1945 to 1970 enabled British governments to continue to adopt a comparatively passive stance on manpower policies. Then, in 1970, the incoming Conservative government led by

Edward Heath decided to restructure the public employment service as part of its effort to make public administration more dynamic. A consultative document *People and Jobs* (Department of Employment, 1971) declared that the employment service needed to be modernized. The employment exchanges were too identified with a limited service to the unemployed.

In modernizing the service, the government was clearly influenced by the Swedish concept of 'active manpower policy', in which the employment service was seen as playing a crucial role in preserving full employment without high inflation. Britain's own problem in swinging rapidly from situations of economic stagnation, when unemployment began to rise, into situations of an 'overheated' economy, bringing inflation and balance of payments difficulties, were seen as at least in part attributable to problems of labour supply. Overheating was associated with difficulties in securing adequately trained skilled labour. It was felt that a more sophisticated employment service, dealing with a much higher proportion of the job placings and able to give more expert attention to training problems, would much more effectively match supply and demand in the labour market, and thus contribute much better to the maintenance of a balanced economy.

A new, active service would seek to have a real impact upon the working of the labour market. In practice, the British manpower initiatives of the early 1970s were brought into operation in a context not just of high inflation but also of rapidly rising unemployment. The modernized employment services had to operate in an economy about which many economists had abandoned the 'Keynesian' belief that there is a direct, simple relationship between unemployment and inflation. While it is easy to sneer that Britain's conversion to an active labour market policy came too late, it is indeed hard to discern whether or not the new service contributed to the mitigation of problems in a very troubled labour market. Certainly the system succeeded in ensuring that it was notified of a better proportion of vacancies than it had been in the past.

However, while *People and Jobs* saw the future of the service in terms of a lesser concern with the unemployed and a greater degree of assistance to those who sought to move between jobs, in fact the stagnation that occurred in the labour market forced the system to give a great deal of attention to the issue of unemployment, and to develop a range of temporary special job-creation and training measures.

On coming to power in 1979, the Thatcher government inherited various special measures to deal with the problem of unemployment from its Labour predecessors. Its initial inclination was to curb these activities as part of its general attack on public expenditure. But it quickly came to realize that the special programmes, particularly those for the young unemployed, offered the cheapest way of providing a response to the problem of growing unemployment. So instead, the early 1980s saw a growth of expenditure on special training schemes and temporary job-creation measures (see Moon and Richardson, 1985).

Certainly some of the measures adopted – in particular, job creation and the use of subsidies – seem to have been influenced by the more active manpower policies of countries like Sweden. Ironically, in Sweden in the 1950s and 1960s such measures were seen as ways of helping the very small minority of the population unable to secure work on the open market when employment was as full as possible. These measures take on a rather different character in an economy characterized by a seriously deficient demand for labour. They have been criticized as inadequate alternatives to the effective management of the economy. One distinguished economist, Lord Vaisey, argued:

> The sum total of these schemes seems to me to be cosmetic rather than genuine in its economic consequences. What they do in effect is to push employment around a bit without much net effect. They are in no sense a substitute for the substantial regeneration of British industry. (House of Commons, 1977, p. 147)

In economic terms, the official answer to Vaisey's argument was that these schemes provided or protected jobs with minimal inflationary effects, by comparison with more direct ways in which the economy might be stimulated. But there is also an interesting social issue here. This is that such policies may be used to influence the impact of a recession on particular groups of people. While they may do little or nothing to change the overall level of employment, they may help to ensure that particular people – the young, the previously long-term unemployed, those resident in certain areas – experience the ill effects of being out of work rather less than other people.

Politicians, when they justify special measures to provide employment, deliberately obfuscate these issues. They want to be able to claim jobs saved or created by government intervention as contributions to the alleviation of unemployment as a whole. The actual macroeconomic effect of these interventions is, happily for them, profoundly obscure.

Since 1980, programmes of assistance to unemployed people and training have gone through a large number of changes. Students will find even quite recent books misleading on detailed schemes, and if they try to trace the changes over recent years, they will be bewildered by the 'alphabet soup' of different schemes each generally identified only by its initials. Undoubtedly this complex evolution – and perhaps, indeed, even the government's willingness to persist with such activities – has been influenced by the changing European Community subsidies available from the European Social Fund.

The government's approach to job-creation and training measures has become one in which the needs of the existing economic system are stressed, and control is very firmly in the hands of private sector employers. There is a strong emphasis on the training of the young. For older, long-term unemployed people there are special programmes, with an increasing requirement of activities as a condition of financial support (even if these do not readily help the individual back into the regular labour market). Over the past fifteen years, governments have blown hot and cold about the desirability of measures of this last kind. One influence has been the considerable sums the government has had to spend on benefits for the unemployed. It has spent with great reluctance, and has increasingly found ways to reduce benefits and prevent individual access to such help.

Britain has moved from a situation in which little was done to try to plan to prevent unemployment in the 1930s, through an era when regional policies were quite prominent, but generally the health of the labour market seemed to make planning unnecessary, between 1945 and 1971, into a brief phase when it was recognized that part of Britain's economic problem stemmed from the lack of an 'active labour market policy', in the 1970s. The rise of unemployment from 1975 onwards then 'hijacked' active labour market policy, concentrating efforts upon special measures for the unemployed. Responses to the problem of unemployment have preoccupied the system ever since.

THE BASIC EMPLOYMENT SERVICES SYSTEM

'Job centres' are the modern successors to the labour exchanges set up in 1908 to do just what their name suggests, to link employers seeking workers with employees. In the 1970s job centres were seen as replacing the large institutional exchanges with modern shop-front offices in commercial and shopping centres. There was an emphasis on self-service, individuals being able to select jobs from open-display advertisements, turning to staff only when advice was necessary. The aim as expressed in 1971 was to counter the problem that 'the Service is regarded by many workers and employers as a service for the unemployed' (Department of Employment, 1971, p. 5). The hopes for this approach have been dashed, however, by the rise in unemployment.

The 1990s have seen an explicit acceptance by the government that this is precisely who the service is for – the long-term unemployed in particular. Accordingly, a visitor from the 1930s would find the modern job centre a puzzling place: on the one hand, all the apparatus of modern consumerism – a pleasant office, courteous staff, ample explanatory material – and on the other, a battery of questions and controls which would seem remarkably familiar.

After a period in which it seemed to want to separate them – and even considered shifting all benefit work to the Benefits Agency – the government has decided to integrate the work of job centres with the work of benefit offices. Hence, whereas the last edition of this book had a special section on 'the policing of the unemployment benefit system', it is now appropriate to put this at the centre of a discussion of the employment service.

In chapter 5 it was shown that the unemployed are supported by the state by the job seeker's allowance. In order to qualify, a person has to make a clear undertaking, signing a job seeker's agreement, on the steps he or she will take to try to get work. Even for those who have been contributing to the national insurance scheme, job seeker's allowance is means-tested after six months. Benefit may also be stopped or reduced if individuals are found to have lost employment unnecessarily or to have failed to take employment opportunities.

The job centres now have a central role to play in relation to the surveillance of the behaviour of the unemployed. The initial job seeker's agreement is subject to regular review (based upon an earlier 'restart' scheme). Particular attention is paid to those who have been out of work for six months or more. At the reviews the individual's efforts to find work are examined, and a variety of other options is explored. These include:

referral to a 'job club', where guidance, training and assistance are offered with job search activities;

a job interview guaranteed by an employer who has agreed to see long-term unemployed people in return for an enhanced recruitment service;

referral to specialized job search assistance at a 'job search seminar', 'job review workshop' or 'job plan workshop';

placement on an appropriate training course (skill training is discussed further in the next section);

referral to special courses, focusing not so much on skill deficiencies as upon personal attributes and attitudes;

work experience in a 'community action programme', offering temporary part-time work;

financial assistance to people to start up a business.

Those who find work may then get a special grant to help them if they have been unemployed for more than two years. There is also a limited scheme whereby employers who give jobs to long-term unemployed people receive subsidies. At the time of writing, the government is piloting new ways to give financial help to the long-term unemployed who get work.

There is, thus, now a substantial, complex battery of measures to encourage the unemployed to seek work. Most of the measures, other than the subsidies, seem premissed upon the view that work is available and that the problem lies in the attitudes and behaviour of unemployed people. Of course, there is a crucial underlying issue here about what kind of work at what level of reward. The emergence of individual subsidies is some kind of recognition by the government that much of the work on offer to the long-term unemployed is very low-paid.

There has been extensive controversy regarding the impact of the social security system on the behaviour of the unemployed. It is alleged that unemployed people have been deterred from seeking work by the high levels of benefit relative to the lowest earnings levels. This has been used as an argument for making sure that the unemployed gain less than any other group from the benefit system. The introduction of the family credit scheme was seen by the government as seeing to it that people with family responsibilities would be better off in work than on benefit. Among the measures introduced in the early 1990s are provisions to try to ensure that administrative problems associated with the shift from out-of-work benefits to in-work benefits like family credit do not lead to temporary falls in income. The particularly harsh treatment of the under 25s under the income support scheme helps to make sure that young people without family responsibilities cannot achieve benefit levels comparable to even exceptionally low wages.

There is also a specific employment service for disabled employees, set up in the 1940s with assistance to injured ex-servicemen very much in mind. This service employs specially trained staff who give advice and help with job placement.

Throughout the 1980s the government tolerated – indeed, partly encouraged – a situation in which people with disabilities were able to leave the unemployment register and receive the long-term, higher-rated invalidity benefit. This contributed to a reduction in the apparent size of the unemployed population. There was a steady growth in the numbers on invalidity benefit, particularly among men in their fifties and early sixties. Then in the 1990s the Department of Social Security became concerned about the cost of supporting this group. In 1995, as shown in chapter 5, invalidity benefit was replaced by incapacity benefit, with its much stricter test of fitness for work. The shift of people back on to the unemployment register may put pressure on the employment services for disabled people.

TRAINING

Young people aged 16 or 17 who have left school but not obtained work are expected to participate in 'youth training'. With certain special exceptions, the only way in which a youngster in this group can get financial help from the state is by participating in this scheme. It is designed to provide both broadly based skills and specific forms of craft training. There is a system of qualifications (NVQs – 'national vocational qualifications' which may be acquired whilst participating in 'youth training'. Just over 270,000 were on the main youth initiative, the 'youth training scheme', in August 1995 (*Employment Trends*, October 1995).

Youth training involves public subsidy to a wide range of schemes – provided by private employers, voluntary organizations and public bodies – offering a mixture of work experience and training. The achievement of qualifications is now strongly emphasized within youth training as a whole. These schemes vary enormously in quality, from elaborate skill training at one extreme to what are little more than 'make work' schemes for lower-ability young people in high-unemployment areas at the other. The better the local demand for young workers, the better the quality of the schemes, in terms of both the training they offer and the real labour market opportunities they lead on to. But it must be recognized

that Britain has (by contrast with most of continental Europe) a very high proportion of young people ending their full-time education and training at the age of 16;

that it used to have a strong pattern of apprenticeship into skilled work in industry, which has now collapsed;

and that before the rise of unemployment in the mid-1970s the labour market for young people aged 16–18 was a thriving one, which has now more or less disappeared.

Youth training may be seen as a necessary means of filling a vacuum in the British education and training system, but it has also contributed to the creation of that vacuum by undermining the incentives to employers to provide work or training for young people at their own expense. The state now pays for most of this, through youth training.

It is worthy of note at this point that the Education and Employment departments were amalgamated in 1995. In the preceding fifteen years the two departments had been to some extent competitors in the provision of measures for young people who were not committed to going on to higher education. Experiments were developed within schools to introduce youngsters to the world of work, and for those just out of school, further education and youth training were sometimes competitors, sometimes linked. Inasmuch as there is controversy about the extent to which efforts for this group should be narrowly vocational or have wider educational objectives, it will be interesting to see what difference the new departmental integration makes. At the end of the last chapter, it was observed that, despite the evident shortage of jobs, there has been a strong tendency to blame youth unemployment on the inadequacies of education. Will the new ministry therefore intensify the training emphasis in modern education?

Turning now to training for the over-18s, a system of skill training, in 'government training centres', pre-dates the modern rise of unemployment. Since that rise, adult training, like all the other employment services, has gone through a bewildering series of changes. In the early 1980s adult training tended to take a back seat as the government concentrated upon the needs of young people. Then, in the later part of that decade, the evidence that people were moving from youth schemes to unemployment generated a renewed attention to adult training, targeted principally at the 18–25 age-group.

In the 1990s the renewed emphasis upon measures for the long-term unemployed has brought about a new concentration on adult training in general. The 'training for work scheme' introduced in 1993 aims to secure places on schemes delivered locally by the training and enterprise councils or local enterprise companies, giving priority to those who have been unemployed for more than six months. The training offered is varied, averaging four to six months, and providing, like youth training, a mixture of general and specific skill training. Participation is voluntary (though departure from a scheme which is not deemed to be justified may lead to benefit penalties). Trainees receive payments £10 above their previous benefit entitlement.

CONCLUSIONS

For many years policies for the relief of unemployment, apart from macro-economic ones, were confined to the provision of benefits and the availability of a relatively passive employment exchange system. The rise of unemployment in the 1970s was met by revitalized public agencies committed to 'active' manpower policy. Initially this led to exploration of the development of job-creation measures, but these measures were undermined by a reluctance to compete with the 'regular' labour market. This led to a concentration upon intervention in the labour market on behalf of specific groups of the unemployed. Such intervention has a strong 'supply side' emphasis, the concern being with 'what is wrong with' the victims of unemployment, rather than upon deficient demand. Workers who are either more highly skilled or more willing to work for very low rewards are seen as less likely to be unemployed. Whilst some rhetoric emphasizes this supply-side activity as the solution to unemployment, politicians may be driven by a more cynical view that competition for work from the unemployed imposes a discipline on the employed. They may also recognize that training and other activities for the unemployed keeps them occupied, prepares them for the hoped-for upturn in the economy, and slims the register of those simply obtaining benefits. There is also a more egalitarian argument for stressing the skill needs of the weakest participants in the labour force: that this may increase their individual prospects of getting work so that, even if aggregate employment cannot be raised, job opportunities can be more widely shared.

There has been a tendency to see these policies as temporary expedients. However, they are beginning to look rather permanent. Pessimism about future prospects for employment is primarily based upon the British economy's diminishing capacity to absorb labour as high-technology industry grows in importance, and Britain competes inadequately with the rest of the world.

Nevertheless, *Employment for the 1990s* (Department of Employment, 1988a) took an optimistic stance on the future of employment, which was quite sharply at variance with what had gone before. The government boasted of its 'great success in creating new jobs and reducing unemployment', and suggested that problems of a labour shortage lie ahead for the British economy as the demographic trends which led to a growth of the labour force begin to be reversed.

There are a number of reasons for scepticism about this perspective. One is that the modest movement out of recession in the early 1990s has had only a slight impact upon the unemployment rate. A second is that the growth in the labour force was fuelled as much by increased female participation in the labour market as by a general demographic trend. It is not clear whether female participation is at its maximum, particularly given the complications which arise from the extent to which it has involved amounts of part-time work which may increasingly be regarded as insufficient. Women's unemployment has always been underestimated by the employment figures. The third reason is that, accompanying predictions of a falling labour force, there have been statements about the burden of the growing elderly population, and some policy changes have taken place to reduce the value of pensions in the future. The period of very high unemployment saw the development of a range of measures to encourage older workers to leave the labour force, but a changing job market could see the reversal of those measures. Furthermore, if job opportunities were good, our increasingly healthy elderly population might feel encouraged to stay in the labour market.

In general, British unemployment data are very unreliable. The changes made to the method of counting the unemployed during the 1980s have been multiple and complex. The most important of the changes involved ceasing to count as unemployed people registering with the Department of Employment for work but not able to claim social security benefit. If the aim of the changes was to ensure that only the *real* unemployed were being counted, this was particularly inappropriate, since anyone registering with no hope of financial gain was manifestly not cheating the system or seeking aid without any interest in getting work! Other changes involved the elimination from the count of people temporarily on work-creation or training schemes and people whom the government wished to encourage to withdraw from the labour force (particularly women and older people). Whilst the government's rationale for changing the counting method was to avoid exaggerating the problem of unemployment (a proposition that its opponents would turn the other way round), it must be recognized that any change in the counting basis tends to lead to a misinterpretation of trends. Elimination from the unemployed count of groups of people whose future labour market behaviour is more than normally difficult to predict – that is, groups like women, the young and the old, whose behaviour in this respect is changing – does tend to make the statistics more difficult to use for planning purposes. In its 1988 paper the Government seemed to be using its own statistics to arrive at peculiarly complacent predictions about the future of unemployment.

Each time I revise this chapter, my feeling grows that much British employment policy is an exercise in rearranging the deck-chairs on the

Titanic, with an overriding concern to increase the discomfort of passengers.

SUGGESTIONS FOR FURTHER READING

This is a topic on which recent policy change has rendered many books rather dated. There have been a large number of books on unemployment, but few have dealt with the measures for the unemployed in any depth. Quite an old book which nevertheless sets out the issues about unemployment and policies for the unemployed very well is Sinfield's *What Unemployment Means* (1981). Up-to-date analyses of policies are contained in the Unemployment Unit's regular bulletin; and one of the staff of that unit has examined policies for the young – Dan Finn, in his *Training without Jobs* (1987). The Unemployment Unit publishes an *Unemployment and Training Rights Handbook* and a *Guide to Training and Benefits for Young People* (there are regular updatings of each; the latest editions came out in 1995).

Considerable use has been made in this chapter of the government's two 1988 publications on employment and training policy. While they do set out the rationale for current policies, as suggested in the chapter, they should be consulted with a sceptical eye. Some more independent, up-to-date books on employment policy are badly needed.

CHAPTER 10

HOUSING

INTRODUCTION

In Great Britain in 1994 the housing stock comprised 23.7 million dwellings. Of these, 19.5 per cent were rented from local authorities; 4 per cent were rented from housing associations; 9.7 per cent were privately rented; and 66.9 per cent were owner-occupied (Department of the Environment, 1996). It will be shown in this chapter that public policies influence all these sectors, if not directly through public provision, then indirectly through tax subsidies (in the case of the owner-occupied sector) or rent regulation (in the privately rented sector).

From the end of the First World War until 1979, the owner-occupier and publicly provided sectors grew dramatically at the expense of the privately rented sector. Since 1979 the growth of owner occupation has continued, but the public rented sector has declined in size as a result of the sale of council houses to their occupiers. Moreover, what was earlier describable as the public rented sector (or 'council housing') is now better described as 'social housing'. It consists of rented housing under a mixture of local authority and housing association ownership. Much of the subsidy for this sector now comes directly to tenants, in the form of housing benefit. This benefit is also available to private tenants, further blurring the private–public distinction.

Developments in the British housing system have been enormously influenced by government intervention. There have also, inevitably, been complex interactions between the sectors as the system has changed. For example, increased opportunities for owner occupation have both diminished the demand for private rented accommodation, and been partly created by landlords' desires to sell houses that seem no longer to offer a satisfactory return if they are let. Later in the chapter fuller attention will be given to some of the interactions of this kind that have policy implications. However, it is clearly simplest to introduce this discussion of policies by examining each sector separately.

THE SOCIAL HOUSING SECTOR

While a small amount of public housing was built earlier, the effective growth of this sector dates from the enactment of legislation after the First World War to enable local authorities to receive central government subsidies towards the provision of housing 'for the working classes'. A long succession of subsequent Acts of Parliament elaborated this initiative, encouraging both the building of large estates designed to meet basic housing needs and the adoption of substantial slum clearance schemes. While the housing no longer has to be specifically 'for the working classes', this sector has become the main provider of houses for those unable to buy their own.

The history of the subsidy system developed in this sector is complicated. There is a need to look at this briefly in order to understand the contemporary situation. For many years the government used, but regularly changed, a system whereby local authorities secured a fixed sum per dwelling annually over a fixed period of years. In the 1960s the Labour government adopted a new approach, without terminating the older subsidies, whereby percentage subsidies were paid to effectively subsidize the rate at which authorities borrowed money. However, in the 1972 Housing Finance Act, the Conservatives sought to sweep away all the continuing older systems of subsidy. The objective was to move to a system in which general-purpose subsidies would eventually be eliminated. They recognized the need to continue to subsidize certain particularly expensive forms of development, in particular slum clearance. They also acknowledged a case for subsidizing low-income tenants by requiring authorities to operate rent rebate schemes which received an element of national subsidy. Otherwise they expected local authorities to move towards balanced housing budgets by raising rents. A national system of 'fair rents', at higher levels than existing rents, was to be developed, which might leave some authorities, those whose housing commitments were particularly costly, with deficits, but these would be met partly out of central government grants. But most authorities were expected to reach a position at which general subsidies would be unnecessary, and some would achieve surpluses.

Naturally this new scheme was designed to be phased in gradually. Rents were to be increased in stages, and a 'transitional subsidy' was paid. Before the transition could be completed, the Conservatives lost power, and the new Labour administration suspended the operation of the Housing Finance Act. It had, however, to put something in its place. In 1975 the Housing Rents and Subsidies Act was enacted as a temporary measure, pending a thorough review of the system. This gave back to the local authorities their power to fix rents. It also maintained the subsidies to the local authorities at the levels operating under the transitional arrangements for the implementation of the 1972 Act, and added some other specific subsidies.

A review of the system was completed in 1977, and a 'consultative document' on housing policy was published (HMSO, 1977). This proposed a system that had some features in common with the Housing Finance Act, but did not directly interfere with the authorities' power to fix their own rents, and did not entail a gradual phasing out of general-purpose subsidies. The general approach offered a potential for manipulation in a variety of ways determined by the ideology of the government operating it. The consultative document described the approach as follows:

1 The starting-point of the calculation of subsidy would be an authority's entitlement to subsidy in the previous year;
2 each year a basis for calculation of the extra expenditure admissible for subsidy – including extra costs of management and maintenance assessed on an appropriate formula – would be settled for the coming year in consultation with local authorities;
3 each year an appropriate level of increase in the 'local contribution' to costs, from rent and rates, would be determined for the coming year, also in consultation with local authorities;
4 if the extra admissible expenditure of an authority exceeded the increase in the 'local contribution', subsidy entitlement would be increased. If on the other hand the extra local contribution exceeded this extra expenditure subsidy entitlement would be correspondingly reduced. (Ibid., p. 83)

The Labour government fell in 1979 before it could enact this system, but the Conservatives' Housing Act of 1980 essentially took it over. Then, what became crucial, since the new government was committed to reducing as far as possible the central government subsidy to council house rents, was the annual assumptions made, under point (3) above, about appropriate levels of rent increases. This was used, particularly after the Local Government and Housing Act of 1989, to drive up rents through reduction of subsidy.

Thus, during the 1980s and 1990s, large numbers of local authorities ceased to be entitled to a subsidy from central government, other than contributions to pay the cost of rent rebates (housing benefit). By the middle of the 1980s, only about a quarter of all local authorities were still getting this subsidy, and over three-quarters of the total sum being paid out was going to London boroughs (Malpass, 1990, pp. 147–8). After this, the numbers of authorities getting the subsidy increased a little. The contemporary picture is confusing; in England and Wales in 1993–4 the government reported a £4,215 million Exchequer contribution to local authorities, but £3,306 million of this was a contribution towards the cost of housing benefit for public sector tenants (Department of the Environment, 1996).

Under the arrangements described above, rents could still be subsidized from local resources (at that time, the 'rate fund'). What in fact happened in the early 1980s was that there was an increased divergence between authorities. The sharp withdrawal of the central subsidy meant that, in aggregate, local subsidies to rents exceeded national subsidies by 1983. However, it was once again only in a small number of authorities, mostly in London, that such contributions were of any significant size (Malpass, 1990, p. 168). In around half of all authorities, no contributions were made at all. At the other extreme, an increasing number of authorities were making contributions *to* the rate fund from rents; that is, council tenants not on housing benefit were subsidizing rate-payers!

In the 1989 Act the government set out to force local authorities to phase out these exchanges between housing accounts and their general accounts. This measure was widely described as 'ring-fencing' the housing revenue accounts. Local authorities were forced to raise rents to replace local contributions. A further complication was that, in determining the rules for these accounts, the government started taking into account a notional income from housing benefit subsidy. What this implies is that authorities may find that they are in effect required to partly subsidize the housing benefit to low-income tenants from the rents of other tenants. This new regime is gradually being phased in; and as before, the actual situation depends upon the government's application to each authority of the formula described above.

As suggested already, as the general subsidy has disappeared and general rents have gone up, so housing benefit has tended to become the dominant form of subsidy going to local authority tenants. This is paid not by the Department of the Environment, but by the Department of Social Security. As its costs went up, the latter department reduced the availability of housing benefit by steepening the rate at which it tapered off with increases in income.

The determination of capital expenditure – that is, primarily the building of new houses – is also based on a system devised in the late

1970s by the Labour government. Before 1977, local councils determined their house-building programmes without consultation with central government. However, to implement those programmes, they had to secure central acceptance, both to enable them to undertake such extensive investment and to obtain subsidies (inasmuch as subsidies were linked to specific building projects). Local government proposed, and central government would dispose. The whole system was relatively haphazard, since central government tried to link its decisions to national, and relative local, priorities, but was dependent upon local initiatives, and did not necessarily have an overall view of national housing needs. Under the system established in 1977, local authorities are required to submit for annual central scrutiny their 'Housing Investment Programmes'. These include not only their plans for the provision of new local authority housing, but also their plans to make loans for house purchase, to give grants for housing improvements, to improve their own stock, to clear unfit houses, to purchase houses and to assist housing associations. Statistical returns from the authorities are required on their own current and future activities, and on their intelligence on local housing needs and problems of private sector building. On the basis of these submissions, the local authorities then, after a process of negotiation through the regional offices of the Department of the Environment or the Scottish or Welsh offices, receive annual expenditure allocations, not in the form of specific permission for particular projects, but in the form of a broad block.

The Thatcher government's impact upon this system in the early 1980s was simply to limit expenditure, particularly on new building. From 1985 onwards, however, there was some relaxation, to allow for the improvement of local authority housing stock. New building remained low. In the late 1970s local authorities in the United Kingdom built a little over 100,000 dwellings each year. In the early 1980s it was down to a little over 30,000 a year, and in the 1990s it has dropped to a very low figure indeed. In 1994 only 1,680 public sector houses were completed. That figure (under 1 per cent of total completions) was dwarfed by the number of completions for housing associations (33,817, or 19 per cent of the total).

These changes in public housing policy in the 1980s, towards the reduction of subsidies and the restriction of new building, need to be seen together with the government's stimulation of the sale of council houses. The role of local authorities in the provision of housing was beginning to be restricted. A Housing Act passed in 1988 aimed to go very much further in marginalizing that role. In a measure misleadingly presented by the government as enabling tenants to choose their landlords, opportunities were presented to housing associations and other independent buyers approved by the government to acquire local authority properties. Initiatives of this kind were bound in practice to come from potential buyers, encouraged by local authorities who wanted to sell their stock, rather than from tenants exercising 'choice'. Such moves could be blocked only if a majority of the tenants concerned vetoed them. Another section of the Act proposed to set up a number of housing action trusts in areas where, according to the government, substantial estate improvements were needed. These trusts would take over local authority properties, spend government money on improvements, and could then pass on the property to new owners.

The housing action trust idea was opposed by tenants in several of the areas where they were planned, and the government backed down or gave pledges that after improvements the properties could be restored to local authority ownership. The 'tenants' choice' proposal led to a limited number of housing association acquisitions from small southern authorities. Whilst the 1988 Act did not work out in the way the government planned, the strict controls over local rent setting and the continuation of limitations on the availability of capital for new building by local authorities have had two effects. One has been the growth of the hitherto small housing association sector, because it has had greater freedom to raise loans for building and rehabilitation work than local government. The other has been the exploration by local authorities of the case for voluntary transfer of their stock to a housing association in order to achieve greater managerial freedom, in particular the freedom to raise money for building and repairs. This latter development is involving not only transfer to existing housing associations, but also the setting-up of new associations, often formed from the staff of the local authority housing department. This is very much an emergent issue at the time of writing, but is being encouraged by the government (in legislation before Parliament) – hence my decision to entitle this section 'the social housing sector' rather than the 'local authority sector' as in the last edition of this book.

It is appropriate, therefore, to interpose here something more about housing associations. Housing associations were important in the nineteenth century, as voluntary, charitable bodies, but declined in relative importance with the growth of the public sector in the first half of the twentieth century. But over the last thirty years, housing association growth has begun to be given increasing government encouragement, being seen as an alternative form of social housing to the large, bureaucratic local authority sector. Housing associations in England may receive grants and subsidies from the government through the Housing Corporation. There is a similar, separate body in Wales. In Scotland, Scottish Homes functions both as a lender of government money and as a direct housing provider. In Northern Ireland (where, incidentally, local authority housing functions have a single Housing Executive directly responsible to the government) there is no intermediary body for housing associations.

In the 1980s and early 1990s the government made more money available to housing associations than to local government (see the impact upon the relative numbers of houses built, figures given on p. 201). Nevertheless, inhibitions on public capital projects have led to curbs on the resources going through the Housing Corporation and related bodies. As suggested above, however, housing associations, unlike local authorities, can raise money on the open market without government permission. Loans from central government have to some extent been replaced in this way, but with inevitable consequences for the rents charged to tenants. The legislation on rents allows new housing association tenants to be charged what are described as 'affordable rents'. What constitutes an 'affordable rent' is not clearly defined by the government, but 'was interpreted by the National Federation of Housing Associations as a rent approximately equal to 20 per cent of the tenant's average net income' (Balchin, 1995, pp. 195–6). Housing benefit is available to low-income tenants, making a formula like this somewhat hypothetical in many cases.

Housing associations vary widely in size, scope and character. Some differ little in their characteristics from private companies; these have grown in size recently, absorbing some smaller associations along the way. Others have distinct charitable aims and objects, and many are specifically local in their coverage. A small number are co-operatives.

Despite the encouragement of housing associations, social housing provision in general has diminished. This has been a product of both council house and housing association sales to tenants (the 'right to buy' legislation extends to housing associations) and the low amounts of new building.

In the 1970s the Labour government had argued that 'There is no longer an absolute shortage of houses. Whereas in 1951 there were about 750,000 more households than houses in England and Wales, by 1976 there were 500,000 more houses than households' (HMSO, 1977, p. 10). This is still broadly the position; in 1994 the alleged surplus of houses was about 600,000 (Central Statistical Office, 1996, p. 176).

Figures like this do not imply a straightforward 'surplus' of houses. A considerable number of houses are temporarily vacant at any time and some people own two houses. There may also be 'suppressed households' – households which would form if suitable accommodation were available. Moreover, an overall national surplus may be accompanied by:

regional and local imbalances in the supply of houses;

the continuing presence of unfit or substandard houses (again unevenly spread across the nation);

the existence of specific groups in the population who have difficulties in securing access to houses adequate for their needs.

In the area of population pressure around London the number of the homeless shows that a straightforward problem of a lack of homes still exists. In other places, however, the central problems are often the deteriorating quality of the housing stock, the existence of local authority dwellings that are difficult or impossible to let, and a lack of appropriate accommodation for people in need.

The whole picture is inevitably complicated, in ways which official housing need assessments do not adequately consider perhaps, by increases in rates of household formation, as young people leave home earlier and couples break up. A characteristic of recent policy has been its explicit disregard of this phenomenon and, indeed, social security policies which attempt to prevent it happening.

These issues regarding homelessness and the deteriorating local authority stock will be discussed further below, after some consideration of what is happening in the other two sectors.

OWNER-OCCUPATION

It has already been suggested that the examination of housing policy raises difficulties for any distinction between social policy and other areas of public policy. It might be imagined that the private market for owner-occupied houses had very little to do with social policy or indeed with government interventions in society. However, such an impression can be readily corrected by examining the attention that housing has been given in the policies of the major parties in the years since the Second World War. A central issue in the general elections of 1950 and 1951 was the performance of the Labour government in 'building' houses, and the claim of the Conservative Opposition to be able to 'build' more houses. The argument was about the building of houses in general, not just building by public authorities. The Conservatives came to power in 1951 committed to 'building' 300,000 houses a year, but many of these were to be built by private enterprise for owner occupation. Indeed, the Conservatives increasingly encouraged the development of this sector during the 1950s. Both parties have been concerned to assist the development of owner occupation, though in rather different ways. They see an aspiration towards owner occupation as having considerable electoral implications.

How, then, do public policies influence the owner-occupied housing sector? Of central importance is the large public subsidy that is given to owner-occupiers through the fact that interest payments on up to the first £30,000 of mortgage loans attract relief from the income tax system. There has been some political debate as to whether it is appropriate to call relief from taxation a subsidy. But what is indisputable is that an allowance of this kind reduces the actual rate of interest paid by mortgage borrowers.

The value of the tax allowance on mortgage interest is dependent on the rate of interest. The higher that is, the more valuable the tax concession. This made it very significant in the 1970s and 1980s, when high rates of interest enormously increased the sum of money lost to taxation. In the 1990s lower rates are changing the picture again.

Mortgage interest relief was originally given when owner-occupied houses attracted a tax called Schedule A tax. But Schedule A tax was abolished in 1963. Owner-occupiers secured help from tax relief to purchase an asset the real cost of which, so long as the price of houses was rising faster than overall inflation, was falling throughout the period of the mortgage. Many existing owner-occupiers have done well out of this process.

Governments support the aspiration to house ownership. They therefore want to help more people become owner-occupiers. However, the peculiar evolution of the British system left them with a device which, while it helps first-time buyers, yields great advantages to owner-occupiers long after they have first started to borrow, and concentrates its help not on low-income but on high-income house-purchasers. Various ideas have been canvassed to reduce what has been called the problem of 'front-loading' of mortgage costs. All require government subsidy to shift the balance of expense. Logically such government expenditure might be offset against some withdrawal of the indiscriminate mortgage subsidy. However, there is a political objection to that. This is that people make decisions to borrow money on the basis of certain expectations of tax relief. In other words, any sudden change would be sharply redistributive, would have its most severe impact upon those whose calculations left least margin for variation, and would therefore be very unpopular in a society where two-thirds of householders are owner-occupiers, most of whom are still repaying mortgages. The government has developed a number of special ways of helping first-time buyers (which limitations of space do not allow me to examine in any detail).

In 1994 and 1995 the government started to phase out tax relief, reducing it in two steps below the then basic tax rate of 25 per cent to 15 per cent. At the time of writing, the depressed state of the housing market has led the government to stop the phasing-out process. While this may be just a temporary situation, there are signs that the wealth accumulation process described above has come to an end. This is discussed further below.

It is not only through subsidies that the government has influenced opportunities for individuals to secure owner-occupied housing. In the period immediately after the Second World War, the government maintained a tight control over building through control over access to building supplies. As it relaxed these controls, it stimulated private building. Then, in the 1950s, as it began to reduce the amount of local authority building, it thereby encouraged a shift of resources into building for sale. During that period of management of a full-employment economy along Keynesian lines, the government came to realize that one of the ways in which it could most easily influence the economic climate was by influencing the demand for new building. While the direct controls of the immediate post-war period no longer exist, there remain a series of factors that influence the scale of building of houses for sale: the extent to which alternative – particularly public sector – opportunities exist for the building industry, the availability of credit – particularly cheap credit – for building enterprises and land speculators, the availability of mortgage funds for home-buyers, and the availability of land.

Government intervention in the land market also has an impact upon owner occupation, by affecting both the availability of building land and its price. Of course, these two are interrelated, and one of the problems for intervention in the land market has been the relative unpredictability of the two effects. A concern about profiteering from land speculation has influenced legislation by all post-war Labour governments, while the Conservatives have sought to reduce the Labour impact upon a free market for land. The actual impact upon private housing of this long-running political battle, through the Town and Country Planning Act of 1947, the repeal of many of its features by the Conservatives in the 1950s, the 1967 Land Commission Act, the Community Land Act of 1975 and its repeal in 1980, is unclear, and cannot be considered here. It is mentioned, however, because it is important not to overlook the significance of land legislation for the housing market.

Until the 1980s the main suppliers of finance for house purchase were the building societies. These were comparatively cautious financial institutions, whose activities had grown slowly. Their origins lie in nineteenth-century self-help and charitable ventures, and they remain in some sense non-profit-making institutions. They depend for their operation on being able to attract money from small investors, influenced by the general range of opportunities open to savers, to lend to house-buyers.

Once the proportion of the population with their own houses was very high, government encouragement of home ownership naturally entailed a concern to open opportunities to borrow money to those who were regarded by the building societies, who have naturally been cautious in these matters, as 'bad risks'. Hence there has been governmental pressure upon these 'private' organizations to lend to more 'marginal' people or for more 'marginal' properties.

During the 1980s the government deregulated the financial market. Restrictions on building societies' activities were removed, and other lenders, including banks, discovered opportunities to move into the domestic mortgage business. There was a boom period when lenders saw the housing market as an ideal source of profits. Mortgages were sold aggressively, and the customary caution about the credit-worthiness of borrowers was abandoned. This further fuelled the boom to which it was a response: owner occupation expanded, and house prices rose rapidly. This boom, pushing up house prices well beyond the overall rate of inflation, eventually collapsed in the recession at the end of the decade. House prices started to fall; the housing market became exceptionally static; and, with rising unemployment, many recent borrowers got into difficulties with their mortgage repayments. At the time of writing, the government faces political difficulties with the frustration of individual expectations and the dispossession of impoverished borrowers occurring. In its search for a solution, it has turned to the lenders, seeking to persuade them to sustain the partly abandoned approach of the building societies of concern for the welfare of their borrowers. Devices are being sought to prevent widespread dispossessions.

One further complication in this situation is that house-owners who are out of work and receiving income support secure some help towards the costs of the repayment of mortgage interest. On the other hand, if they have low, earned incomes from full-time work, they are disqualified from income support, and cannot get any help with their housing costs from housing benefit. In this respect, they differ from workers who are renting, who can get housing benefit. The government has been concerned about this situation, which forms – in their eyes – a benefits 'trap', which discourages some people from seeking work. They have severely curbed the help available to house-buyers from income support. An alternative way of dealing with this situation would have been to extend housing benefit to low-income owner-occupiers, perhaps trading off this concession against the more indiscriminate subsidy to all house-buyers provided by tax relief on mortgage interest.

It is still too early to give a clear verdict on the comparative collapse of the housing market. It may be simply that financial institutions, egged on by politicians, encouraged wild speculation in owner-occupied housing that was bound to lead to personal disasters in a recession. Slumps have occurred in the housing market before, but their effects have tended to be masked by high inflation, so that a fall in the relative price of houses was not accompanied by a fall in their cash prices. On the other hand, overall demand for new owner-occupied houses may be falling, because of the size of the existing housing stock, a fall in the rate of new household formation, and the greater economic difficulties faced by young people at the household-formation stage. The situation in which owner-occupied housing has been seen as the safest investment for middle-income people – a feature of British society regarded by many economists as amongst the reasons for low investments in economic activity – may be coming to an end. This does not necessarily mean that there will be widespread losses by owner-occupiers – these will probably be confined to the unfortunate low-income buyers enticed into over-committing themselves in the late 1980s boom – but that housing will cease to be a source of widespread capital gains. Of course, few people enjoy those gains themselves; mostly they pass them on to the next generation. In considering this issue as a whole, there is a connection to be made here with the discussion of the care costs of elderly people (p. 148), since capital assets are taken into account in the means-testing process.

THE PRIVATE RENTED SECTOR

The private rented sector (excluding the housing association sector) now houses about 10 per cent of the population. Since, however, its decline to this position is a relatively recent phenomenon (in 1951, over half the households in England and Wales were in this sector, and in 1918 probably about 90 per cent were renting privately), it is important to consider the causes of this decline.

There has been a political, but now rather academic, argument about this. Was the decline of the private rented sector inevitable, as better outlets for investment opened up? Or was it produced by government-imposed controls? From 1916 onwards there were rent controls of various kinds, applied with varying degrees of stringency. Controversy raged over the protection of private tenants from both eviction and high rents. Between 1965 and 1988 the fair rent principle was adopted for most forms of private tenure. This represented a political compromise based on a comparatively nonsensical formula according to which rent officers were expected to assume that properties were let in a market in which there was no scarcity. The reality was that rents were determined by a system of comparisons at levels some way below what the market might be expected to bear. At the same time, many landlords sought to evade the rent controls altogether by legal devices such as the granting of a 'licence to occupy' rather than a tenancy. The 1988 Housing Act effectively abandoned rent control, apart from various rather complex measures of protection for tenants with agreements dating from earlier rent control regimes.

In decontrolling this sector, the government argued that returning it to the market-place would arrest its decline. But this depends upon the alternative opportunities available to renters. In particular, in the context of a tax system which subsidizes house purchase (as described above), owning is often a better prospect than renting for most people with the resources to pay market rents and proposing to stay in the same district for some time.

Excluding temporary residents of an area, amongst whom students figure as a significant group, this means that private tenants will tend to be low-income earners and recipients of social security benefits. To enable them to pay market rents, the government has had to allow them access to the housing benefit scheme. However, the problem with this scheme is that receipt of benefit removes any incentive to the renter to behave like a free market participant. The cost of the rent falls upon the state. To cope with this problem for the social security budget, a complex procedure has been adopted, requiring rent officers to rule whether rents should be regarded as excessive for benefit purposes and the hapless tenant (or sometimes the local authority) to find the balance, rather than central government. In other words, a special system of benefit control has replaced rent control.

The private rented sector is unevenly distributed across the country. In some areas, particularly in the north, there are still old, poor-quality houses occupied by elderly tenants who have been in them for many years. With this property the main public concern has been about conditions. Elsewhere, the private sector may have rather different characteristics. In London in particular, but also in many other big cities, much of this accommodation is in the form of flats created out of large old houses. These areas tend to accommodate people whom local authorities do not see as their responsibility (or at least place very low on their scales of priorities): in particular, newcomers to the area and the young single. The decline in the rate at which social housing is provided (discussed above) intensifies the pressure on this sector. As other housing problems have been solved, the gap between the good housing conditions of the majority and the often very poor conditions experienced in this part of the private sector has become increasingly evident.

HOMELESSNESS

Homelessness has increased as a result of a combination of a decline in the supply of new accommodation with mobility in search of work in the overcrowded south and family breakdown. It also has causes outside the direct control of housing policy, in the unwillingness of the social security system to pay adequate benefits to some groups (in particular, the young). Finally, it must be noted that many amongst the homeless are in need of health and social care, to assist with problems of mental illness, alcoholism and drug abuse.

In 1977 the Housing (Homeless Persons) Act imposed a duty upon local housing authorities to provide accommodation for homeless persons in certain 'priority' groups. These priority groups are, broadly, families with children or elderly or sick persons, together with those made homeless by disasters such as flood or fire. However, authorities need not help families who are deemed to have become homeless 'intentionally'. This controversial provision was added to the Act by an amendment, and may be used to justify refusal of help to someone who has been evicted for not paying rent.

The 1977 Act makes it mandatory for an authority to give temporary help, and for more permanent help to be given where a homeless person has a (carefully defined) local connection. It is implicit in the Act that the homeless must be rehoused, except on a very temporary basis, in permanent homes, and not herded into inadequate accommodation. Thus they are in competition with those being rehoused by the housing departments from their waiting lists. In practice, many authorities, particularly in London, use poor-quality temporary accommodation to house homeless people for long periods of time. Recently, central government have been unwilling to pressure reluctant local authorities to fulfil their responsibilities better; and at the time of writing, amending legislation is being enacted which will limit local authority responsibility in respect of homelessness to the provision of time-limited temporary accommodation (normally for one year).

It must be emphasized, in conclusion, that the policy response described above is principally for families. Local authority obligations to the single are simply to give advice! It is single homelessness which has grown visibly, particularly in London, during the 1980s. It has already been suggested that the roots of this problem lie in a complex of factors, only some of which concern housing policy. Certainly, however, the hard-pressed, under-resourced local authority housing departments are unable to pay much attention to the needs of this group, particularly if the individuals need some combination of housing and social care.

SOCIAL HOUSING ALLOCATION PROCEDURES

Wherever there is competition for social housing, the determination of rules to govern priorities is an emotive matter. As local authority housing became big business, most authorities changed from systems that depended upon the judgements, or whims, of councillors or officials to waiting lists based upon some queuing principles. The main issues were:

first, the extent to which a simple queuing approach should be modified by the development of 'points systems' enabling individual priorities to be weighted;

second, the balance in such systems between needs and waiting time;

third, whether a preference should be given to those who had resided in the area for some time.

It should be noted that these issues apply to social housing in general. There are arrangements between local authorities and housing associations which give the former nomination rights to accommodation belonging to the latter.

Central government became critical of local schemes that did not give overwhelming importance to need. Local authorities were urged to abandon residence requirements, both because they may have an impact upon labour mobility and because they may facilitate a covert form of racial discrimination. An official advisory committee, the Cullingworth Committee (Central Housing Advisory Committee, 1969) strongly urged the adoption of need-based points schemes. There has been a distinct move towards the development of points schemes; this was particularly enhanced by the abolition of many smaller housing authorities when local government was reformed in 1974. Nevertheless, local commitments to residence rules die hard.

However much a local authority endeavours to govern its allocation policies by fair, open points schemes, it must also make allowance for housing priorities that do not fit those schemes. Homelessness has already been mentioned as an example of this. Individual unfit houses may also require immediate responses. Demolitions because of new roads or slum clearance schemes bring rehousing responsibilities that may cut across waiting list allocation in a major way. With low levels of new house building, such commitments may bring movement from waiting lists almost to a standstill. Finally, some authorities recognize special categories of need, which cannot readily be translated into housing 'points', determined by health or social work priorities, and allow other agencies to make special recommendations. These call for discretionary judgement by housing officials and by doctors or social workers, and there is an inevitable tension between maintenance of the rules and special arguments for 'queue-jumping'.

HARD-TO-LET HOMES

Allocation of social housing involves achieving a balance between what people want, what they are deemed to need, and what is available. Under conditions of housing scarcity, individuals are in a weak position to assert their wants, unless their co-operation is required with a redevelopment scheme. Housing authorities allocate on the basis of assessments of need, attempting to make the most efficient use of the housing stock. But they often, in the past, gave attention to capacity to pay, and many were also disposed to make judgements about potential tenants' suitability for 'good' houses.

The Cullingworth Committee (Central Housing Advisory Committee, 1969) attacked this aspect of housing management. Housing authorities have become increasingly sensitive to the problems entailed in, and following from, policies of this kind. However, as the number of families who are desperate for help declines in some areas, so the balance of power between housing officers who judge needs and potential tenants who express their wishes inevitably shifts. Now, in some areas, poorer houses are often only easily allocated to, for example, the homeless. Nevertheless, a reshuffling of tenants proceeds all the while, and those allocated the 'bad' houses seek transfers to better ones. Often they secure such transfers only if they have been 'good' tenants, and in particular if they have been regular rent-payers. The only people who shift in the opposite direction are those who are punished for rent arrears or strikingly non-conforming behaviour, by eviction from 'good' houses and allocation of 'bad' ones.

Local authorities now have stocks of houses and flats of various kinds: in particular, pre-war semi-detached houses, post-war 'semis' built when standards were very low, modern houses built to very high standards, flats in blocks of various sizes, good old houses acquired from private owners, and patched houses with short lives pending demolition. Of course, these dwellings vary in popularity, with perhaps high-rise flats and short-life houses as the least popular. If through allocation and transfer policies there are various forms of segregation within an authority's housing stock, then the 'hierarchy of popularity' will have been influenced by social as well as architectural considerations. Indeed, these social factors may well complicate the hierarchy as certain estates, not necessarily characterized by severe design problems, also acquire reputations as 'rough' or 'respectable', perhaps as a result of some really rather complex accidents of history. This can obviously tend to involve differentiation by income, particularly if accessibility to employment opportunities influences tenant choices. Thus the unpopular areas may contain substantial proportions of households dependent on social security benefits. The sale of council houses (see next section) further enhances the social divisions, since houses on popular estates and on estates in which the more prosperous tenants live will be more likely to be sold.

As a result of this mixture of factors, local authorities now find that, where the demand for housing is falling, they have 'hard-to-let houses'. Families still in quite poor conditions in the private sector regard their existing situation as preferable to rehousing in, for example, a badly vandalized tower block. Authorities' problems may be compounded, moreover, by the fact that those families least able or likely to object to these undesirable dwellings may be the very families who, rightly or wrongly, are identified in the eyes of others as contributing to the stigma attached to them. Further, some aspects of this vicious circle have already been identified above. What do the authorities do about applications for transfers out of unpopular dwellings? And if an authority does not want to create homelessness, what weapon can it use against bad rent-payers other than 'demotion' to less desirable accommodation?

Authorities resort to a variety of devices in these situations. Some halt transfers, and seek to allocate unwary 'good' tenants to unfavourable property; but this is unpopular, and may have political repercussions. In some cases architectural and environmental improvements may help. In some areas a group whom local authorities have largely ignored hitherto, the young single, are accommodated in unpopular properties, particularly high-rise flats. Some authorities have sold some blocks of flats cheaply to private owners. But in some cases demolition, even of relatively modern property, has been seen as the only answer. In many places local authorities are worried about the extent to which they are becoming new kinds of 'slum landlords'.

THE SELLING OF SOCIAL HOUSING

The Conservatives came to power in 1979 determined to stimulate the sale of local authority and housing association houses to their tenants.

Their Housing Act of 1980 provided a statutory right to most tenants to buy their own houses, at market prices less a discount based on length of tenancy ranging from 33 to 50 per cent. Subsequently the government put pressure on Labour-controlled authorities which dragged their feet in implementing this provision, going so far in one case, Norwich, as to put in a special commissioner to do the job.

Social Trends 22 describes the impact of this policy as follows:

> As a result of this legislation, almost 1.5 million local authority and new town tenants bought their homes during the 1980s. Annual sales peaked at 226 thousand in 1982, but fell to less than half this level in 1985 and 1986. Between 1986 and 1989 sales increased in each year before falling again in 1990 when only 140 thousand dwellings were sold. (Central Statistical Office, 1992, p. 147)

By 1994 the number of sales was down to about 80,000 (Central Statistical Office, 1996, p. 178). Since social housing tenants are, generally speaking, low-income people, sales will have been affected by unemployment, which was particularly high in the middle and at the end of this period. Moreover, the number with the resources to buy will ultimately be finite, so some falling away in numbers is to be expected. In fact, the recovery from the sales slump in 1985–6 was helped by increased discounts and an increase in the range of properties which could be bought. It is also the case that the success of the policy varies markedly from area to area, according to levels of prosperity (see Forrest and Murie, 1991, ch. 6).

There has been a debate about the justification for selling social housing. This is partly a technical one about the actual effect of such sale upon the housing effort as a whole and partly an ideological one about tenants' rights. There is a trade-off here between the rights of actual tenants and the interests of potential future tenants whose needs may not be met so easily because public authorities have lost control over some of their stock. The trade-off has been made more evident by the refusal of the government to let all the proceeds of sales be recycled into new investment in housing.

This debate must also be seen in the light of what was said in the last section about hard-to-let houses. The houses that tenants are likely to buy will be in 'good' popular estates. The development within these of a mixture of owner occupation and renting may be seen as desirable for the future of such estates, in the long run extending social mixing and social diversity to those estates. But such a development reinforces the growing gap between the 'good' estates and the 'bad'. In this way it reinforces a future for social housing in which renting (even from a public authority or housing association) will be seen as a much inferior option to ownership. Britain is moving to a situation, like that in the United States, in which social housing is not even 'housing for the working classes', as it was required to be in the original legislation, but housing for the poor. By 1993–4, more than 60 per cent of local authority tenants were on means-tested benefits (Green and Hansbro, 1995, p. 69). This development has been influenced by government policies which push rent levels up, leaving subsidy to the benefit system. This increases the incentive for those required to pay full rents to seek to buy. The problem is that owner occupation is popular, and its growth seems desirable; but this growth leaves a minority behind in possibly decreasingly satisfactory circumstances.

It is significant that in order to enhance the sale of social housing the government has been forced to provide large discounts. The provision of discounts weakens the economic arguments for sales; older houses that are, perhaps quite reasonably, sold to long-term sitting tenants at low prices still have to be replaced, if there is outstanding housing need, by new, expensive houses. This issue draws our attention to a variation of the same anomaly as exists within the owner-occupied sector: there is a vast gap between the original, 'historic' costs of housing and modern 'replacement' costs. In the owner-occupied sector, someone who bought a house, say in the 1960s, for £2,000 may today be repaying a minute (by modern standards) mortgage. If he or she dies, heirs will receive an asset worth many times the original price. In the local authority sector, a similar house may today, assuming rents have moved in line with prices, be yielding the local authority a 'profit', which it returns to the rent pool to subsidize newer houses. What is a fair rent (in the true sense, not in the sense in which the term is used in the Rent Acts) for such a house? And if the occupier wants to buy, what is a fair price? There are no right answers to these questions; the whole situation is riddled with anomalies. To treat such a tenant well is to give a privilege relative to those who are still seeking local authority accommodation. To treat him or her harshly is to emphasize his or her disadvantage relative to the long-term owner-occupier.

CONCLUSIONS

The latter part of this chapter has particularly emphasized the issues that have arisen from the interaction between Britain's various housing sectors with the growth of owner occupation and the decline of private renting. The interactions here are complex. Studies of housing have given attention to movement between the sectors, examining the filtering hypothesis which suggests that the benefits of new houses, even at the top of the owner-occupier market, filter down to contribute to the reduction of housing need. Superficially this seems plausible. However, the 'chains' that have been traced resulting from new houses at the 'top' end of the system are often short. Typically, they extend down only to a young new entrant to owner occupation, perhaps from that part of the private rented sector where the needs of the young mobile middle class are met, perhaps merely forming a new separate household for the first time (Murie et al., 1976; Forrest et al., 1990). The same seems to be true of purchased social housing when it is later sold by the original buyer.

At least three very different kinds of housing 'career' can be detected. One involves movement into or entirely within the owner-occupied sector as described above. Another involves movement, either on separation from a parental home or via the private rented sector, to social housing, but then stops there for the rest of life. And a third, of diminishing significance, involves difficulty in moving from the private rented sector to either of the other more privileged sectors. The argument in this chapter has entailed the assumption that the last of these careers is likely to remain rare. If this is correct, then some of the peculiar problems that have been identified regarding different expectations within the two major sectors become of increased importance. At the moment, interchange between them takes the form of movement out of social housing (often by purchase of a rented house).

What are the implications for social segregation in Britain if this remains the case? But equally, what are the implications of those interchanges that do occur, since they may, as the examination of the sale of social housing implied, reinforce this new form of social segregation. It is a division in our society that does not precisely correspond to the social class division between manual and non-manual work which has received so much attention in the past. Yet it is a division that may have equally serious implications for the allocation of opportunities and for territorial justice in our society. Since, furthermore, owner occupation conveys benefits which are passed on through inheritance, whilst the other sectors do not, these social divisions may be reinforced across time (this is an issue which is attracting increasing attention; see, for example, Hamnett, 1991). However, the divisions may be becoming more complex; owner occupation is increasingly stratified in terms of the age and quality of the housing and in terms of when individuals achieved that status. As suggested above, many recent buyers may not have secured appreciating assets comparable to those bought by earlier generations.

SUGGESTIONS FOR FURTHER READING

Balchin (latest edition, 1995) provides a good general introduction to housing policy. The many issues about housing finance are well discussed in Gibb and Munro's *Housing Finance in the UK* (1991) and in Malpass's *Reshaping Housing Policy* (1990). Two books which deal with contemporary developments are Malpass and Murie's *Housing Policy and Practice* (4th edition, 1994) and the collection of essays edited by Malpass, *The Housing Crisis* (1986). A thorough account of the 'right to buy' legislation is contained in Forrest and Murie (1991).

SOCIAL POLICY, POLITICS AND SOCIETY

INTRODUCTION

This book has given attention to the major policy areas that are conventionally labelled 'social policy'. It has shown that within these areas the state is responsible for a wide range of activities. In the chapters on individual policies a number of weaknesses were noted in the pattern of provision. Yet it is widely suggested today that the state takes on too much, and that the public service sector, of which the social policy areas account for a large proportion, is too large. We need therefore to look, in this final chapter, at some of the general issues regarding the role of social policy in society and at some of the attempts to make social policy, as a whole, more effective and more responsive to popular needs and attitudes.

SOCIAL EXPENDITURE IN THE CONTEXT OF NATIONAL PUBLIC EXPENDITURE

Table 11.1 provides figures setting out expenditure under the main functional headings with which this book has been concerned, together with some other functions, for the purposes of comparison. It gives information on expenditure in a year early in the period of Conservative rule (1981), in one ten years later (1991) and in the most recent year for which official information has been published (1994). The figures for the expenditure totals are what are called 'real terms' figures: that is, figures adjusted to common price levels at a single point in time, in this case 1994.

These figures show a rise in expenditure in real terms of 27 per cent. Since, of the social policy expenditure categories set out above, only housing has fallen in proportionate terms, we may conclude that all the

Table 11.1 General government expenditure by function: percentages

Function	1981	1991	1994
Social security	27	32	34
Health	11	14	14
Education	12	13	13
Housing and community amenities	6	4	4
Defence	11	10	8
Public order and safety	4	6	5
All expenditure (£ billion at 1994 prices)	224.6	250.9	285.7

Source: Central Statistical Office (1996)

rest have risen in real terms, and that social security expenditure has risen very substantially since 1991. Indeed, the social policy percentage indicated in the above table increased from 56 per cent in 1981 to 65 per cent in 1994.

The level of public expenditure was about 43 per cent of the Gross Domestic Product (an estimate of the total economic output of the nation) in 1994 (Central Statistical Office, 1995b). Social policy expenditure (not including expenditure on employment services) at about 65 per cent of all public expenditure is thus about 28 per cent of GDP. Of course, the relationship of public and social expenditure to GDP depends upon *both* the level of public expenditure and the level of productive output.

Politicians pay attention to the relationship between public expenditure and GDP, and some critiques of the welfare state suggest that it is dangerously high. However, much public expenditure involves no more in practice than transfers between citizens (as in social security payments). Hence the notion, sometimes expressed, that a large part of the output of the nation is being absorbed into the 'unproductive' public sector is rather misleading. Nevertheless, this perspective will be examined in more detail in the next section.

ALTERNATIVE PERSPECTIVES ON SOCIAL POLICY AND THE STATE

The financing of extensive public expenditure requires heavy taxation. It is argued that the size of the redistributive exercise via taxation into public expenditure undertaken by the British government has a disincentive impact upon private initiative, and has contributed towards low productivity. It is also suggested that the scale and scope of the state 'bureaucracy' are such that public resources are inevitably used inefficiently. The British people are alleged to be overtaxed and overgoverned. These propositions about public expenditure are found in the attack upon the welfare state which comes from the political Right (Harris and Seldon, 1979; Minford, 1984).

One way of examining propositions of this kind is to compare Britain with other countries. Newspaper articles regularly attempt to do this, skating nonchalantly over the many problems entailed in making such comparisons – in particular, different definitions of public expenditure and GDP. Nevertheless, such comparisons tend to show that, while in the United States public authorities proportionately tax less and spend less, Britain's position in league tables of comparable European countries is low (see Hills, 1993). Perhaps this merely proves that 'overgovernment' is a shared European problem. Alternatively, it may be suggested that the important comparisons concern not overall taxation and expenditure, but kinds of taxation – in particular, differences in the use made of direct and indirect taxation – and kinds of expenditure. There are some very clear differences in the extent to which different nations use insurance devices in relation to expenditure on social security and health; and widely differing uses are made of means tests to control spending on all the major services. In the last resort, it is welfare outcomes which are important.

Hence, while comparison between overall levels of public expenditure may not be very revealing, a more detailed examination of ways of providing social policies introduces us to some of the main standpoints in the political debate. Government in modern industrialized societies is unlikely to be indifferent to the need to provide cash for those unable to earn, education for the young, and health care for all. But it may choose various options for their provision. It may seek to encourage, regulate and strengthen broadly private provisions. It may devise very mixed forms of private and public services. Or it may stress public services, and in so doing endorse the possibility of extensive social engineering towards egalitarian goals.

Certainly political theorists on the Right see the provision of health and social care, housing and education, together perhaps with social security (beyond some bare minimum), as the responsibility of the individual. It is asserted that, instead of depending upon a paternalistic state, people should be free to make choices about amounts and kinds of social benefits, just as they make choices about the purchase of ordinary consumer goods. This perspective is likely to embrace the view that a protective welfare state is undesirable, and that individual initiative and independence are desirable characteristics of society which are undermined by welfare measures. People of this persuasion generally regard the existing range of social policies as already too developed. They argue, therefore, in favour of the maintenance of private sectors in health and education, and of the rationing of services through charging policies.

The advocates of less government involvement, and of the extension of the role of the market, generally have a stance on social equality too. While it could be the case that bureaucratic rigidity and lack of choice in the present social welfare system might be reduced by an extension of the free market system, changes to such a system might well leave vulnerable low-income groups unprotected. In theory, this might be countered by government interventions to enhance the incomes of the poor and decrease inequality. Hence the poor would gain both more income and more choice. The difficulty with such compensating changes is that they would entail very extensive government intervention to equalize incomes. These would be anathema to those who expound the virtues of free enterprise. The latter require, instead, the distribution of incomes to be determined by the 'hidden hand' of the market. Modern British society is today an enormous distance away from such a free market. Clearly, political realists among the exponents of this view have a gradual programme of moves towards their ideal society. They look to means of enhancing private social policies, using state policies to play underpinning roles.

The clearest alternative to this perspective sees social policies as potentially able to contribute to the redistribution of income in Britain. As Titmuss and his colleagues developed the study of social policy in Britain in the 1950s, they were concerned to attack the complacent belief that the creation of the welfare state, particularly through the social policy reforms of the 1940s, had secured a very much more equal society. It was pointed out that the main beneficiaries of some of the key reforms were the relatively well-to-do. The free health service extended benefits to all, but was used more by the higher social classes. The middle classes could now send their children to grammar schools without having to pay fees. Even the main extensions of the social security system gave the better-off access to benefits from which they were previously excluded. At the same time, while it was true that the tax burden had considerably increased for higher earners, a wide range of concessions and untaxed fringe benefits offset this or provided compensating benefits (Titmuss, 1962; Atkinson, 1975; see also Le Grand, 1982, and George and Wilding, 1984, for more recent explorations of this issue).

In the early 1960s, researchers, including notably Abel-Smith and Townsend (1965), showed that extensive poverty was still present in Britain. Not only were there large numbers of people dependent upon that subsistence level guaranteed by national assistance, but there were also many, a considerable proportion of whom were in families containing a full-time wage-earner, with incomes below or only a little above that level. More recent data present an even bleaker picture of poverty and inequality (Oppenheim and Harker, 1995; Commission on Social Justice, 1994, ch. 1; Joseph Rowntree Foundation, 1995; Philo (ed.), 1995).

Hence it has been shown that the welfare state never has been either markedly redistributive or particularly effective at eradicating poverty. Studies of the overall distribution of income and wealth suggest that a degree of equalization occurred earlier in the twentieth century, particularly between 1939 and 1975. Since 1975, however, inequality has increased considerably; and whilst the continuation of the growth of social expenditure has contributed to blunting this, its impact has been increasingly weak (see Glennerster, 1995, ch. 10).

But should social policy be redistributive? Is the prevailing degree of inequality acceptable? And is the extent and nature of the poverty that exists tolerable? Students of poverty (Townsend, 1979; Mack and Lansley, 1985; Veit-Wilson, 1994) have tended to shift their attention away from consideration of a definition in terms of the minimum income necessary to sustain life, to one concerned with capacity to achieve a widely accepted standard of living and share in everyday social life. Probably most people in Britain today, no matter how tough their attitude to poverty, would accept some version of this. Few would argue for a 'bowl of rice a day' level of nutrition or be content to see the children of the poor in our society without shoes. However, what is clearly more controversial is how such a poverty standard should be identified. Should the politically determined income support level (described in chapter 5) be such a standard? Should the standard be related to average wages? Should the lowest quartile in the income distribution be deemed to be in poverty, whatever the nature of that distribution?

Clearly, how you answer these questions will determine how you answer the wider questions about the success of the government's interventions into social policy. They will determine whether you regard it as sufficient to ensure that all citizens secure access to free education, free primary health care and subsistence-level benefits when they are unable to work; or whether you believe that social policy should be a powerful engine for social equality. It is quite likely that neither of these extreme statements fits your requirements for social policy, in which case you will be faced by rather more complicated questions about policy adequacy and the extent to which an element of redistribution should be built into social policy.

Here, then, are two rather different perspectives on the role of social policy in society. On the Right are those who see the provision of social services as the responsibility of the individual and who reject the idea that such services should be redistributive. The role of the state is merely to alleviate the most extreme forms of hardship, but otherwise to stand back from interfering in the market. Alternatively, on the Left are those who evaluate social policy in relation to its commitment to equality.

But there is also a centrist position of considerable importance for British politics. Not only does it have its adherents in both major parties, but there are also strong political forces which lead to the adoption of this stance by governments regardless of their initial ideological inclinations. Labour governments have become inhibited from developing policies that expand the public sector, particularly the social policy sector, for fear of its impact upon either inflation or taxation. It has been argued that public expenditure draws in so many resources that it inhibits investment in industry (Bacon and Eltis, 1976; see also the discussion in Hill and Bramley, 1986, ch. 5).

The Conservatives came to power in 1979 committed to cuts in public expenditure, other than for defence and law and order, claiming that this would enable the economy to recover. They were, apparently, successful in curbing public expenditure on housing, but that success was not as great as it appears to be, because housing support for low-income people has increasingly been given through the housing benefit scheme (some of which is classified as social security expenditure). Otherwise, they failed in their goal of cutting social expenditure. Expenditure under social policy headings other than housing has increased, markedly so in the case of social security. As far as health expenditure is concerned, the government has been inhibited from making cuts by the continuing popularity of the service. Nevertheless, as was suggested in chapter 6, the actual growth level has been sufficiently low for it to be regarded by many as involving a decline in the standard of service provided.

Hence, while governments in the period 1979–95 have seen themselves, and been seen, as engaged in an attack on social expenditure, what we actually find are some rather confusing changes. They have gone to considerable lengths to cut social security benefits, but the following have each contributed to upward pressure for more social security expenditure:

demographic trends (increased numbers of the elderly),

economic trends (increased unemployment),

a tendency to shift other social expenses on to income maintenance (housing support, in particular, but also some of the costs of care of the elderly – see chapter 7).

Education and health expenditure have been attacked, but there has still been a considerable rise in real expenditure, albeit a rise insufficient to meet rising demands or expectations. The one big success has been in cutting *direct* expenditure on *public* housing (Hills (ed.), 1990).

Inevitably, in a situation in which social policy expenditure consumes a high proportion of national income and provides little room for political manoeuvre, yet leaves ample scope for dissatisfaction about what is provided, there is a search for better ways of delivering the social services. Political parties unable markedly to influence the overall pattern of public services will seek other ways of modifying their performance and enhancing the 'value for money' provided. The various forms this search has taken are the subject of the next section.

THE QUEST FOR EFFICIENT AND RESPONSIVE MODES OF SOCIAL POLICY DELIVERY

The view that social policy interventions have not achieved the success that might have been expected from the effort put into them has been accepted by many politicians and public servants. It has been recognized that a complex bureaucracy has been developed to provide social services, and that efforts are therefore needed to overcome the resulting institutional problems with the system.

In the 1960s and 1970s governments devoted a considerable amount of attention to the organization of both central and local government. There was a search for the most rational form of organization. The search was always made difficult by a wide range of political considerations: reorganization might change the balance of power, and alter opportunities and career prospects of individuals. Moreover, established patterns of organization develop supporting sentiments and loyalties. In any case, the rationalization of government is not an easy process. There are often competing criteria for rationalization which are hard to assess. For example, there is a conflict between the achievement of uniformity through centralization and the maximization of flexibility through decentralization. The close integration of particular services – for example, health and the personal social services – may weaken links between those services and other related activities – for example, the provision of housing and the achievement of high environmental standards. Rationalization seems to involve a search for the best arrangement, when perhaps in reality there are merely alternative arrangements, each carrying costs and benefits. These are hard to evaluate. Finally, there are informal aspects to organizational arrangements which develop within formal structures. While, in theory, formal arrangements may be sought to maximize effective informal links, these are particularly hard to predict. Moreover, one of the effects of a formal reorganization is to distort – and perhaps undermine – informal links operating prior to reorganization.

At central government level there was, between the mid-1960s and the mid-1970s, a move towards super-departments embracing many different policy areas. The 1980s saw some backing away from this approach. The largest of the social policy departments, the Department of Health and Social Security was broken into two. On the other hand, in 1995, Education and Employment were joined together. But probably more important than this has been the 'next steps' initiative whereby small policy-making departments are gradually being achieved which delegate to executive agencies their day-to-day policy delivery tasks. The significance of this change for social security and for employment services has been discussed in chapter 4.

This new model enables the policy departments to set policy output goals and targets to which agencies can be held accountable. It is too early to judge whether this managerial approach to accountability is superior – in its outcomes and in its ultimate public accountability – to the older doctrines of ministerial responsibility.

A more radical innovation in respect of accountability involves trying to get away from a situation in which one agency is the sole provider of a publicly required service. This is the model being developed for the health and personal social services, discussed in chapter 4 and further explored in chapters 6 and 7, in which purchasers (health or local authorities) give contracts to providers. The theory is that providers are placed in a market or quasi-market situation in which they may be in competition with each other, and in which failure to deliver contracted services can lead to non-renewal of a contract. This model also allows for the possibility that the provider may be a private body, even a profit-making body. Once again, it is too early to evaluate this development. Its proponents see it as increasing efficiency, with competition driving down costs, whilst accountability is maintained, because contracts can specify standards of work and amounts of output. Its opponents argue that quantitative output criteria will dominate at the expense of qualitative considerations, or that much of the competition will be illusory. To many on the Left, it is seen as the thin end of a wedge of privatization in which subsequent steps will be to enable multinational companies to make profits out of British social services or compel consumers to become purchasers of what were hitherto public services. At the time of writing, Labour Party pronouncements on policy show an ambivalence about this development, recognizing what has been achieved in increased visibility of costs, but critical of the insecurity engendered and the lack of longer-run policy planning.

As pointed out above, the New Right advocate shifting, as far as possible, to arrangements for individuals to purchase social services, using vouchers if necessary towards that end. For them, real public accountability must surely involve not purchasing agencies, but rather situations in which individuals buy services for themselves and their families. Education has been seen as an area in which this market approach can be more easily advanced. So far, apart from a scheme to meet some of the costs of pre-school education, the government has resisted the voucher approach, which would be principally a subsidy to private education. Rather, it has aimed to produce a system in which parents are supplied with information on schools' 'outputs' and are free to choose where their children will go. In practice, the costs of establishing and altering schools and the extent to which geographical considerations limit choices impose severe limits upon the realization of a real market situation here. Furthermore, as was noted in the chapter on education, this development occurs at the expense of the planned use of educational resources, and is enhancing various forms of social and racial segregation and inequality.

The Conservative governments between 1979 and 1995 thus developed two, not necessarily compatible, approaches as important for the control of public services. One of these has been a managerialist quest for means of control by creating accountable subdivisions within large organizations and by delegating services to accountable agencies. This process of delegation has involved strong budgetary controls and demands for the achievement of specific quantitative outputs (see Pollitt, 1990, for further discussion of this). The other has involved the search for devices which mimic markets, and thus, as described above, use competition and choice as control devices. Since the fall of Margaret Thatcher, the new Conservative regime led by John Major has put a strong emphasis on consumerism. Major's approach to consumerism entails stressing the importance of information about service outputs to enable people to exercise choice and exploring ways to provide financial compensation when services fail to deliver outputs or to deal with problems within a specific time-span. This is central to Major's 'citizens' charter'.

It is important to contrast these approaches to public policy with an alternative which has been more popular on the Left. This is to see the key problem for public accountability as not public monopoly *per se*, but rather the absence of devices for popular participation in decision-making (Donnison, 1991). The chief characteristic of this approach is to seek to establish ways of decentralizing decision-making. In the late 1970s and early 1980s the lead in this decentralization movement was provided by Labour- (and sometimes Liberal-) controlled local authorities (Gyford, 1985, 1991). Decentralization took the form of the breakdown of some authorities into sub-areas with local offices and local committees, the development of tenants' participation in housing management, and so on.

Arguments for greater participation have developed against the backcloth of the elimination of the smaller organs of local government and an increased centralization of decision-making. Accordingly, in those areas where governments, or local authorities, have been willing to countenance the development of participatory devices, there have been grounds for regarding this as tokenism designed to disguise the retreat of the real locus of power. To put it a little more neutrally, there is a significant conflict between the desire for centralized uniformity and the suspicion of particularistic local interests, on the one hand, and real local accountability on the other.

Perhaps the most significant area in which participation rights have been extended is in strategic and local land-use planning, areas of policy outside the scope of this book. Within social policy two examples have been discussed in earlier chapters: community health councils (CHCs) in the health service and school governors and managers in education. In the first of these, actual power is very limited, CHCs being merely officially supported pressure groups. In the case of school management, significant steps have been taken to ensure parents' representatives an equal share with local authority nominees in a context of increasingly devolved powers over school arrangements, though not over the curriculum.

The very considerable hostility of the Conservative government to local government has had the effect of increasing centralization, and perhaps making local delegations of power – like that in education – fairly meaningless (see Glennerster et al., 1991). In chapter 3, the way in which the Conservatives have very firmly controlled local government finance was discussed. In health policy the Conservatives have removed the last vestiges of local authority participation in district decision-making. In community care policy local authorities are being forced to transfer services to private and voluntary providers. In education, as has been shown, local authority autonomy is now very limited. Local government aspirations to participate in employment policy have been almost totally suppressed.

An unfortunate feature of the political polarization of Britain in the 1980s was the conflict between the largely Labour-controlled governments of the major urban authorities and the central Conservative government, led by a woman who openly made war against local government part of her strategy for eliminating 'socialism' in Britain. Of course, it did not help local government's cause that some Labour authorities matched Margaret Thatcher's extremism with a 'leftist' extremism of their own; but the damage done over this period to local government as a building-block for genuine local democratic accountability was out of all proportion to the modest attempts to establish local socialist strongholds.

It is now necessary for Britain to look again at its whole structure of local government, and at the relationship between central and local government. Both Labour and the Conservatives now recognize the case for simplifying the local government structure. Interestingly, the purchaser–provider principle allows the possibility that purchasers may represent quite small areas and be able to buy services from specialist providers outside their own geographical patch. More difficult is the question of whether there is a need to look at the structure of government for the United Kingdom as a whole, conceding social policy responsibilities to elected bodies within the constituent nations, and perhaps within the English regions as well.

Fortunately, through all this conflict over local democracy and despite the search for new methods of delivering services, mechanisms have survived that enable citizens to take action over individual grievances. In principle, the two categories into which grievance procedures fall are nearly as old as the nation-state itself: appeals to courts and complaints to elected representatives. In practice, they take modern forms very different from these traditional grievance procedures. In centuries past, litigation *vis-à-vis* dissatisfaction with an administrative agency depended upon an elaborate, costly legal procedure whereby the royal prerogative was invoked on behalf of the aggrieved citizen. These 'prerogative remedies' are still used from time to time, and today individuals may secure legal aid or the assistance of a voluntary organization to enable them to take grievances against public authorities to the High Court. But for everyday purposes what is much more important is that a large number of lower 'courts', generally known as 'tribunals', have been set up to deal with appeals against decisions of public agencies. Furthermore, in many cases there may be direct appeals to the courts or a supervisory tribunal against the decisions of these bodies.

The area of social policy in which tribunals are most important is social security. Individuals may appeal against most decisions taken by social security officials. There is a two-tier appeal system for social security benefits, with commissioners who operate at the top level, whose decisions are regarded as precedents for lower-tier decisions. Special systems, less detached from day-to-day decision-makers, exist to deal with claimants dissatisfied with social fund and housing benefit decisions.

In the housing sector, tribunals deal only with a limited range of disputes over rent levels and security of tenure in the private sector. Disputes between tenants and local authorities are not covered. These have to go to county courts.

There are tribunals to deal with complaints against family practitioners, but not against other parts of the health service. There are tribunals that review cases of compulsory detention under the Mental Health Acts. There is also a tribunal system to deal with disputes about the licensing of private residential and nursing homes.

Parents may appeal against the refusal of admission of a child to a school and against a child's exclusion from a school. A weakness of these procedures is that the appeal system is run by the very bodies whose decisions are contested. On the other hand, disputes regarding decisions about the appropriate schooling for a child with learning difficulties are heard by an independent tribunal.

The case for tribunals is that they provide for separate (and, in the best cases, independent) review of decisions, particularly those involving official discretion. They are less important for the control of policy itself; it is comparatively rare for tribunal decisions to indicate a significant defect in policy. To aggrieved individuals they offer not so much a chance to change policy as an opportunity to check a controversial application of policy.

The system of tribunals in Britain has been improved considerably in recent years. As a result of the Franks Committee (HMSO, 1957), attempts have been made to make tribunal proceedings more consistent and impartial. A Council on Tribunals maintains an oversight of tribunal arrangement, and reports (if necessary, publicly) its observations to the government. There is still, nevertheless, a suspicion that some tribunals are too closely identified with the government agencies whose decisions they are expected to examine. For example, the committees that adjudicate on complaints against doctors have been seen as rather too closely identified with the administration of the family practitioner services.

In the Scandinavian countries there are officials known as 'ombudsmen' who investigate complaints against the administration. When the appointment of such officials was first proposed for Britain, one of the arguments used against it was that elected representatives perform this function. Eventually, in 1967, the office of Parliamentary Commissioner was set up, but only to investigate individual public grievances passed on by Members of Parliament. Later, when local government and the health service were reorganized, Local Government and Health Service Commissioners were appointed. Complaints against local authorities were to be presented by councillors, but a provision was included to enable the Local Government Commissioners to investigate direct complaints when they were satisfied that a member of the public might have had difficulty in securing a councillor's backing (presumably because of involvement in the decision at issue). However, in the absence of elected representatives within the health service, direct access was allowed to the Health Service Commissioner. Hence there is a curious mixture of direct and indirect access to these British 'ombudsmen'. Perhaps in due course direct access will become the rule for all.

The Commissioners are concerned solely with maladministration. They do not deal with policy, so long as that policy has a clear statutory foundation. Nor do they deal with decisions that involve statutorily legitimate discretion or professional judgement. They provide, therefore, like the tribunals, only a limited protection for citizens against the worst abuses of administrative behaviour, not an opportunity to participate in policy formulation or to comment upon its overall implementation.

The underlying issue throughout this section concerns the extent to which Britain has a political and administrative system which tends to exclude meaningful participation, except through representative political institutions or through very specific devices to deal with individual grievances for consumers of social services. Concerns about participation, as we have seen, tend to be channelled into two, often distinct, ideological streams. For some, the key to control lies in the marketplace. Services should be privatized, and consumers put in a position in which they can make choices as the free purchasers of services. For others, decentralization of public provision to the local level, breaking up big bureaucracies and offering local participation in service control, is the preferred approach to this problem.

CONCLUSIONS

This chapter has looked at the issue of social policy and society by considering, first, some of the political perspectives on the level and character of social service expenditure, then some government or local authority-inspired attempts to improve social policy implementation or enable citizens to have some slight influence upon the impact of policy upon themselves. It has thus concentrated primarily upon some of the more detailed questions about the relationship between policy and society. It could, however, have developed an entirely different level of analysis, in which attention was focused upon the functions of social policy in our society and its relationship to our social structure.

Many of the propositions discussed in this chapter presuppose that social policy has developed out of a concern to protect, and to offer services to, weak and vulnerable groups in our society. For some writers on social policy, such state activities have an integrative function, serving to unite us in one mutually dependent community. Within such a community, developments to enhance social equality may occur. A welfare state advances us towards an egalitarian society. But the development of social policy may also be seen very differently. Perhaps the clearest alternative view is provided by Marxists (as was suggested in chapter 1). Of course, they argue, various social benefits have been extended to the poor. These are designed to increase their productive efficiency, by educating them and keeping them in good health, and to stave off revolution by meeting their most salient grievances. But they are never likely to advance a capitalist society far along the road to social equality. Thus democratic socialists are likely only to secure social policies that help to preserve the *status quo*, while radical free marketeers on the Right are likely to be restrained by the fact that a return to the open market-place would accelerate the drift towards the class warfare that Marx originally predicted. Modern variants of this viewpoint (which often eschew the label 'Marxist') reject historical inevitability, arguing instead about capitalism's capacity to retain its dominance in a changing society. They may well draw attention to the 'global' nature of economic forces.

This argument secures credence from the fact that social policy has not so far been proved to be a powerful source of social change. At the level of the interpretation of political motives and political behaviour, the Marxian position cannot be disregarded. Most political conflicts in a society like our own are battles between those who seek to gain from social change and those who benefit from the *status quo*. Those who seek change are always likely to be most successful when the defenders of the existing order see advantages in making concessions. Conservative politicians have at various times in the past spoken openly of the need to win popular support through specific measures. Countless government reports have drawn attention to the inefficiency of a society which is insufficiently fit to work hard or fight wars and insufficiently educated to provide the skills needed for industry. Social reformers with unquestionable humanitarian and altruistic motives have always fought alongside politicians who see new policies as expedient to protect the *status quo* and to win popular support.

The most difficult part of this argument to evaluate is dealing with the role played by mass political movements. Marxist theorists have long been split between those who believe that the working class can force capitalism to change peacefully and gradually and those who believe that real change will be achieved only by revolution. Clearly, in twentieth-century Britain the organized working class has sought to secure gradual social change. How successful has it been? And how much more success is it likely to achieve?

These are questions to which readers will want to choose their own answers. Clearly they raise issues that go far beyond the scope of the policies discussed in this book. However, there is one rather complicated answer to these questions which has a considerable bearing upon the interpretation of the making of social policy. This is that the organized working class has achieved quite considerable political success in Britain, forcing concessions from capitalism that nevertheless fall short of the transformation of Britain into a 'socialist society'. Moreover, those concessions are much more marked in some areas of social life than in others, and serve to benefit the better-organized segments of the working class more clearly than anyone else. These gains have thus been more likely to advantage males than females, and to favour the long-established indigenous population, as opposed to more recent immigrants and their families. Hence, while it is true that the overall distribution of income and wealth has been affected but little, and in particular has changed little at the extremes, some groups of manual workers have advanced significantly in income relative to some groups of non-manual workers and small entrepreneurs. These new middle-income workers are also significant beneficiaries from the advancements in the health and education services, and from income maintenance reforms which provide good short-term benefits.

However, their gains have done very little to benefit those who are less well organized, who remain low-paid and highly vulnerable to unemployment. The more powerful groups of workers also have relatively little interest in some of the problems for social policy that have been described in this book (such as homelessness, mental handicap, racial disadvantage). Those most in need of help from the welfare state are likely to be correspondingly ill-equipped to secure concessions from it. We have increasingly to face the phenomenon which, in the European Union context, has been called 'social exclusion'.

That is a personal, and inevitably contentious, suggestion of the way in which an interpretation of the development of social policy that has its roots originally in the Marxian perspective may be of relevance. It is an argument about power in the social structure, which sees capitalist interests as still of considerable importance, though forced to compromise with some better-off, male, white sections of the organized working class. It is important to recognize that political action in our complex society is enormously complicated. In no way is it a simple confrontation between twin forces of capital and labour. Both these forces tend to be segmented in various ways. In addition, the role of the state has grown to such an extent that it employs, at various levels and with various interests, a great army of people who are not necessarily readily aligned with any other forces in our society. In explaining social policy, it is necessary to examine the impact of such groups of state employees as doctors, teachers and central administrators. In sum, readers are asked to accept that social policies are not merely derived from humanitarian aspirations, but are also products of power conflicts in our society.

However, the disturbing evidence for those who, like myself, regard the developments set out above as progress is that the forces which contributed to these gains seem to be becoming progressively weakened. As suggested in chapter 9, high levels of unemployment have continued for twenty years, and there seems little prospect of change. Those who are in work have increasingly to accept poor rewards and low levels of job security. Many can get only part-time work. Even in the public sector low levels of security for many have been seen as necessary in the interests of efficiency. While many women have gained new employment opportunities, these are largely in these disadvantaged parts of the work-force. Hutton has persuasively described Britain as a 30/30/40 society, in which 30 per cent are seriously deprived and another 30 per cent insecure (Hutton, 1995). This is a society in which a progressive welfare state is both desperately needed and equally hard to achieve, since the 'comfortable' 40 per cent are inclined to look the other way.

Britain's situation needs to be seen in a global context. On the one hand, comparisons with nations close by (in the European Union) suggest that the performance of the British welfare state could be better. On the other hand, the economic forces which make full employment difficult to sustain and low-wage sectors endemic are creating problems for even the most progressive welfare states. Economic elites – through international organizations like the Organization for Economic Co-operation and Development and the World Bank – warn governments that high public expenditure levels will have adverse consequences for competitiveness.

Hence the struggle for better social policy is an increasingly difficult one. Great gains were made when humanitarian aspirations and political and economic forces were moving in the same direction. This is no longer the case. In this book I have tried to explore what has been achieved and the complex edifice of social policy institutions which is in place and which does a great deal to advance welfare. But I would be dishonest if I tried to end on an upbeat note. There is much still to be done, in an economic and political environment which makes social policy advance very difficult.

SUGGESTIONS FOR FURTHER READING

The government's 'public expenditure White Papers' are the most thorough up-to-date sources on expenditure patterns. They are published early in each calendar year. *Social Trends* also provides a valuable collection of official statistics, much used in this book. A collection edited by Hills (1990) provides a most authoritative examination of the impact of the Thatcher governments on public expenditure. Hills has also produced an admirable guide to the case against those who see social policy growth as impossible in his *The Future of Welfare* (1993). The book by Hutton cited in the text and the report of the Commission on Social Justice (1994) offer progressive agendas for social and other public policy.

The two sides in the debate on social policy provision have been well put together in a collection edited by Loney (1987); other important contributions are Deakin's *The Politics of Welfare* (1994), George and Wilding's *Welfare and Ideology* (1994), and Donnison's *A Radical Agenda* (1991).

Recommendations on the emergent literature on institutional change were included at the end of chapter 4.

There is a growing literature which puts Britain's welfare state in a wider context: notably Ginsberg's *Divisions of Welfare* (1992) and Gould's *Capitalist Welfare Systems* (1993). My own contribution to this literature is *Social Policy: A Comparative Analysis* (Hill, 1996).

BIBLIOGRAPHY

Abel-Smith, B. (1976) *Value for Money in Health Services*. London: Heinemann.
Abel-Smith, B. and Townsend, P. (1965) *The Poor and the Poorest*. London: Bell.
Alcock, P. (1993) *Understanding Poverty*. Basingstoke: Macmillan
Argyris, C. (1960) *Understanding Organisational Behaviour*. London: Tavistock.
Ashford, D. E. (1986) *The Emergence of the Welfare States*. Oxford: Blackwell.
Atkinson, A. B. (1975) 'Income Distribution and Social Change Revisited'. *Journal of Social Policy*, 4(1), 57–68.
Audit Commission (1986) *Making a Reality of Community Care*. London: HMSO.
Bachrach, P. (1969) *The Theory of Democratic Elitism*. London: University of London Press.
Bacon, R. and Eltis, W. (1976) *Britain's Economic Problem: Too Few Producers*. London: Macmillan.
Balchin, N. (1995) *Housing Policy: An Introduction*. London: Routledge and Kegan Paul.
Baldwin, P. (1990) *The Politics of Social Solidarity*. Cambridge: Cambridge University Press.
Ball, S. J. (1990) *Politics and Policy Making in Education*. London: Routledge.
Barclay, P. (1982) *Social Workers: Their Roles and Tasks* (Report of a Working Party). London: Bedford Square Press.
Bardach, E. (1977) *The Implementation Game*. Cambridge Mass: MIT Press.
Barnes, J. and Barr, N. A. (1988) *Strategies for Higher Education*. Aberdeen: University Press.
Barr, N. A. (1981) 'Empirical Definitions of the Poverty Line'. *Policy and Politics*, 9(1), 1–21.
Barrett, S. and Fudge C. (eds) (1981) *Policy and Action*. London: Methuen.
Becker, S. and Macpherson, S. (1988) *Public Issues, Private Pain*. London: Social Services Insight Books.
Beer, S. H. (1965) *Modern British Politics*. London: Faber & Faber.
Beveridge, W. (1942) *Social Insurance and Allied Services*, Cmnd 6404. London: HMSO.
Booth, C. (1889–1903) *Life and Labour of the People in London*, 17 vols. London: Macmillan.
Bosanquet, N. (1983) *After the New Right*. London: Heinemann.

Bottomley, A. K. (1973) *Decisions in the Penal Process*. London: Martin Robertson.

Bottomore, T. B. (1966) *Elites and Society*. Penguin: Harmondsworth.

Bowe, R. and Ball, S. J. (1992) *Reforming Education and Changing Schools*. London: Routledge.

Braybrooke, D. and Lindblom, C. E. (1963) *A Strategy of Decision*. New York: Free Press.

British Association of Social Workers (1977) *The Social Work Task*. Birmingham: BASW.

Brittan, S. (1971) *Steering the Economy*. Penguin: Harmondsworth.

Bryson, L. (1992) *Welfare and the State*. Basingstoke: Macmillan.

Butcher, T. (1995) *Delivering Welfare: The Governance of the Social Services in the 1990s*. Buckingham: Open University Press.

Butler, D., Adonis, A. and Travers, T. (1994) *Failure in British Government: The Politics of the Poll Tax*. Oxford: Oxford University Press.

Butrym, Z. T. (1976) *The Nature of Social Work*. London: Macmillan.

Byrne, T. (1994) *Local Government in Britain*, 6th edn. Penguin: Harmondsworth.

Cahill, M. (1994) *The New Social Policy*. Oxford: Blackwell.

Cairncross, A. (1985) *Years of Recovery: British Economic Policy 1945–51*. London: Methuen.

Campbell, C. and Wilson, G. K. (1995) *The End of Whitehall: Death of a Paradigm*. Oxford: Blackwell.

Central Advisory Council for Education (1954) *Early Leaving*. London: HMSO.

— (1959) *Fifteen to Eighteen* (Crowther Report). London: HMSO.

— (1963) *Half Our Future* (Newson Report). London: HMSO.

— (1967) *Children and their Primary Schools* (Plowden Report). London: HMSO.

Central Housing Advisory Committee (1969) *Council Housing Purposes, Procedures and Priorities* (Ninth Report of the Housing Management Sub-Committee: The Cullingworth Report). London: HMSO.

Central Statistical Office (1992) *Social Trends 22*. London: HMSO.

— (1995a) *Population Trends*, winter issue. London: HMSO.

— (1995b) *Public Finance Trends*. London: HMSO.

— (1996) *Social Trends 26*. London: HMSO.

Clark, B. R. (1956) 'Organizational Adaptation and Precarious Values'. *American Sociological Review*, 21, 32–6.

Clarke, J., Cochrane, A. and McLaughlin, E. (1994) *Managing Social Policy*. London: Sage.

Cole, D. and Utting, J. (1962) *The Economic Circumstances of Old People*. London: Codicote.

Commission of the European Communities (1993) *European Social Policy: Options for the Union*. Luxembourg: Official Publications of the European Communities.

Commission on Social Justice (1994) *Social Justice: Strategies for National Renewal*. London: Vintage.

Corrigan, P. and Leonard, P. (1978) *Social Work Practice under Capitalism*. London: Macmillan.

Crossman, R. H. S. (1975–7) *Diaries of a Cabinet Minister*, 3 vols. London: Hamish Hamilton and Jonathan Cape.

Crozier, M. (1964) *The Bureaucratic Phenomenon*. Chicago: University of Chicago Press.

Dahl, R. A. (1961) *Who Governs?* New Haven: Yale University Press.

Dale, J. and Foster, P. (1986) *Feminists and State Welfare.* London: Routledge and Kegan Paul.

Dawtrey, L. et al. (eds) (1995) *Equality and Inequality in Education Policy.* Buckingham: Open University Press.

Deacon, A. (1976) *In Search of the Scrounger.* London: Bell.

Deacon, A. and Bradshaw, J. (1983) *Reserved for the Poor.* Oxford: Martin Robertson.

Deakin, N. (1994) *The Politics of Welfare: Continuities and Change.* Hemel Hempstead: Harvester Wheatsheaf.

Dearlove, J. and Saunders, P. (1991) *Introduction to British Politics.* Cambridge: Polity Press.

Department of Education and Science (1985) *Education for All* (a brief guide by Lord Swann to the Report of the Committee of Inquiry into the Education of Children from Ethnic Minority Groups). London: HMSO.

Department of Employment (1971) *People and Jobs.* London: HMSO.

— (1988a) *Employment for the 1990s,* Cmnd 540. London: HMSO.

— (1988b) *Training for Employment,* Cmnd 316. London: HMSO.

Department of the Environment (1996) *Housing and Construction Statistics.* London: HMSO.

Department of Health (1995) *Health and Personal Social Services Statistics.* London: HMSO.

Department of Health and Social Security (1974) *Social Work Support for the Health Service.* London: HMSO.

— (1976) *Priorities for Health and Personal Social Services.* London: HMSO.

Department of Social Security (1995) *Social Security Statistics.* London: HMSO.

Dicey, A. V. (1905) *Lectures on the Relations between Law and Public Opinion.* London: Macmillan.

Dilnot, A. W., Kay, J. A. and Morris, C. N. (1984) *The Reform of Social Security.* Oxford: Clarendon Press.

Donnison, D. (1991) *A Radical Agenda.* London: Rivers Oram.

Douglas, J. W. B. (1964) *The Home and the School.* London: Macgibbon and Kee.

Dunleavy, P. (1981) *The Politics of Mass Housing in Britain.* London: Oxford University Press.

Eckstein, H. (1960) *Pressure Group Politics.* London: Allen and Unwin.

Edgell, S. and Duke, V. (1991) *A Measure of Thatcherism.* Glasgow: HarperCollins.

Esping-Andersen, G. (1990) *The Three Worlds of Welfare Capitalism.* Cambridge: Polity Press.

Etzioni, A. (1961) *A Comparative Analysis of Complex Organisations.* New York: Free Press.

— (1969) *The Semi Professions and their Organization.* New York: Free Press.

Fimister, G. (1986) *Welfare Rights in Social Services.* London: Macmillan.

— (1995) *Social Security and Community Care in the 1990s.* Sunderland: Business Education Publishers.

Finch, J. (1984) *Education and Social Policy.* London: Longman.

Finer, S. E. (1958) *Anonymous Empire.* London: Pall Mall.

Finn, D. (1987) *Training without Jobs.* London: Macmillan.

Floud, J., Halsey, A. H. and Martin, F. M. (1956) *Social Class and Education Opportunity.* London: Heinemann.

238   *Bibliography*

Ford, J. (1969) *Social Class and the Comprehensive School*. London: Routledge and Kegan Paul.
Forrest, R. and Murie, A. (1991) *Selling the Welfare State*. London: Routledge.
Forrest, R., Murie, A. and Williams, P. (1990) *Home Ownership: Fragmentation and Differentiation*. London: Unwin Hyman.
Foster, P. (1983) *Access to Welfare*. London: Macmillan.
Fox, A. (1974) *Beyond Contract: Work, Power and Trust Relations*. London: Faber.
Fraser, D. (1973, latest edn 1984) *The Evolution of the British Welfare State*. London: Macmillan.
Friedman, M. (1962) *Capitalism and Freedom*. Chicago: University of Chicago Press.
— (1977) *Inflation and Unemployment: A New Dimension of Politics*. London: Institute of Economic Affairs.
Friedson, E. (1970) *Professional Dominance*. New York: Atherton.
Friend, J. K., Power, J. M. and Yewlett, C. J. L. (1974) *Public Planning: The Inter-Corporate Dimension*. London: Tavistock.
George, V. and Wilding, P. (1984) *The Impact of Social Policy*. London: Routledge and Kegan Paul.
— (1994) *Welfare and Ideology*, 2nd edn. Hemel Hempstead: Harvester Wheatsheaf.
Gewirtz, S., Ball, S. J. and Bowe, R. (1995) *Markets, Choice and Equity in Education*. Buckingham: Open University Press.
Gibb, K. and Munro, M. (1991) *Housing Finance in the UK*. London: Macmillan.
Gilbert, B. B. (1970) *British Social Policy 1914–39*. London: Batsford.
Gilbert, R. (1989) *Employment in the 1990s*. London: Macmillan.
Ginsberg, N. (1992) *Divisions of Welfare*. London: Sage.
Glennerster, H. (1992) *Paying for Welfare*. Oxford: Blackwell.
— (1995) *British Social Policy since 1945*. Oxford: Blackwell.
Glennerster, H., Matsaganis, M. and Owens, P. (1994) *Implementing Fundholding*. Buckingham: Open University Press.
Glennerster, H., Power, A. and Travers, T. (1991) 'A New Era for Social Policy: A New Enlightenment or a New Leviathan?' *Journal of Social Policy*, 20(3), 389–414.
Gold, M. (ed.) (1993) *The Social Dimension*. Basingstoke: Macmillan.
Goldberg, E. M. and Warburton, R. W. (1979) *Ends and Means in Social Work*. London: Allen and Unwin.
Gough, I. (1979) *The Political Economy of the Welfare State*. London: Macmillan.
Gould, A. (1993) *Capitalist Welfare Systems: A Comparison of Japan, Britain and Sweden*. London: Longman.
Green, H. and Hansbro, J. (1995) *Housing in England 1993–94*. London: HMSO.
Gunningham, N. (1974) *Pollution, Social Interest and the Law*. London: Martin Robertson.
Gyford, J. (1985) *The Politics of Local Socialism*. London: Allen and Unwin.
— (1991) *Citizens, Consumers and Councils*. London: Macmillan.
Hall, P. (1976) *Reforming the Welfare*. London: Heinemann.
Hallett, C. (1982) *The Personal Social Services in Local Government*. London: Allen and Unwin.
Hallett, C. and Stevenson, O. (1979) *Child Abuse: Aspects of Interprofessional Communication*. London: Allen and Unwin.
Halsey, A. H. (ed.) (1972) *Educational Priority*, vol. 1. London: HMSO.

Ham, C. (1992) *Health Policy in Britain*. London: Macmillan.

— and Hill, M. (1993) *The Policy Process in the Modern Capitalist State*. Brighton: Wheatsheaf.

Hamnett, C. (1991) 'A Nation of Inheritors? Housing Inheritance, Wealth and Inequality in Britain'. *Journal of Social Policy*, 20(4), 509–36.

Handler, J. (1973) *The Coercive Social Worker*. Chicago: Rand McNally.

Hanson, A. H. and Walles, M. (1990) *Governing Britain*. Glasgow: Fontana.

Harris, J. (1972) *Unemployment and Politics*. London: Oxford University Press.

— (1977) *William Beveridge: A Biography*. Oxford: Oxford University Press.

Harris, R. and Seldon, A. (1976) *Pricing or Taxing*. London: Institute of Economic Affairs.

— (1979) *Overruled on Welfare*. London: Institute of Economic Affairs.

Harrison, S., Hunter D. J. and Pollitt, C. (1990) *The Dynamics of British Health Policy*. London: Unwin Hyman.

Heclo, H. H. (1974) *Modern Social Politics in Britain and Sweden*. New Haven: Yale University Press.

— and A. Wildavsky (1981) *The Private Government of Public Money*. London: Macmillan.

Hennessy, P. (1992) *Never Again: Britain 1945–51*. London: Cape.

Higgins, J. (1988) *The Business of Medicine: Private Health Care in Britain*. London: Macmillan.

Hill, M. (1972) *The Sociology of Public Administration*. London: Weidenfeld & Nicolson.

— (1990) *Social Security Policy in Britain*. Aldershot: Edward Elgar.

— (1993a) *The Policy Process: A Reader*. Hemel Hempstead: Harvester Wheatsheaf.

— (1993b) *The Welfare State in Britain*. Aldershot: Edward Elgar.

— (1996) *Social Policy: A Comparative Analysis*. Hemel Hempstead: Harvester Wheatsheaf.

Hill, M. and Bramley, G. (1986) *Analysing Social Policy*. Oxford: Blackwell.

Hill, M. and Laing, P. (1979) *Social Work and Money*. London: Allen and Unwin.

Hills, J. (ed.) (1990) *The State of Welfare*. Oxford: Clarendon Press.

Hills, J. (1993) *The Future of Welfare: A Guide to the Debate*. York: Joseph Rowntree Foundation.

HMSO (1957) *Report of the Committee on Administrative Tribunals and Enquiries*. (Franks Report), Cmnd 218. London: HMSO.

— (1967) *The Future Structure of the National Health Service*. London: HMSO.

— (1968a) *The Administrative Structure of Medical and Related Services in England and Wales*. London: HMSO.

— (1968b) *Report of the Committee on Local Authority and Allied Personal Social Services* (Seebohm Report), Cmnd 3703. London: HMSO.

— (1969) *Report of the Royal Commission on Local Government in England* (Redcliffe Maud Report), Cmnd 4040. London: HMSO.

— (1972) *Proposals for a Tax-Credits System*, Cmnd 5116. London: HMSO.

— (1975) *Royal Commission on the Distribution of Income and Wealth, Initial Report on the Standing Reference*, Cmnd 6171. London: HMSO.

— (1977) *Housing Policy: A Consultative Document*, Cmnd 6851. London: HMSO.

— (1979) *Report of the Royal Commission on the National Health Service* (Merrison Report), Cmnd 7615. London: HMSO.

HMSO (1985) *Reform of Social Security: Programme for Action*, Cmnd 9691. London: HMSO.

— (1989) *Caring for People: Community Care in the Next Decade and Beyond.* Cmnd 849. London: HMSO.

— (1995) *The Government's Expenditure Plans: Employment Department Group*, Cmnd 2805. London: HMSO.

Holman, R. (1978) *Poverty*. London: Martin Robertson.

Holme, A. and Maizels, J. (1978) *Volunteers in Social Work*. London: Allen and Unwin.

House of Commons (1977) *Seventh Report from the Expenditure Committee: The Job Creation Programme*. London: HMSO.

Hudson, B. (1994) *Making Sense of Markets in Health and Social Care*. Sunderland: Business Education Publishers.

Hutton, W. (1995) *The State We're In*. London: Cape.

Jackson, B. and Marsden, D. (1962) *Education and the Working Class*. London: Routledge and Kegan Paul.

Jackson, P. and Lavender, M. (1995) *The Public Services Yearbook 1995/96*. London: Chapman and Hall.

Jenkins, W. I. (1978) *Policy Analysis*. London: Martin Robertson.

Jones, B. et al. (1991) *Politics UK*. Hemel Hempstead: Harvester Wheatsheaf.

Jordan, A. G. and Richardson, J. J. (1987) *British Politics and the Policy Process*. London: Unwin Hyman.

Jordan, B. (1974) *Poor Parents*. London: Routledge and Kegan Paul.

Joseph Rowntree Foundation (1995) *Inquiry into Income and Wealth*. York: Joseph Rowntree Foundation.

Jowell, J. (1973) 'The Legal Control of Administrative Discretion'. *Public Law*, no. 178, 178–220.

Judge, K. (1982) 'The Public Purchase of Social Care'. *Policy and Politics*, 10(4), 397–416.

— (1987) *Rationing Social Services*. London: Heinemann.

Keynes, J. M. (1936) *The General Theory of Employment Interest and Money*. London: Macmillan.

Klein, R. (1995) *The Politics of the NHS*. London: Longman.

Kohli, M. et al. (1991) *Time for Retirement: Comparative Studies of Early Exit from the Labour Force*. Cambridge: Cambridge University Press.

Land, H. and Rose, H. (1985) 'Compulsory Altruism for Some or an Altruistic Society for All'. In P. Bean, J. Ferris and D. Whynes (eds), *In Defence of Welfare*, London: Tavistock, 74–96.

Le Grand, J. (1982) *The Strategy of Equality*. London: Allen and Unwin.

— (1990) *Quasi-Markets and Social Policy*. Bristol: School for Advanced Urban Studies.

Lindsey, A. (1962) *Socialised Medicine in England and Wales*. Chapel Hill: University of North Carolina Press.

Lipsky, M. (1980) *Street-Level Bureaucracy*. New York: Russell Sage.

Loney, M. (ed.) (1987) *The State or the Market*. London: Sage.

Loughlin, M. (1986) *Local Government in the Modern State*. London: Sweet and Maxwell.

Lowe, R. (1993) *The Welfare State in Britain since 1945*. London: Macmillan.

Lynes, T. (1962) *National Assistance and National Prosperity*. London: Codicote.

Mack, J. and Lansley, S. (1985) *Poor Britain*. London: Allen and Unwin.
Malpass, P. (ed.) (1986) *The Housing Crisis*. London: Croom Helm.
Malpass, P. (1990) *Reshaping Housing Policy*. London: Routledge.
Malpass, P. and Murie, A. (1994) *Housing Policy and Practice*, 4th edn. London: Macmillan.
Marsden, D. (1973) *Mothers Alone*. Penguin: Harmondsworth.
Marsh, D. and Rhodes, R. A. W. (1992a) *Implementing Thatcherite Policies*. Buckingham: Open University Press.
— (1992b) *Policy Networks in British Government*. Oxford: Oxford University Press.
McCarthy, M. (1986) *Campaigning for the Poor*. Beckenham: Croom Helm.
McKeown, T. (1980) *The Role of Medicine*. Oxford: Blackwell.
Means, R. and Smith, R. (1994) *Community Care: Policy and Practice*. Basingstoke: Macmillan.
Minford, P. (1984) 'State Expenditure: A Study in Waste'. *Economic Affairs*, (April–June).
Mishra, R. (1977) *Society and Social Policy*. London: Macmillan.
— (1984) *The Welfare State in Crisis*. Brighton: Wheatsheaf.
Moon, J. and Richardson, J. J. (1985) *Unemployment in the U.K.* Aldershot: Gower.
Morgan, K. O. (1984) *Labour in Power 1945–51*. Oxford: Oxford University Press.
— (1990) *The People's Peace: British History 1945–89*. Oxford: Oxford University Press.
Moynihan, D. P. (1969) *Maximum Feasible Misunderstanding*. New York: Free Press.
Mukherjee, S. (1972) *Making Labour Markets Work*. London: PEP.
Murie, A., Niner, P. and Watson, C. (1976) *Housing Policy and the Housing System*. London: Allen and Unwin.
Murray, C. (1984) *Losing Ground*. New York: Basic Books.
O'Connor, J. (1973) *The Fiscal Crisis of the State*. New York: St Martin's Press.
Oppenheim, C. and Harker, L. (1995) *Poverty: The Facts*. London: Child Poverty Action Group.
Packman, J. (1975) *The Child's Generation*. Oxford: Blackwell.
Parker, H. (1989) *Instead of the Dole*. London: Routledge.
Pater, J. E. (1981) *The Making of the National Health Service*. London: King's Fund.
Peters, T. and Waterman, R. (1982) *In Search of Excellence*. New York: Harper Collins.
Phillimore, P., Beattie, A. and Townsend, P. (1994) 'Widening Inequality in Health in Northern England 1981–91'. *British Medical Journal*, 308, 1125–8.
Philo, C. (ed.) (1995) *Off the Map: The Social Geography of Poverty in the UK*. London: CPAG.
Piven, F. F. and Cloward, R. A. (1972) *Regulating the Poor*. London: Tavistock.
Pollitt, C. (1990) *Managerialism and the Public Services*. Oxford: Blackwell.
Pressman, G. and Wildavsky, A. (1973) *Implementation*. Berkeley: University of California Press.
Ralphs, Sir F. Lincoln (1973) *The Role and Training of Education Welfare Officers*. Luton: Local Government Training Board.
Ranade, W. (1994) *A Future for the NHS: Health Care in the 1990s*. London: Longman.

Rex, J. and Tomlinson, S. (1979) *Colonial Immigrants in a British City*. London: Routledge and Kegan Paul.

Roberts, D. (1960) *Victorian Origins of the British Welfare State*. New Haven: Yale University Press.

Roberts, G. K. (1970) *Political Parties and Pressure Groups in Britain*. London: Weidenfeld & Nicolson.

Robins Committee (1963) *Higher Education*, Cmnd 2154. London: HMSO.

Robinson, R. and Judge, K. (1987) *Public Expenditure and the NHS: Trends and Prospects*. London: King's Fund Institute.

Rose, H. (1981) 'Rereading Titmuss: The Social Division of Welfare'. *Journal of Social Policy*, 10(4), 477–502.

Rowntree, B. S. (1901) *Poverty: A Study of Town Life*. London: Macmillan.

Sabatier, P. (1986) 'Top-Down and Bottom-Up Approaches to Implementation Research: A Critical Analysis and Suggested Synthesis'. *Journal of Public Policy*, 6(1), 21–48.

Sanderson, M. (1991) 'Social Equality and Industrial Need: A Dilemma of English Education since 1945'. In T. Gourvish and A. O'Day (eds), *Britain since 1945*, London: Macmillan, 159–82.

Savage, S. P., Atkinson, R. and Robins, L. (eds) (1994) *Public Policy in Britain*. London: Macmillan.

Schattschneider, E. E. (1960) *The Semi-Sovereign People*. New York: Holt, Rinehart and Winston.

Schon, D. (1971) *Beyond the Stable State*. London: Maurice Temple Smith.

Schumpeter, J. (1950) *Capitalism, Socialism and Democracy*. New York: Harper and Row.

Selznick, P. (1949) *TVA and the Grass Roots*. Berkeley: University of California Press.

Semmel, B. (1961) *Imperialism and Social Reform*. London: Oxford University Press.

Simon, B. (1988) *Bending the Rules*. London: Lawrence and Wishart.

Sinfield, R. A. (1969) *Which Way for Social Work?* London: Fabian Society.

— (1978) 'Analysis in the Social Division of Welfare'. *Journal of Social Policy*, 7(2), 129–56.

— (1981) *What Unemployment Means*. Oxford: Martin Robertson.

Smith, B. C. (1976) *Policy Making in British Government*. London: Martin Robertson.

Smith, M. J. (1993) *Pressure, Power and Policy*. Hemel Hempstead: Harvester Wheatsheaf.

Specht, H. and Vickery, A. (1977) *Integrating Social Work Methods*. London: Allen and Unwin.

Stacey, M. (1988) *The Sociology of Health and Healing*. London: Unwin Hyman.

Stanworth, P. and Giddens, A. (1974) *Elites and Power in British Society*. Cambridge: Cambridge University Press.

Stone, M. (1981) *The Education of the Black Child in Britain*. Glasgow: Fontana.

Taylor-Gooby, P. (1985) *Public Opinion, Ideology and State Welfare*. London: Routledge and Kegan Paul.

Thane, P. (1982) *The Foundations of the Welfare State*. London: Longman.

Therborn, G. (1986) *Why Some Peoples are More Unemployed than Others*. London: Verso.

Titmuss, R. M. (1958) *Essays on the Welfare State*. London: Allen and Unwin.
— (1962) *Income Distribution and Social Change*. London: Allen and Unwin.
Townsend, P. (1954) 'Measuring Poverty'. *British Journal of Sociology*, 5(2), 130–7.
— (1979) *Poverty in the United Kingdom*. Harmondsworth: Penguin.
— (ed.) (1970) *The Concept of Poverty*. London: Heinemann.
Townsend, P., Davidson, N. and Whitehead, M. (eds) (1988) *Inequalities in Health*. Harmondsworth: Penguin.
Unemployment Unit (1992), *Working Brief* (issued monthly). London: Unemployment Unit.
Urry, J. and Wakeford, J. (eds) (1973) *Power in Britain*. London: Heinemann.
Veit-Wilson, J. (1994) *Dignity not Poverty*. London: Institute for Public Policy Research.
Wall, A. (1996) 'Mine, Yours or Theirs? Accountability in the New NHS'. *Policy and Politics*, 24(1), 73–84.
Walter, J. A. (1988) *Basic Income: Escape from the Poverty Trap*. London: Marion Boyars.
Webb, A. (1985) 'Alternative Futures for Social Policy and State Welfare'. In R. Berthoud (ed.), *Challenges to Social Policy*, Aldershot: Gower, 46–71.
Webb, A. and Wistow, G. (1986) *Planning, Need and Scarcity*. London: Allen and Unwin.
— (1987) *Social Work, Social Care and Social Planning: The Personal Social Services since Seebohm*. London: Longman.
Weber, M. (1947) *The Theory of Social and Economic Organization*, trans. A. M. Henderson and T. Parsons. Glencoe, Ill: Free Press.
Wilding, P. (1982) *Professional Power and Social Welfare*. London: Routledge.
Williams, F. (1989) *Social Policy: A Critical Introduction*. Cambridge: Polity Press.
Willis, P. (1977) *Learning to Labour*. Westmead: Saxon House.
Wootton, B. (1959) *Social Science and Social Pathology*. London: Allen and Unwin.
Wootton, G. (1970) *Interest Groups*. Englewood Cliffs, NJ: Prentice-Hall.

Index